RHETORIC
and ETHNICITY

Edited by
Keith Gilyard and Vorris Nunley

New Perspectives in Rhetoric and Composition

CHARLES I. SCHUSTER, SERIES EDITOR

Boynton/Cook
HEINEMANN
Portsmouth, NH

To Edna Edet and Elloville Nunley, in memory

Boynton/Cook Publishers, Inc.
A subsidiary of Reed Elsevier Inc.
361 Hanover Street
Portsmouth, NH 03801–3912
www.boyntoncook.com

Offices and agents throughout the world

© 2004 by Boynton/Cook Publishers, Inc.

Library of Congress Cataloging-in-Publication Data
Rhetoric and ethnicity / edited by Keith Gilyard and Vorris Nunley.
   p. cm.
   Papers presented at a conference on American ethnic rhetorics held at Pennsylvania State University in 2001.
   Includes bibliographical references.
   ISBN 0-86709-575-X   (alk. paper)
  1. Ethnicity.   2. Rhetoric.   3. Discourse analysis, Narrative.   I. Gilyard, Keith, 1952–
II. Nunley, Vorris.   III. Title.

   GN495.6.R47 2004
   305.8—dc22

                                   2004002386

Editor: Charles I. Schuster
Production service: Barbara Stabb, TechBooks
Production coordinator: Sonja S. Chapman
Typesetter: TechBooks
Cover design: Jenny Jensen Greenleaf
Manufacturing: Jamie Carter

Printed in the United States of America on acid-free paper
08 07 06 05 04 VP 1 2 3 4 5

Contents

Preface

Serious attention to the rhetorics employed by an ethnically diverse populace constitutes a wise investment of time, energy, and resources in a national quest to realize a critical democracy. If such form of political organization is indeed our nation's goal, then we are compelled as part of our work to examine continually the wide range of ethnic discourses used in our country to fashion knowledge, participate in public affairs, and engage in formal education. The greater is our collective comprehension of this multiplicity, the better are our chances of elevating the import of our civic deliberations and maximizing the potential of students in our academic institutions. However correct or suspect, this is the reasoning that drives me to some extent and led me to convene a conference at Penn State in 2001 organized around the theme of "American Ethnic Rhetorics." The present volume is a selection of papers derived from that event.

The broad idea I just outlined, plus my basic curiosity about contemporary conceptions of ethnicity held by scholars in rhetoric and composition, led me to prod participants on specific issues of verbal forms, identity, politics, pedagogy, and canon formation. In other words, I aimed to foreground questions of how ethnic rhetorics might function as generative sites of difference, how they intersect with social movements, how they might shape composition instruction, and how they should relate to presentations of the rhetorical tradition.

Although no single conception of *rhetoric* or *ethnicity* was forced on conference participants, nor does uniformity about the meaning of these terms exist, I offer definitions as a way to suggest how one might begin to read or reread the field at large concerning the issues I raise. Naturally, I am explaining in the process something about how I read as well.

Roderick Hart's definition offered in *Modern Rhetorical Criticism* (1996) is particularly useful. *Rhetoric,* to him, is "the art of using language to help people narrow their choices among specifiable, if not specified, policy options" (4). Ethnic rhetoric, to extend the idea, may be seen as this sort of language use inflected with an ethnic difference. This second definition can signal at least two directions for study: (1) attention to ethnic people employing any style of rhetoric, and (2) concern for verbal forms and discursive strategies unique or characteristic of particular ethnic assemblages. I lean toward the latter. I certainly see value in mapping the advocacy efforts of any ethnic group regardless of the rhetoric utilized, but the dominant forms of persuasive discourse sometimes employed are in no imminent danger of being erased. I am thus more intrigued at this point by the distinctive forms of discourse generated by ethnic groups—and the knowledge encoded in those forms—that can be preserved, retrieved, revitalized, and efficiently used in progressive social, political, and educational campaigns.

For a working definition of *ethnicity,* I turn to Joseph Hraba's (1979) view that ethnic groups are "self-conscious collectivities of people, who on the basis of a common origin or a separate subculture, maintain a distinction between themselves and outsiders" (27). Stephen Cornell (2000) sharpens this notion by pointing out that sometimes the "outsiders" assign the designation. In addition, Paul Spickard and W. Jeffrey Burroughs (2000) stress the narrative and rhetorical aspects of ethnicity. They emphasize that, like all assertions of identity, ethnicity is an argument about significance that involves selection, plotting, and interpretation (51). Of course, there is theoretical leakage. How common, for example, are the origins? How separate is the subculture? Some would argue that in the United States *Latino/a, Asian American,* and *Indian* are not really ethnic groups but political coalitions that include subgroups that do not necessarily share a strong sense of commonality. And I remember that it was often remarked by street-corner sociologists in New York City, my hometown, that waves of Jamaicans, Barbadians, and Trinidadians did not become "West Indian" until they arrived in Brooklyn. Furthermore, all the labels referenced here can fall into disuse. So my objective is not to reach an inviolable formulation. I point out the contingent, dynamic, and narrative to highlight that ethnicity is a social and political process. As such, I angle for discussions of, say, a *critical ethnicity,* discourse that would be several steps beyond both the mere affirmation of cultural difference, on the one hand, and, on the other hand, the logjam of theorists who cannot figure out quite what to do after they have deconstructed *race.*

Consider a reflective moment, one that may seem familiar. The import is basically this: "Race is a fiction as demonstrated by biologists and anthropologists. Phenotype, therefore, is a weak intellectual rationale for affiliation. Furthermore, identity is shifting and multiple and one really cannot say who is what—or what is who. Why, after all is said and done, I of Ethnicity A could just as easily be you of Ethnicity B, and you could be me." Then, heady with enthusiasm, our hypothetical thinker realizes that he or she has solved the race problem in America, having theorized it out of existence.

To be fair, there is worth in the aforementioned line of reasoning insofar as it can direct attention to the social and political elements that have shaped racialized disparities. However, this mental exercise does not represent or yield the most forceful and positive argument to be made given the circumstances. After all, what materiality is altered by race deconstruction? It is not as though you can flip a switch on a social projector, send the reel in reverse, and, because you have deconstructed race, you have undone all the ramifications of racism. The problematic materiality remains problematic.

So, the most important question relative to ethnicity and curriculum is what conceptions of ethnicity (and the race conversation) can we circulate that best contribute to social justice efforts.

In being unsympathetic toward a strong deconstructionist position (I'll compromise on a weaker version), I am not indicating a desire to create any more fissures in our society than already exist. But I am concerned that a facile fusion, or a discursive papering over of ethnic differences may undermine enrollment in ethnic narratives that historically have been sustaining and transformative. For example, as C. Eric Lincoln (1996) observed, the formation of expressly African-American identities never hinged on whether those psychic constructions corresponded to any "pure" Africanity. That question was immaterial. In the absence of social justice, an embrace of African heritage proved to be powerful and sustaining for the founders of the first Black cultural institutions, who habitually included the word African in the titles of those institutions even as direct experience or memory of the African continent was receding further into the past. The question for them was not simply genetics but commitment to collective Black progress.

In formulating this argument, I am not essentializing, nor am I minimizing the complexity of identity formation or ignoring its somewhat individual nature. As Toi Derricotte (1997) expresses it, "sometimes I think that eventually every identity breaks down to some self that has to learn to live between loneliness and connection" (78). That is a legitimate story. However, I also understand, along with Cornell (2000), and no doubt with Derricotte as well, that her story is situated within a particular group story, whether she wraps the group's tale tightly around herself or not. As an individual, she is nonetheless historically located within an ethnic group narrative. And as Cornell notes, "in the struggle to construct ethnic narratives, to assert authorship, to control selection, plot, and meaning, and to give the narrative currency or dominance in the group's conception of itself and in wider conceptions of the group, much is at stake" (51). He is making reference, in part, to moral and legal claims that gain rhetorical force because they stem from ethnic stories that assert a special social significance. In my view, the best thing to do with these various ethnic narratives, even as we assess each claim to uniqueness, is to mine them for what they can contribute to positive social struggle. In other words, what positive, radical, even revolutionary, difference can ethnic difference make? This concern contrasts to what is often manifested in academe, that is, a surface celebration of diversity while there is an accompanying rhetorical undertow that suggests that everything is diversity anyway, which deprivileges the surface celebration. The real message conveyed, then, is that a group's story is so highly permeable, so ragged at the edges, so open to border crossers that it lacks potential as a productive organizing mechanism.

Allow me to press this point with an example from popular culture because these dynamics were actually on my mind as I recently viewed the movie *Barbershop* and listened to and read some of the controversial commentary in the media, which mainly revolved around script references to Rosa Parks and Martin Luther King, Jr., with particular emphasis on King's sexual habits. I will refrain from commenting on those aspects or advise anyone at this point how to celebrate King's birthday. More curious to me, more disturbing, was how African-American identity as a whole was destabilized in the film. The one White barber in the shop has Blackness conferred on him by consensus. Apparently, he has earned the honor because he wears baggy clothes (I guess that's what the Black guys do), he plays loud hip hop music while driving (I guess that's what the Black guys do), and he lewdly fondles his African-American girlfriend in public (I guess that's what the Black guys do and what the Black gals invite and allow). For these performances he is deemed more Black than an African-American college student who has fairly standardized diction and a penchant for designer coffee. The two actually come close to exchanging blows, but by the end of the movie, the college brother allows his opposite number to trim his hair for him, the acknowledgment that his now former adversary is worthy of acceptance, not as Euro-American but, following the logic of the film, as Black. What is the message being pushed here? Who would embrace it? Who would promote it? Who would recycle it?

Fortunately—a mistake maybe, a stroke of unintentional brilliance?—an important reality is revealed. This White barber has no customers in the film, never has had any. So, on one question of identity, is he really even a barber? I mean, he don't cut no hair, and he don't because for the community at large, the community beyond the contrived barbershop set-up, simply performative or commodified Blackness is not enough. Could a White barber actually catch on in the "hood"? Perhaps. But not that one, who shows no positive political embrace of the African-American group story, of a legacy of advocacy and struggle around issues pertinent to the group's well-being.

Critical ethnicity reads all of these representational dynamics. Critical ethnicity goes to the movies and everywhere else. Critical ethnicity could not ignore what material bodies or phenotypes or cultural histories mean in our society and, in gesturing toward social justice (the reason to be critical in the first place), would presuppose a factoring in of these realities alongside any other contemporary understandings about racial and ethnic configurations.

This approach links to my prior work (Gilyard 1999), most notably the preface to *Race, Rhetoric, and Composition* and my chapter in that collection titled "Higher Learning: Composition's Racialized Reflection." In essence, I called for an increasingly critical inspection of race as a concept but did not entirely dismiss the notion of race itself. In an attempt to illustrate how cultural codes often operate implicitly yet powerfully, to show how ideology, exploitative or otherwise, is embedded in discourses, and because talk about race consumed so much time in classrooms, I aimed to promote a discussion about race that was clarifying. The ultimate goal was to get students to understand, manipulate, and resist certain dominant discourses. This involved the historicizing of race, a project that, of course, highlighted its constructed and contingent nature. But while acknowledging that race is rhetorical, I asserted that it is not *merely* so. Race, constructed or not, is real in its effects. Furthermore, the conversations about racism that I remain interested in having with people beyond the academy often revolve around the terminology of "race." In most instances, it has been more productive to keep the conversation moving along in old, familiar vocabulary rather than to digress so I can prove that we are not really talking about race at all. For this last choice, I would be labeled a racializationist by Spickard and Burroughs (2000). Their specific charge would be that even as I argue against racism I adopt the oppressive terminology of pseudoscientific racists and, therefore, do not contest racial reasoning. This is inaccurate. Although I have no problem with the fact that Spickard and Burroughs always prefer the term *ethnicity* over *race,* what I imply by *critical ethnicity* is a culling, if not a synthesis, of the best of both ethnicist and racializationist traditions. In other words, I accept intellectually the social scientific analysis of Spickard and Burroughs and their accompanying emphasis on race as a social and political category, one that they do acknowledge has serious consequences. Simultaneously, I understand that American society is shot through with racial reasoning; if not, scholars like Spickard and Burroughs would never have been moved to pursue an ethnicist project. It seems to me, therefore, given how saturated with conceptions of race our society is, that utilizing the semantic term *race* is unavoidable if one is truly interested in communicating with large numbers of people not only to contest racial reasoning but also to contest, in a concrete way, racial hierarchies. In the overall scheme of things, I fail to discern how antiracist activity is compromised by any theorizing that, along the plane of the everyday, helps to clarify social reality. I trust, furthermore, that as I merge insights from several strands of antiracist thought to engage a variety of people, I will not be mistaken for a pseudoscientific oppressor.

Ultimately, critical ethnicity is a search for the elements in various ethnic narratives that have the most political potential in a push for a more humane society, and it represents an impulse to share the fruits of that search with our students. It is a project of examination, but also one of reclamation, and reflects the idea that the most generative ethnic activity, at this point, amid talk about decentering and indeterminancy, is the building outward from subcultural understandings.

All the authors in this volume walk along the theoretical path with me to some degree. Some part ways with me fairly quickly; others hang out for a long stroll. I helped to establish the agenda for the conference but did not seek sameness of intellection as an outcome. Nor did I speak at the event, which is mainly why I have presently gone on at length. When we solicited feedback about the conference, several respondents suggested that I should have explained "where we are with all this." So I have added my voice to this collection, which I hope has been illuminating, though I am certainly not claiming to speak for "we."

The essays are distributed across two sections: (1) History and (2) Identity and Pedagogy. The categories overlap, and legitimate arguments exist for moving certain essays from one section to another. Where Vorris and I placed them was based on our sense of whether the focus seemed to be on general historical trends, political moments, or reminiscences—thus, a placement in History—or on specific questions of identity *per se* and of classroom practice.

The consensus among conference participants is that the event constituted an exciting and energetic intellectual moment. We hope to have represented the moment with distinction.

—Keith Gilyard

Works Cited

Cornell, Stephen. 2000. "That's the Story of Our Life." In *We Are a People: Narrative and Multiplicity in Constructing Ethnic Identity*, edited by Paul Spickard and W. Jeffrey Burroughs, 41–53. Philadelphia: Temple University Press.

Derricotte, Toi. 1997. *The Black Notebooks: An Interior Journey*. New York: W. W. Norton.

Gilyard, Keith. 1999. "Higher Learning: Composition's Racialized Reflection." In *Race, Rhetoric, and Composition,* edited by Keith Gilyard, 44–52. Portsmouth, NH: Heinemann-Boynton/Cook.

———. 1999. "Preface." In *Race, Rhetoric, and Composition,* edited by Keith Gilyard, ix–x. Portsmouth, NH: Heinemann-Boynton/Cook.

Hart, Roderick P. 1996. *Modern Rhetorical Criticism. 2d ed.* Glenview, IL: Scott, Foresman and Company.

Hraba, Joseph. 1979. *American Ethnicity*. Itasca, IL: Peacock Publishers.

Lincoln, C. Eric. 1996. *Coming Through the Fire: Surviving Race and Place in America.* Durham, NC: Duke University Press.

Spickard, Paul, and W. Jeffrey Burroughs. 2000. "We Are a People." In *We Are a People: Narrative and Multiplicity in Constructing Ethnic Identity,* edited by Paul Spickard and W. Jeffrey Burroughs, 1–19. Philadelphia: Temple University Press.

Acknowledgments

Much thanks to Cheryl Glenn, Meredith Kramer, Avis Kunz, Andrea Berlin, and Meredith Kramer for their assistance with the conference that led to this book. Our gratitude extends to Lita Cunningham for her help in pulling together the manuscript. Also, we thank the Rhetoric Group at Penn State for trying to keep us sharp in our thinking about rhetoric and culture. Finally, we wish to acknowledge Joyce Johnson for friendship and support over the years.

Part I

History

1

Meditations on Language, Pedagogy, and a Life of Struggle

Geneva Smitherman

Author's note: At the conference, this essay was presented in a reader's theatre format. The sections in italics were read by Elaine Richardson, Adam Banks, Les Knotts, and Mursalata Muhammad. Shoutouts to them and many thanks for their participation.

I have always been fascinated by words and the way people use them. I remember hearing intriguing phrases from my granmomma, who would say things like, "Gal, if you don't git to that store, or wash dem dishes [or whatever it was that she had done tole me to do, and I ain done it], uhm gon beat you from Amazing Grace to Floating Opportunity." Or sometime it would be "from Genesis to Revelation." When I got in ninth grade and started studying Latin, I became even more intrigued as I tried to master those sounds, wondering why in the worl the Romans confused they v's and w's; no wonder the Roman Empire crumbled.

As a high school senior, I worked in the school library and came across Richard Wright's *Native Son* (1940). In those days, the school librarian kept it in the classified section; you had to have a note from your teacher to check this book out. I would read a lil bit of *Native Son* each day. I thought I could hear the rhythms of Bigger Thomas's Black Dialect: "There go a rat . . . git im!" I identified with Bigger's pain and with his language. I too had done battle with rats in our broken-down house on Detroit's lower eastside ghetto in a house with only one way in and out. But it wasn't until I was forced to take speech correction as a university student because I didn't talk "right" that I knew language research was gon be something I'd be involved in for a long

time. Of course, that was before I discovered the streets and the lure and
promise of amassing mad Dead Presidents for those smart enough to manipulate and wheel and deal. Making loot by any means necessary would
become my goal before I came to myself and found the Black Liberation
Movement. That Movement began in the 1960s, spanning, as political
scientist Ron Walters argues, the period from 1960 to 1980. The Movement
was a catalytic force that brought about fundamental changes in a whole lot
of people.

There was a time when—as poet and literary critic Haki Madhubuti
(1969) once wrote—"if somebody had da called us black, we woulda broke
his right eye out, jumped into his chest, talked bout his momma, lied on his
sister and dared him to say it again." But since the days of the Black Liberation Movement, like the old Bluesmen sang, the thangs we usta do, we don't
do no mo.

On December 18, 1996, the Oakland, California, School Board issued
its Resolution on Ebonics, and all hell broke loose. From my position as the
chief advocate for the parents and children in the 1977–79 *Martin Luther
King Junior Elementary School Children, et. al., v. Ann Arbor School District Board* (popularly known as the "Black English Case"), the sound and
fury over Ebonics made me say and later write, "Ain we done been here
befo?" Since the 1960s, there has been an overwhelming body of research
and publication on the language of African Americans, demonstrating that
this language follows systematic, ordered linguistic rules as do all human languages. Contrary to what some critics charge, this research has not been the
purview of one particular group. Rather, the work has been done by language
arts scholars of all persuasions—male and female; Black, White, Latino; gay,
lesbian, straight; young and old; lame and hip. But as Cornel West said, "race
matters." The issue of Ebonics, like that of bilingualism, goes far beyond language, invoking a racialized discourse. In fact, when it comes to issues of
language and education, linguists and educators are often sidelined in favor
of people like California's rich businessman, Ron Unz, author of Proposition
227, California's anti-bilingual education bill, or the late Eldridge Cleaver, a
former Black Panther, who told us in 1997 to just say "no" to Ebonics.
Cleaver's pronouncements in the media were only one of numerous instances
of "sound and fury" that came from so-called "leaders" and the established
"elite."

> I am Maya Angelou: "I am incensed. The idea that African Americans speak
> something other than English is very threatening. It could say to our young
> people that they don't have to learn to speak properly."

> I am Jesse Jackson: "The Oakland School Board has become the laugh-
> ingstock of the nation. This proposal is unacceptable surrender, borderlin-
> ing on disgrace."

I am Ward Connerly, University of California Regent and anti-affirmative action advocate: "[This proposal] is tragic . . . These are kids that have had every opportunity to acclimate themselves to American society, and they have gotten themselves into this trap of speaking this language—this slang, really—that people can't understand. Now we're going to legitimize it."

I am Walter Williams: "Black English is an attempted cover-up of school corruption and capitulation to mediocrity. It's not simply a matter of Black English being hard on the ears. Poor command of language is devastating to learning potential and reasoning skills. If I were conspiracy-minded, I'd believe that undercover Klansmen have infiltrated the Oakland School Board . . ."

The program that the Oakland School Board put forth wasn't radical. Not even. They were simply proposing to teach the students literacy and communication skills in the Language of Wider Communication in the United States, also known as "standard English," or more accurately, following Clark and Ivanič (1997) in *The Politics of Writing*, we should say "standardized English." The Oakland Board's proposal was that teachers would use the students' home language as a bridge to move them to competence in "standardized English." The "Ebonics Resolution" was based on the success of students at Oakland's Prescott Elementary School, the only school in the District where the teachers were participants in something called the "Standard English Proficiency Program," a statewide program in which Ebonics is recognized as legitimate and systematic and used to teach literacy skills in "School English." The Oakland School Board sought to extend the educational success students were achieving at Prescott to the entire District.

The Board was addressing a familiar crisis throughout the land—same song, different verse. In Oakland, the tune went like this:

White grade point average 2.7

Asian grade point average 2.4

Black grade point average 1.8

Blacks were 53 percent of the student population, but 80 percent of the suspensions and 71 percent of the "special needs" students. Nationally, the tune is also off key. During the 1997 U.S. Senate hearings on Ebonics, the national data on reading that were presented indicated that at age nine, African American kids are twenty-nine points behind their European American counterparts. At age thirteen, they are thirty-one points behind. And by age seventeen, they are thirty-seven points behind. The longer Black kids stay in school, the further behind they get. Addressing the language issue is one significant way to step to this pedagogical challenge. We need to move the language conversation to a higher level.

> *I am Thomas Sowell, economist at the Hoover Institute, Stanford University: "From what African language did 'ain't' come? . . . Phony history has been backed up by phony claims about the present. You would think the Oakland School Board's program about 'black English'— 'ebonics'" they call it—would have died of ridicule after so many saw it for the nonsense that it is."*

> *I am former Secretary of Education Richard Riley: "Elevating Black English to the status of a language is not the way to raise standards of achievement in our schools and for our students. Federal funds cannot be used to support this proposal."*

> *I am an editor at* Vibe *magazine: "Is ebonics California's way of telling us they want African-American children to be null and void for the new millennium? And by the way, who thought up that ignorant name, anyway?"*

The name "Ebonics" was not coined by the Oakland, California, School Board in 1996. Rather, the term has been around since 1973, having emerged during a caucus of Black scholars at a conference, "Language and the Urban Child," convened in St. Louis, Missouri, by Dr. Robert Williams, who was then head of the Institute of Black Studies in St. Louis. Now Professor Emeritus at Washington University, Dr. Williams, a clinical psychologist, coined the term. In *Ebonics: The True Language of Black Folks,* his 1975 publication of the conference papers, Williams captures the thinking of that historical moment:

> The Black conferees were so critical of the work on the subject done by white researchers, many of whom also happened to be [at the conference] that they decided to caucus among themselves and define black language from a black perspective. It was in this caucus that the term ***Ebonics*** was created. (3)

Evidence for an African language background in African American speech and for making U.S. Blacks a part of the linguistic continuum from Africa to the so-called "New World" is the legacy of Black linguist, Lorenzo Dow Turner (1949), who learned several West African languages in the course of his research on Gullah. In work that consumed over two decades of his life, Turner uncovered surviving grammatical patterns and word formations from African languages in the speech of slave descendants in the Sea Island communities off the coast of South Carolina. He published this research in *Africanisms in the Gullah Dialect* in 1949. Now, it is unfortunate that Turner used the term "dialect" in his title, for there is plenty of evidence that Gullah was fundamentally more than a "dialect" of English. For example, the speakers themselves refer to it as "Gullah Language."

The *linguistic,* not *dialect,* status of Gullah was implicit in Williams' formulation of "Ebonics," as was the *linguistic,* not *dialect,* status of African American speech in non-Gullah areas of the United States. Theoretical linguistic debates aside, it is the case, as linguist Ralph Fasold (2001) argues, that the speech of Africans in America can be a language if Black people declare it and then act on that declaration. And we don't need no Government approval! For the record, note that Williams, writing in 1973, is African American, and Fasold, writing a generation later, is, to use Fasold's own words, "an old white man." Linguists recognize that there is no hard and fast empirical way to distinguish a "language" from a "dialect." As the Linguistic Society of America noted in its resolution supporting Oakland on the issue of Ebonics: ". . . different varieties of Chinese are popularly regarded as 'dialects,' though their speakers cannot understand each other, but speakers of Swedish and Norwegian, which are regarded as separate 'languages,' generally understand each other." Thus, more often than not, the language–dialect distinction is social and political, not linguistic.

The language spoken here in the U.S. Black community can be considered but one variety of Ebonics, what I call United States Ebonics, or USEB. The Gullah that Turner studied, then, should be considered a subvariety of USEB. In other words, Ebonics is not to be subsumed under "English." Rather, it should be considered a "parent" language in its own right, with "descendant" languages in a number of regions of the world. Just as English has a number of varieties around the globe, what linguists are these days calling "World Englishes"—Australian, Indian, South African, and so forth—so too there are Ebonics language varieties around the world—Jamaican, Haitian, Surinam, West African Pidgin, and so forth.

"Ebonics," then, was conceived of as a superordinate term, covering all the African–European language mixtures developed in various African–European language contact situations throughout the world. As Williams noted back in 1973, Ebonics is the language of "Black people, especially those who have been forced to adapt to colonial circumstances." This conceptualization opens up a window to comparative studies of language use throughout the entire African Diaspora. We have barely scratched the surface in terms of these kinds of studies—in great measure because we have been so mired in linguistic–cognitive deficit and bell curve-type debates. Williams and his colleagues were on to something, but they got cut off at the pass.

I am a New York Times *editor: "By labeling Oakland Black students linguistic foreigners in their own country, the new policy will actually stigmatize African American children—while validating habits of speech that bar them from the cultural mainstream and decent jobs . . . Inner-city speech is best viewed as a variant of Standard English that is colorful in its place, but dangerously limiting to young people who embrace it too fully."*

I am Bill Cosby: "Before the city of Oakland, California starts to teach its teachers Ebonics, or what I call 'Igno-Ebonics,' the school board should study all the ramifications of endorsing an urbanized version of the English language. The first thing people ask when they are pulled over by a policeman is: 'Why did you stop me, officer?' Imagine an Ebonics-speaking Oakland teenager being stopped on the freeway by a non-Ebonics-speaking California highway patrol officer. The teenager would begin by saying, "Lemme ax you . . ." The patrolman, fearing he is about to be hacked to death, could charge the kid with threatening a police officer." (1997)

If it is true that police and citizens in a community are not intelligible to one another, then a *White* teenager could also be charged because the pronunciation "axe" exists among White youth—as well as among various and sundry groups of English speakers. In any case, as linguist Thomas Kochman pointed out on the Oprah Winfrey show on Black English back in 1987, "axe" was used in Old English and was the original formation.

There was a time when some educators believed that "Negro Dialect was the last barrier to integration," which was the title of an article that appeared in the *Journal of Negro Education* in 1963. Subscribing to this belief during that era, many Blacks advocated and worked for the eradication of Black Language, but they discovered that the barrier to equity, first-class citizenship, and the "decent jobs" that the *New York Times* editor is so concerned about was not really language, but racism and White power. And so the thangs Black people usta do, they don do no mo.

As I meditate on my role in the Language Struggle, often on the front lines of battle, I feel like shouting with Toni Morrison (1981) when she say:

> The language, only the language . . . It is the thing that black people love so much—the saying of words, holding them on the tongue, experimenting with them, playing with them. It's a love, a passion. Its function is like a preacher's: to make you stand up out of your seat, make you lose yourself and hear yourself.

At the same time, there is value in bilingualism and multilingualism—not just for African Americans or Latinos, but for everybody in our global community. Speaking more than one language has never been threatening to people of African descent, whether here in the United States or elsewhere in the African Diaspora. In fact, on the Continent, you would have to search high and low to find someone, regardless of educational or literacy level, who speaks only one African language.

I am Helen Halyard, assistant national secretary of the Socialist Equality Party in the United States: "Those who base themselves on the permanence of capitalism are seizing upon racial differences in order to make them a barrier to unifying working people in the struggle to change society. The growth of poverty in capitalist society is not a race but a class problem. In major capitalist countries throughout the world, the welfare state is being dismantled and funding for public education drastically reduced. The main beneficiaries of the Oakland Resolution on 'Ebonics' are not the youth, but a small privileged layer of Blacks. Black nationalists accept the status quo of an economic and social system based on exploitation, inequality and oppression. They have seized upon the misuse of grammar to be found in more impoverished neighborhoods in order to invent a new language that they claim is racially determined." (1997)

There was a time when as a child growing up amidst the poverty of South Side Chicago and East Side Detroit, we would drive past Cadillac cars—we called them "Rada's" and "Rada Dog's" in those days. We would be in my father's old beat-up Chevy that smoked and sometime caught a flat. I remember thinking Ima go to college so I can get a good job and drive a big, fine car like that. This is the way of life under capitalist commodification; material consumerism shapes your thinking and your values. But as an adult reading W. E. B. Du Bois in a study group, I learned that the goal of education is not to make a living but to make a life, and that the role of the educator, the linguist, the intellectual is not just to understand the world, but to change it. The fundamental question is: how do we make the change happen? It's way past time to move the language conversation to higher ground.

As studies have demonstrated time and again—most recently in the American Book Award-winning *Spoken Soul* by Rickford and Rickford (2000)—the speakers of USEB are not just Black youth, nor Black youth who wear baggy clothes and listen to Hip Hop on head phones, nor even stereotypical gangsta Black males chillin with 40s in they hands in front of the many liquor stores that blight Black communities across the nation. The speakers of USEB are persons of African descent on all levels throughout the African American community, including the Black middle class. This latter group, however, is generally bilingual, conversant in both USEB and "standardized English." The linguistic and literacy role models for Black students, then, become the professionals, the educated members of the community, the race men and women. This gets us away from the notion that "standardized English" is "talkin white." How do these role models weave in and out of language codes, playing all the notes on the linguistic scale? Keith Gilyard's sociolinguistic autobiography, *Voices of the Self* (1991), winner of an American Book Award, was the first to explore this fascinating phenomenon, the African American version of what linguists call "code switching." But we need more work in this area. We need to understand how and when the speaker or writer makes the decision to change the linguistic flow. Linguist Marcyliena Morgan recently asked me, how do I, myself, make the decision to move in and out of language codes. This has been an intuitive process for me, but she was pushing for conscious apprehension of these linguistic moves. When we bilingual Blacks shift codes, is there some kind of cognitive traffic signal that says, "Look out, something crucial is up ahead?"

Another area of need is systematic study of the language of Black women; this is long overdue. I am particularly struck these days by the communicative practices of Black women preachers, who have emerged in this postmodern era in unprecedented numbers. In 2000, we witnessed the election of Reverend Dr. Vashti McKenzie, the first woman to head the African Methodist Episcopal (A.M.E) Church, the oldest Black church in our history. At the same time, there is now emerging a strong presence of Black women preachers on national television. I would like to see studies of the linguistics of these Sista preachers.

An Ebonics framework allows us to appreciate the linguistic virtuosity of Hip Hop. Musical genius Quincy Jones, in an interview with Tavis Smiley, said that late Hip Hop artist Tupac Shakur once asked him, "What do the singers and musicians think of us?" Quincy said that's when it occurred to him that Hip Hop is a "third force." This AfroDiasporic cultural production combines new technologies, Oral Tradition rhythms, and lyrics, with Afrocentric and ghettocentric themes. We have not even begun to understand the artistic genius of this polyrhythmic, polysyllabic "third force," with its interlocking and intricate rhymes, and artists like E40 bustin rhymes and spittin verses faster than you can blink your eye. Yes, some Hip Hop musical content is problematic, but no more than the low-down dirty Blues once was. African American popular culture, music especially, has always been a resistance culture, operating way outside of the norms and conventions of White mainstream society.

We need new thought, new pedagogies, and a new vision. As we move on up a lil higher, the people on the ground, as they say in South Africa, will be with us. It was clear during the Ebonics controversy that among the ordinary, everyday folk, the work of linguists and educators had indeed made some impact—which was clearly not the case during the *King* ("Black English") controversy of the late 1970s. In several community forums, everyday people indicated that it made sense for Blacks to keep "our lingo" (as one community leader put it) as we learn other languages. Linguist Ralph Fasold (2001) recounts his experience on a Washington, D.C., radio talk show, with an African American talk show host and a predominantly African American-listening audience. Four of the seven callers showed that they understood the issues. The following conversation, though not framed in the jargon of academic linguists and educators, illustrates that our labor in the vineyard has borne fruit among everyday people.

Caller: Ms. Johnson, I think when you hear a replay of your comments concerning this discussion, I think you will surprise yourself. I think you are a very intelligent woman. But I think you, like Senator Specter, don't have a clue to the very simple statements that have been and are being made that Ebonics is now being touted as some second, third, tenth, twelfth language. It is a language. It is language. It is a starting point that teachers are encouraged to move from where the student is, to standard English. And I wish you would open your mind to that.

Host: My mind is fully open to that, but the question is this. When you have children that are speaking a language that is not going to assist them in getting through this society successfully, and we know it as a corrupted form of standard English, do you elevate this particular language? I mean, you recognize it, it exists, people are speaking it. But it doesn't necessarily mean that you give it a formality.

Caller: I don't mean to offend you, or anything. I'm going to call you "sister" anyway. I want you to listen to what one of your callers said. You should take a tape of this program and listen to what you're saying. Because I can see you looking down your nose at this whole discussion about Ebonics. Because the first thing you said is you used adjectives like "ghetto" language and all that kind of stuff.

Host: It is ghetto language!

Caller: Well, that's your attitude. OK?

Host: It was in the ghetto I came from; that's the language we spoke.

Caller: You're looking down your nose again, sister.

As the Ebonics controversy was surfacing in late 1996, the Language Policy Committee of the Conference on College Composition and Communication—also known as CCCC—was preparing to launch its national survey of language attitudes, practices, and training among secondary and college teachers who are members of the National Council of Teachers of English (NCTE) and CCCC. The Language Policy Committee's charge was to assess current attitudes and the current state of knowledge of the membership about language diversity and about NCTE and CCCC organizational language policies. These views are crucial because NCTE and CCCC are leading language arts organizations. Further, teacher language attitudes are crucial in the new millennium because of the burgeoning linguistic diversity in high school and college classrooms. Paradoxically, this school population increase exists alongside its opposite: a high rate of school force-outs among students of Color. The good news from the Language Policy Committee membership survey is that, yes, we've come a long way since the 1970s when the membership engaged in profound and often bitter struggle about the "Students' Right to Their Own Language." Teachers today have come to accept the idea of language and cultural diversity: 95.5% of the teachers in the survey stated that a college course in language diversity was necessary for anyone preparing for a career in teaching. However—and here is the bad news—universities are not preparing or requiring teachers to have training in language diversity. Nearly a third of the teachers surveyed reported having had no college course in language diversity. For those who had had such training, it clearly had a positive effect on their attitudes. The lack of training sharply distinguished secondary from college teachers. In a recent article, the author commented that the gap between schools and colleges dates back to the establishment of the public high school in the late nineteenth century and that Harvard University President Charles Eliot complained about this gap in 1890 at a National Education Association meeting. Well, we shouldn't take any comfort in the fact that the gap between high school and college existed long before we were born. The fact that it's been around so long is all the more reason we need to change up things, right here, right now.

The immediate change that's needed to help high school (and elementary) teachers prepare for students of this new millennium is training in language diversity. We need to push for national credentialing standards for all teachers—both those in training and those already in the profession—to have at least one course focused on language diversity. This would be in addition to whatever other language courses might be required, such as history of the English language.

My meditations on language, pedagogy, and a life of struggle bear witness that change and transformation, both social and personal, can happen—indeed *will* happen if we struggle. There was a time when NCTE spearheaded a campaign called "Better Speech Week" (see Gawthrop 1965), the aim of which was to improve speech through posters, parades, and short skits like "Mr. Dictionary defeats the villain 'ain't.'" As part of this campaign, a language pledge was developed for daily recitation by students. Included in that pledge were statements like: "I love the United States of America. I love my country's flag. I love my country's language. I promise that I will not dishonor my country's speech by leaving off the last syllable of words [and] that I will say a good American "yes" and "no" in place of an Indian grunt "um-hum" and "nup-um" or a foreign "ya" or "yeh" and "nope." That was NCTE from 1917 to 1929. But like the Bluesmen sang, the thangs NCTE usta do, it don do no mo.

There was a time when the educational system made me feel ashamed of the way I and my family and friends spoke. We talked too "loud" and sounded "country," even those of us who had never lived in the "country" South. We "dropped" word endings and "broke" verbs. But then I stumbled into the Black Liberation Movement and learned that language is a people's identity, culture, and history, that with words you could not only "empty the riverbeds of their content" but also even "raise the dead" (Reed 1970). And so the thangs I usta thank, I didn thank no mo.

Works Cited

"20 Questions." *Vibe,* April, 1997, 146.

Angelou, Maya. *Talk Back Live,* CNN, December 20, 1996.

Clark, Romy, and Roz Ivanič. 1997. "Issues of Correctness and Standardisation in Writing." In *The Politics of Writing,* 187–216. New York: Routledge.

Connerly, Ward. As quoted in Elliot Diringer and Lori Olszewski, "Critics May Not Understand Oakland's Ebonics Plan, Goal is to teach black kids standard English," *San Francisco Chronicle,* December 21, 1996.

Cosby, Bill. "Elements of Igno-Ebonics Style." *The Wall Street Journal,* January 10, 1997.

Fasold, Ralph. 2001. "Ebonic [sic] Need Not Be English." In *Georgetown University Round Table on Languages and Linguistics 1999: Language in Our Time: Bilingual Education and Official English, Ebonics and Standard English, Immigration and the Unz Initiative,* edited by James E. Alatis and Ai-Hui Tan. Washington, DC: Georgetown University Press.

Gilyard, Keith. 1991. *Voices of the Self: A Study of Language Competence.* Detroit: Wayne State University Press.

Gawthrop, Betty. 1965. "1911–1929." In *An Examination of the Attitudes of the NCTE Toward Language,* edited by Raven McDavid, Jr., 7–15. Urbana, IL: National Council of Teachers of English.

Halyard, Helen. 1997. "Ebonics and the Danger of Racial Politics." International Committee of the Fourth International, World Socialist Web Site, http://www.wsws.org/polemics/1997/apr1997/ebonics1.shtml.

"Linguistic Confusion." *The New York Times,* December, 1996.

Green, Gordon C. 1963. "Negro Dialect, the Last Barrier to Integration." *The Journal of Negro Education* 32 (Winter): 81–3.

Kochman, Thomas. *The Oprah Winfrey Show.* November, 1987.

Linguistic Society of America. 1997. "Resolution on the Oakland 'Ebonics' Issue." January 3, 1997, Chicago. Reprinted in a number of collections, including Theresa Perry and Lisa Delpit, *The Real Ebonics Debate: Power, Language, and the Education of African-American Children,* 160–61. Boston: Beacon Press, 1998 and in John Baugh, *Beyond Ebonics: Linguistic Pride and Racial Prejudice,* 117–18. New York: Oxford University Press, 2000.

Madhubuti, Haki. 1969. "In a Period of Growth." In *Don't Cry Scream.* Detroit: Broadside Press.

Morrison, Toni. "A Conversation with Toni Morrison: 'The Language Must Not Sweat.'" By Thomas LeClair, *New Republic,* March 21, 1981, 25–29.

Reed, Ishmael. 1970. *19 Necromancers From Now.* New York: Doubleday.

Riechmann, Deb. "Furor Over Black English Grows." *Detroit Free Press,* December 25, 1996.

Rickford, John R., and Russell J. Rickford. 2000. *Spoken Soul: The Story of Black English.* New York: John Wiley.

Smitherman, Geneva. 2000. *Talkin That Talk: Language, Culture and Education in African America*. New York: Routledge.

Sowell, Thomas. "Black English (ebonics) Is An Obsolete White Dialect." *Detroit News,* January 19, 1997.

Turner, Lorenzo Dow. 1949. *Africanisms in the Gullah Dialect*. Chicago: University of Chicago Press.

Williams, Robert L., ed. 1975. *Ebonics: The True Language of Black Folks*. St. Louis: Robert L. Williams and Associates.

Williams, Walter. "Ebonics Talk Has No Ties to Any African Heritage." *Detroit Free Press,* December 26, 1996.

2

Enslaved Women as Autobiographical Narrators: The Case of Louisa Picquet

Joycelyn K. Moody

As a rule, autobiography scholars ignore narratives dictated by enslaved men and women. They argue that because illiterate slaves could not control how their lives were reconstructed or represented, the narrative accounts of their lives amount merely to acts of "literary ventriloquism," in one unfortunate phrase, or they amount to "black messages inside white envelopes," to cite a second.[1] Consequently, these scholars disregard details about slavery presented by thousands of Black people who lived in bondage between 1760 and 1865. In my own work, I am unwilling to disregard what dictated slave narratives have to offer us, even if they pose difficult, even sometimes insurmountable, issues for literary critics.

In this essay, I focus on the rhetorical situation implicit in *Louisa Picquet, The Octoroon,* a slave narrative dictated in 1859 to Rev. Hiram Mattison, pastor of Union Chapel in New York. This extraordinary text (1861/1988) illuminates critical differences between men and women, between free people and bound people, between victims and agents, between White persons and Black persons, between literate and "illiterate," between orality and literacy, and finally between spirituality and physicality. Mattison's representations of his own rhetoric contrast sharply with his representations of Picquet's rhetoric, elucidating differences between what Ann duCille calls "discourse and dat course" (1996, 120–35). Specifically, the contrasts reveal the relationships of slaves' "ethnic rhetoric" to race, gender, and religion; to the U.S. abolitionist movement; and to politics and power imbalances operative across the spectrum of antebellum American life.

Before I turn to *Louisa Picquet, The Octoroon*, however, let me try to articulate what I find to be the crucial issues in the study of dictated slave narratives. First, there is the question of who controls the narrative: the bound narrator or the free interlocutor? Can a person confined to orality accurately be said to control a written text? Then there is the matter of the extent to which a slave narrator can "disrupt" the figure of slavery as the amanuensis draws it. Given that an amanuensis finally determines, inscribes, and edits the contents of a text, can an illiterate person be said to influence the text in any meaningful way? Third, to what extent do slave narrators and amanuenses share a common language? To the degree that the two are separated by such fundamental chasms as freedom and self-possession, can readers rightly assume that the discourse of the one obtains as the discourse of the Other?

What especially interests me as I formulate such questions is precisely how much they privilege literacy. That is, the very questions I am inclined to pose as a veteran literary critic betray our discipline's privileging of literacy over orality. An article by Sam Worley (1997) on the 1853 dictated slave narrative of Solomon Northup illustrates the case. Worley begins his essay by condemning the scholarly practice of neglecting dictated narratives simply because the slaves who dictated them were illiterate. He argues that were it self-authored, Northup's autobiography would not have been "treated as a narrative of the second rank" (243). And yet as he continues, Worley himself unwittingly privileges literacy, as when he argues, "The act of *writing* the narrative becomes the ultimate act of self-redemption, for by *writing* of his own origins the ex-slave can make himself his own author in a sense. . . . The act of reflecting on and representing moments of victimization or subjection allows the author to master them, to make them, at least symbolically, the effects of his own consciousness" (246, my emphasis). Ultimately, I hope to establish that Louisa Picquet's "mastery" over moments of vulnerability and victimization in her life does not depend on her own ability literally to inscribe her story.

In a way not unlike Worley, DoVeanna Fulton (1998) unfortunately ends up implying that the failure of Picquet's project lies in its narrator's lack of literacy. This development is highly ironical, for Fulton focuses on the triumph of orality in Picquet's narrative (98). No less than literate women, her article "Speak Sister, Speak" argues, illiterate women "employed verbal communication and orality to exert authorial control within a discourse that would normally exclude them" (98). Fulton persuasively explicates the primacy of orality—*telling,* or as I prefer to think of it, *tattling*—as a key concept in Picquet's story. She rightly insists that "if one carefully examines [dictated] texts, there are spaces and tensions, which I term windows of opportunity, that contain moments of orality or oral resistance in which the nonliterate freedwoman wrests narrative agency from the amanuensis and creates a subjective representation" (102). Yet in the end her essay is unconvincing because it relies too much on a *reading* of Mattison's text; that is, the essay privileges Mattison's skill over that of Picquet, though it explicitly says one should not. Moreover, Fulton concedes that despite "Picquet's empowerment through oral resistance, the agency in her oral narrative is problematized by the fact that *Louisa Picquet* is ultimately written by the amanuensis" (102). Another feminist critic, Shelli Fowler (1997), must make a similar confession—er, concession. Fowler's deployment of rhetorical and linguistic theory is inadequate to prove her contention that the text "ultimately grant[s] agency and authority to the historically black female slave" (470). These critical studies manifest the same double bind in which I find myself caught as I struggle to articulate the complexities of Picquet's story and my concurrence that Picquet manipulates Mattison into producing a narrative the multivalency of which he himself cannot discern.

Ironically, at the root of my project is a desire to dismantle the foundations of *literary* studies inasmuch as they constitute *literacy* studies. I want to take issue with Black feminist scholars like Jacqueline Jones Royster (2000), who has brilliantly shown the importance of literacy to enslaved women, and cogently argued for early Black women's arduous, steadfast pursuit of literacy. As a rhetoric scholar, Royster has proved that bound women "recognized that literacy was a skill, a talent, an ability appropriate to their new environment [in the New World]" (114), and that after Emancipation Black women brandished the tools of literacy in splendid ways to insert themselves into American life and society. And yet I think stubbornly of Toni Morrison's *Beloved* (1987), which posits Sethe Suggs as evidence of enslaved women who perceived the devastation that the hieroglyphics of alleged intellectuals like schoolteacher could cause. Sethe's haunting echo, "I made the ink" (271), attests to her horror at the idea of her complicity in literacy's hold on Black people. The fictive Sethe functions as ancestor to the real women interviewed by social scientist Patricia Hill Collins in *Black Feminist Thought* (1990). Collins joins Morrison in depicting the many African-American women who remain(ed) suspicious of literacy well into the present, both disdainful and mistrustful of the capacity of the written word to document their truths with precision and faithfulness. These Black women scorn literacy and invest instead in the survival of an African-American oral tradition. Among them, "book learning and written documents are believed to be limited in what they can convey and teach" (Smitherman 1994, 8), especially when it comes to Black women's experiences. In short, as one of my colleagues has wryly observed, what I am really about is putting myself out of business as a literary critic.

Let me turn now to Picquet's autobiography, which Mattison published in 1861, the same year as the appearance of the now better known *Incidents in the Life of a Slave Girl,* by Harriet Ann Jacobs. Like Jacobs' narrative, Picquet's documents issues such as estranged motherhood, familial loss, physical brutality, and psychosexual abuse within the context of slavery. Unlike Jacobs, Picquet was forced to rely on a White man's sympathy and morality to verbalize slavery's unspeakable acts. However, the resultant narrative, riddled with the narrator's authorial anxiety and self-protective obfuscation, shows the figure of Mattison to be as lecherous and prurient as Dr. Flint, the man who harasses the eponymous Slave Girl in *Incidents*. Moreover, he proves an unreliable author whose rhetorical skill Picquet must alternately trust, deflect, and extort. Although Mattison emphasizes the linguistic differences between himself and his subject, Picquet clearly hopes both (1) that she and her amanuensis speak the same language and (2) that she can manipulate him into transcribing a discourse that he cannot comprehend.

"Black" Talk

Geneva Smitherman has described the discourses of African Americans as cross-cultural: "Black Talk crosses boundaries—of sex, age, region, religion, social class" (1994, 2). I find that in *Louisa Picquet,* Black talk crosses additional boundaries of race, gender, and caste. The narrative constitutes Mattison's (1861/1988) interlocution of Picquet's speech. As mediated discourse, it verifies Smitherman's claim concerning the transmutability of Black talk. Yet because the text is mediated through and by Mattison, Picquet's speech is his, not hers. That is, although the text allegedly consists of Picquet's own Black talk, the abolitionist emphasizes his control over that talk and the crucial differences between his verbality and her orality.

One of the chief ways that Mattison (1861/1988) distinguishes himself from Picquet is by delineating their speech patterns differently. For example, he sometimes uses a question-and-answer format to tell Picquet's story; thus, he insinuates the authenticity of his interviews with the ex-slave. In these sections Mattison consistently represents his own speech in standard English and Picquet's in so-called Black dialect. Her transcribed speech abounds with subject–verb disagreements, contractions, and dropped final consonants. At the beginning of the narrative, Mattison explains that although Picquet's physical appearance may lead one to regard her as White and thus free, her formerly enslaved status becomes unmistakable when she speaks. He writes: "But a few minutes' conversation with her will convince almost any one that she has, at least, spent most of her life in the South. A certain menial-like diffidence, her plantation expression and pronunciation, her inability to read or write, together with her familiarity with and readiness in describing plantation scenes and sorrows, all attest to the truthfulness of her declaration that she has been most of her life a slave" (5). Thus, he locates bondage not only in what he deems a servile demeanor and a predilection for lambasting slavery but also in a Southern accent, in a regional dialect, and in illiteracy as well. So, she might look as White as he does, but, he underscores, she is not. His emphasis on her "readiness" to describe her life in slavery seems intended to substantiate both the self-portrait she offers and his relentless questioning. That is, he assures us that we can trust the words he attributes to her because she shares the abolitionist's desire to enumerate slavery's atrocities. His description of her servility, measured by her orality, provides any necessary authentication of her enslaved status, her honest testimony, and his own accurate I-witnessing.

I do not mean to imply that Mattison (1861/1988) casts Picquet's speech in the kind of gross dialect that Harriet Beecher Stowe deployed for Black characters in *Uncle Tom's Cabin*. To briefly illustrate the dropped consonants he repeatedly gives her, I refer to the story of Mary White, another former slave whose escape story Picquet inserts into her own.[2] Picquet concludes the embedded narrative by reporting that she "got a couple of letters from [Mary], returning thanks to us all for helpin' her on her way" (29). Mattison lops off the *g* at the end of *helping,* as if to remind readers that he *heard* the assertion, that it was dictated (thus oral, thus unlettered). In this way he underscores the irony of Picquet's reference to Mary's letters, which imply a (Black) readership that does not include her. For although Picquet presumably cannot read Mary's letters, it stands to reason that someone among "us all" *is* literate, or Mary would not have written to them. That Mary's letters may have been dictated to or read by a White person is another issue.

To be sure, however, Mattison's (1861/1988) reconstruction of Picquet's life does include a series of letters the bondswoman received from her mother, Elizabeth, but which Mattison maintains were actually written by a White person. These letters, too, form an embedded narrative within Picquet's story, and add yet another level of mediation to the text. In the first of the letters, dated March 8, 1859, Elizabeth grieves not having heard from her daughter:

> I a gane take my pen in hand to drop you a few lines. I have written to you twice, but I hav not yet received an answer from you[.] I can not imagin why you do not writ[e.] I feel very much troubel I fear you hav [not] recived my letters or you would hav written. . . . (30)

Mattison contradicts the mother's assertion that she has taken "pen in hand" to write her daughter. He counters that "The letter is, of course, written by some white person, and is printed exactly as it is written" (32). Furthermore, when Picquet says that on receiving Elizabeth's March 8 letter, "Then I wrote a letter," Mattison parenthetically corrects the alleged direct discourse with the note that Picquet instead "got one written" (32). He seems to take every textual opportunity to accentuate the differences between himself and his subject, to remind readers of Picquet's limited literacy and of her dependence on his mediation. In addition, an ironical elitism undercuts Mattison's claim that "some white person" wrote the mother's letters directed to Louisa. Though the reconstruction of Louisa Picquet's life bears his name, Mattison attributes Elizabeth's letter(s) to Picquet as written not by herself but by an anonymous and unskilled White person. Does he mean to imply that Louisa Picquet's autobiography by his hand is better than Elizabeth's letter(s) because he makes his identity known, whereas his White counterpart does not? Or does he rather intend the statement to critique Elizabeth's illiteracy, or more precisely, to critique the slaveocracy's laws responsible for her illiteracy?

"Who's Zoomin' Who?"

Despite Mattison's (1861/1988) emphasis on his own privileges in contrast to those of Picquet, literacy chief among them, it is Louisa Picquet who ends up rhetorically besting her interlocutor. Although it is arguable that the author of *Louisa Picquet* purposefully shows the former slave woman as smarter than himself, such a reading depends on attributing to Mattison a humility that the text does not sustain. Instead, Picquet's Black talk, her verbal dexterity is lost on the arrogant Mattison. For example, Chapter 5 eloquently illuminates the difference between privileged persons and subjugated ones. Very few critics have analyzed this narrative, but virtually all of those few have concentrated on Chapter 5, because of its clear and inadvertent depictions of the Rev. Mattison's sexual deviance.[3] Yet, although Mattison strives to get Picquet to detail her concubinage, what emerges is not a struggle between the privileged and the powerless. Instead, the chapter illustrates the broad (rhetorical) power that an "illiterate" Black woman *can* wield over a literate White man.

In Chapter 5, Picquet slyly corrects Mattison's depiction of her as sexual victim. She redirects his invasive questions and invalidates his presumptions about (read stereotypes of) enslaved women. In the text's most glaring example of Mattison's transgressive inquiry, Picquet recounts being whipped by her master after evading his efforts to lure her, at age thirteen, into his bed. Arguably seeking to depict the interconnections of psychic dominance, sexual violence, and physical brutality that enslaved women suffered, Mattison asks Picquet to describe the beating, and in the process he crosses the line between propriety and impropriety:

Q. —"Well, how did he whip you?"

A. —"With the cowhide."

Q. —"Around your shoulders, or how?"

A. —"That day he did."

Q. —"How were you dressed—with thin clothes, or how?"

A. —"Oh, very thin; with low-neck'd dress. In the summertime we never wore but two pieces—only the one under, and the blue homespun over. It is a striped cloth they make in Georgia just for the colored people." (12)

Mattison is apparently frustrated by Picquet's deft digression from talk of her lascivious owner to chitchat about the attire worn by Georgia's bondspeople. His next question is, "Did he whip you hard, so as to raise marks?" and later, "Did he cut through your skin?" (12, 13) To conclude the chapter, Mattison transcribes Picquet's report that the slaver "came to me in the ironin'-room, downstairs, where I was, and whip me with the cowhide, naked, so I 'spect I'll take some of the marks with me to the grave" (14–15). But the horror of this disclosure is not enough for the interlocutor, who parenthetically notes, "[Here Mrs. P. declines explaining further how he whipped her, though she had told our hostess where this was written; but it is too horrible and indelicate to be read in a civilized country.]" (15). Mattison's allusion to delicacy and decorum ironically document his own depravity. Moreover, he seems oblivious to Picquet's obfuscation of his invasive inquiry. Indeed, the passage goes a long way toward establishing the ability of the ex-slavewoman to subvert the lascivious rhetorical intentions of the powerful, free White man.

Picquet's signifyin' act argues also for the power of orality to conceal what literacy would coarsely expose. Geneva Smitherman has located the genesis of this kind of Black verbal subversion "in enslavement, where it was necessary to have a language that would mean one thing to Africans but another to Europeans. Forced to use the English of Ole Massa, Africans in enslavement had to devise a system of *talking* to each other about Black affairs and about the MAN right in front of his face" (1994, 26, my emphasis). There's irony, of course in the fact that the obtuse Mattison is not a slaveholder but an abolitionist, so it seems absurd that Picquet would (have to) engage in double-speak when narrating her story to him. But their power struggle for control over the narrative is, from the beginning, one of the text's signature features. For as Gillian Whitlock writes in her study of women's autobiography, *The Intimate Empire* (2000), "By convention an amanuensis remains unnamed, appropriately so in that the appearance of a proper name on the title page suggests authorship, the cohering of identity and style of narration" (18). Yet Mattison's name on the title page of an "autobiography" called *Louisa Picquet* verifies his desire to possess—to control—her story. The redundancy of avowals of authorship in titles that emphatically end in "Written by Herself" or "Written by Himself" illustrates enslaved people's anxiety about self-possession amid self-representation. Mattison's inattention to such a convention ironically divulges his vying for power over the slave narrative under his name.

Examining the psychosexual abuse that one enslaved woman endured and that her amanuensis was thus compelled to transcribe, Whitlock asks, "How is decency preserved here?" She concludes that, "The constraints of what might be said and heard [within the confines of both accuracy and civility] were figured out right there in the intimacy of the narrator-amanuensis relationship" (2000, 20). What a stunning contrast to Mattison's barely concealed efforts to unveil Picquet and expose the wounds she suffered as a pretty pubescent girl. Clearly, Mattison lacks any comprehension that "The relationship between the amanuensis and narrator, ear and voice [,] must be carefully managed, for the distinctions between permissible entrance into the ear and invasive impropriety are subtle" (21). Ultimately, antebellum (White) readers forced Louisa Picquet and countless other enslaved women who spoke their life stories into print to expose the literal marks of slavery etched onto their bodies. For all her verbal machinations, for all that she *would* not say to Mattison, there are some things Picquet must have known she could *not* say. She would have needed to demonstrate "her abiding concern with self-respect and privacy" (Castronovo 1999, 44). However modest she may have been, naturally or culturally, Picquet clearly knew that by answering Mattison's grotesque questions about the sexual violations perpetrated on her own body and her mother's (and the other slavewomen whose stories she succinctly relates), she would risk alienating her readership, whose double standard salaciously demanded both her chastity (i.e., the sign of her worthiness as a True Woman) and her defilement (i.e., the sign of her authenticity as an enslaved woman). Until the reading public could gaze upon the textual representation of slavery writ familiarly upon her body, witnessed by a Northern, White man of God, her narrative lacks authenticity and Picquet fails as a "genuine article" of bound humanity. Her truthfulness depends on the turning of the amanuensis into spectator.

Worley defines a slave "as a creature whose life cannot be construed as a narrative, whose days and works are merely submoments of the master's biography and cannot be, according to the ideology of the slaveholder, meaningful or coherent in themselves" (1997, 245). When Mattison decides to transcribe Picquet's story—or better, when Picquet agrees to dictate her story to Mattison—she insists on the narrative structure that her life can have and on the primacy of her experience, in and outside of bondage. Although the "peculiar institution" of slavery robbed her life of the kind of coherence and control that slaveholders' lives possessed, her rehearsal of her life events restores the meaning with which she endowed her own experience. It may seem that as Mattison literally transcribes such moments, Picquet is mastered by the experiences, by her "owner," and by Mattison. But I hold that Picquet is never "victimized" because she understands all along the impropriety, injustice, immorality, and criminality of acts of violence visited on her by the slavers who held her and her family in bondage, who sold them and sold them apart from each other, and who attempted to sexually exploit her and so many other slave women. Counter to victimhood is agency, which depends not just on the capacity to resist oppression, but on the capacity to perceive and name it, as we see Picquet struggling to do in Mattison's written transcription of her oral autobiography.

Acknowledgments

For inestimable help with this paper, I offer thanks to members of my feminist writing group at the University of Washington: Professors Kathie Friedman, Caroline Chung Simpson, and Shirley J. Yee.

Notes

1. Both phrases were developed by Andrews. The first appears in *To Tell a Free Story* (1986, 35) and the second in "Narrating Slavery" (1997, 16).

2. It is convention of accounts bearing the name of a single slave to narrate the stories of multiple slaves. Cf. Jacobs, *Incidents in the Life of a Slave Girl, Written by Herself.*

3. Cf. Andrews, *To Tell a Free Story* (1986, 243–47), as well as the texts by Fulton (1998) and Fowler (1997).

Works Cited

Andrews, William L. 1997. "Narrating Slavery." In *Teaching African American Literature: Theory and Practice,* edited by Maryemma Graham et al., 12–30. New York: Routledge.

———. 1986. *To Tell a Free Story: The First Century of Afro-American Autobiography, 1760–1865.* Urbana: University of Illinois Press.

Andrews, William L., ed. 1988. *Memoir of Old Elizabeth. Six Women's Slave Narratives.* New York: Oxford University Press.

Castronovo, Russ. 1999. "Framing the Slave Narrative/Framing Discussion." In *Approaches to Teaching "Narrative of the Life of Frederick Douglass,"* edited by James C. Hall, 42–48. New York: MLA.

Collins, Patricia Hill. 1990. *Black Feminist Thought: Knowledge, Consciousness, and the Politics of Empowerment.* New York: Routledge.

duCille, Ann. 1996. *Skin Trade.* Cambridge, MA: Harvard University Press.

Fleischner, Jennifer. 1996. *Mastering Slavery: Memory, Family, and Identity in Women's Slave Narratives.* New York: New York University Press.

Fowler, Shelli B. 1997. "Marking the Body, Demarcating the Body Politic: Issues of Agency and Identity in *Louisa Picquet* and *Dessa Rose.*" *College Language Association Journal* 40 (4): 467–78.

Fulton, DoVeanna S. 1998. "Speak Sister, Speak: Oral Empowerment in *Louisa Picquet: The Octoroon.*" *Legacy* 15 (1): 98–103.

Jacobs, Harriet. 1988. *Incidents in the Life of a Slave Girl. Written by Herself,* edited by Valerie Smith. New York: Oxford University Press.

Mattison, H. 1861/1988. *Louisa Picquet, The Octoroon: Or Inside Views of Southern Domestic Life.* In *Collected Black Women's Narratives,* edited by Anthony Barthelemy. New York: Oxford University Press.

Morrison, Toni. 1987. *Beloved.* New York: Knopf.

Royster, Jacqueline Jones. 2000. *Traces of a Stream: Literacy and Social Change Among African American Women.* Pittsburgh: University of Pittsburgh Press.

Smitherman, Geneva. 1994. *Black Talk: Words and Phrases from the Hood to the Amen Corner.* Boston: Houghton Mifflin.

Whitlock, Gillian. 2000. *The Intimate Empire: Reading Women's Autobiography.* London: Cassell.

Worley, Sam. 1997. "Solomon Northup and the Sly Philosophy of the Slave Pen." *Callaloo* 20 (1): 243–59.

3

"Semblances of Civilization": Zitkala Sa's Resistance to White Education[1]

Jessica Enoch

As we open this twenty-first century, Native American literature still remains the red sheep, as it were, of the current multicultural diversity university. More than thirty years after Momaday's Pulitzer, it is not at all clear that red matters in the academic or day-to-day life of this country.

Arnold Krupat
"Red Matters"

Arnold Krupat's statement (2001, 657) challenges the multicultural ease that twenty-first-century educators may feel when they incorporate the work of Native-American writer Zitkala-Sa into their curriculums. Bringing Zitkala-Sa's autobiographical essays into the classroom is not difficult; she has already been officially inducted into the canon of American literature. Her three autobiographical essays, "Impressions of an Indian Childhood" (1900a), "The School Days of an Indian Girl" (1900c), and "An Indian Teacher among Indians" (1900b) appear in a number of contemporary anthologies and readers, including *The Heath Anthology of American Literature, The Norton Anthology of American Literature, American Local Color Writing 1880–1920,* and *Writing Lives: Exploring Literacy and Community.* Through these texts, present-day educators and students both teach and learn that Zitkala-Sa, or Gertrude Simmons Bonnin,[2] was a nineteenth-century Yankton Sioux; a student at the Quaker missionary school in Wabash, Indiana; a teacher at the

Carlisle Indian School; an activist for Indian causes; and a writer, whose work reflects, in the words of the *Heath,* her "struggles with issues of cultural dislocation and injustice" (Herzog 1998, 859). Collections like these prompt discussions of Zitkala-Sa's life and the exchanges she was forced to make as an off-reservation student and teacher. Her presence in these anthologies seems to be a positive step that signals the material effects of multiculturalism and the entrance of an Indian woman's work into the canon. But Krupat's statement, which opens my essay, troubles any complacency about multiculturalism as he calls on educators to conceive of pedagogical practices that would make her work "matter."

In this essay, I present a way for Zitkala-Sa's work to "matter" by recontextualizing her autobiographical essays so that twenty-first-century educators and students discover a much more politicized and resistant Zitkala-Sa than the one found in contemporary anthologies. When these texts decontextualize Zitkala-Sa's writings, they dilute the force of her work by not taking into account the political and cultural conversation in which Zitkala-Sa was engaged. Taken out of context and anthologized next to works like Crane's "The Open Boat," Frost's "Fire and Ice," and James's *Daisy Miller,* Zitkala-Sa's autobiographical essays recount her life on the reservation and her experience as both a student and a teacher at off-reservation boarding schools. But within its original context, her work presents itself in three controversial installments of the January, February, and March issues of the *Atlantic Monthly* in 1900 and engages in a popular and pressing debate concerning the education of Indian children—a debate that rarely left any discursive space for an Indian voice.

My argument here is that when Zitkala-Sa's writings are recontextualized, they do more than reflect her individual "struggles with cultural dislocation and injustice" as the *Heath* suggests. Instead, her work becomes an overt act of resistance to the dominant (i.e., "White") narratives that justified the off-reservation schooling system. Through her essays, Zitkala-Sa deploys her own rhetoric of resistance in which she inscribes her Indian ethnicity in opposition to and defiance of White educational narratives. In so doing, Zitkala-Sa argues for what Scott Lyons (2000) calls "rhetorical sovereignty," or "the inherent right and ability of [Indian] peoples to determine their own communicative needs and desires [. . .], to decide for themselves the goals, modes, styles, and languages of public discourse" and, in Zitkala-Sa's case, of education (449–450). Zitkala-Sa implicitly calls for the right of Native-American people to control how, where, and what they will learn when she asks her *Atlantic Monthly* audience to read the dominant educational script from an Indian perspective and to discontinue their support of White education for Indian students. But even though her essays level a strategic critique against White educational discourses for Indian students in general, they target one school's discourse more particularly—the discourse at Zitkala-Sa's former place of employment, the Indian Industrial School in Carlisle, Pennsylvania.[3]

When Zitkala-Sa moves toward rhetorical sovereignty in her essays by addressing and then undoing the dominant narratives that validated off-reservation schools, she had the Carlisle Indian school in mind. Zitkala-Sa received her off-reservation schooling at White's Manual Institute in Wabash, Indiana, but she was a teacher at Carlisle just one year before she published her essays in the *Atlantic Monthly* in 1900.[4] In addition, her letters to her fiancé Carlos Montezuma[5] indicate that Zitkala-Sa was not only frustrated with the school, its newspapers, and its president and founder, Colonel Richard Pratt, but that she was also troubled by Carlisle and Pratt as she wrote and published her essays. In her correspondences, she repeatedly mentions Pratt and the publications of the school, calling Pratt "woefully small" and "bigoted" (March 5, 1901) and writing that she "imagines Carlisle will rear up on its haunches" after one of her stories is published (Summer 1901). Her final autobiographical essay, "An Indian Teacher among Indians," compounds this connection as she alludes to the fact that it is her experience at Carlisle that has opened her eyes to the wrongs of Indian education:

> As months passed over me, I slowly comprehended that the large army of white teachers in Indian schools had a larger missionary creed than I had suspected. It was one which included self-preservation quite as much as Indian education. (1900b, 385)

Zitkala-Sa refrains from explicitly naming Carlisle in her autobiographical essays, but her personal letters and essays suggest that this particular school was the target of her critique. Because the off-reservation Indian School at Carlisle was undoubtedly the most successful and well known of these schools (Adams 1995, 51–59), Zitkala-Sa chose to take on a particularly important and prestigious force.

To investigate the ways in which Zitkala-Sa undoes or at least threatens to undo the master narrative of Indian education, I juxtapose Zitkala-Sa's autobiographical essays with the articles, anecdotes, and letters published in Carlisle's newspapers, the *Indian Helper* and the *Red Man*.[6] These publications promoted the school's program to "quietly, peacefully, surely and as rapidly as possible break down tribal barriers and induce the Indian to live with us as part of one great family" (*Indian Helper*, March 4, 1898).[7] By juxtaposing Zitkala-Sa's work with Carlisle's primary modes of communication, I illuminate the ways in which Zitkala-Sa's work stood in protest to Carlisle's educational rhetoric that legitimated, produced, and reproduced an education that was culturally destructive to its Indian students.

* * * * *

Begun in 1880 and headed by Pratt, Carlisle was the first of its kind—the prototype for all off-reservation schools in the United States. U.S. educational officials came to prefer schools like Carlisle over their on-reservation coun-terparts because at on-reservation schools, Indian children were in close prox-imity to their homes, and it was thought that anything taught to students during school hours was un-taught once the students went home. Carlisle's greatest pride and strength, then, was that it took the children off the reser-vation and relocated students in central Pennsylvania, thousands of miles from their homes on Western reservations. By distancing students from the tribal environment, Carlisle was able to meet the objectives of Indian school-ing, which were, according to Carlisle supporter O. B. Super, "to make of the Indians thrifty, industrious, capable, American citizens" (1895, 228). Carlisle met these objectives through pedagogical practices that "American-ized" Indian students, distanced them from their tribes, and civilized their "savage" ways. These goals littered the pages of the *Indian Helper* and the *Red Man*, where mantras such as "Kill the Indian; Save the man" and "Out of savagery into civilization and citizenship" informed readers of the "good" work Carlisle had accomplished.

Although these newspapers were geared toward three main audi-ences—current Carlisle students, alumni, and White readers—the patron-age of White readership was vitally important to Carlisle's success. If these White supporters chose not to sponsor the work done at schools like Carlisle, their discontent could persuade the government to alter educa-tional polices and funding allocations for Indian education. Even though the government had spent $45 million on the education of 20,000 Indian students from 1880 to 1900, there was a growing sense of unrest and doubt concerning the success of these institutions as the century came to its close (Adams 1995, 307). As J. W. Powell writes in his 1895 article, the time had come to assess whether or not Indian education was a success or failure:

> These experiments have now been going on a sufficiently long time to enable us to reach something like a clear conclusion as to whether any con-siderable proportion of the North American Indians may ever be expected to merge themselves into our American life as civilized men, or whether these agencies for educating and civilizing them will at most do only a good service for a few individuals—an inconsiderable number of the whole—and the great mass of Indians will be left gradually to disappear as civilization presses in around them in an ever-narrowing circle[.] (623)

As this quotation suggests, the turn of the century brought with it more ques-tions than support. Carlisle, of course, felt the brunt of this discontent and used its *Indian Helper* and *Red Man* to convince readers of the schools' worth, producing and reproducing a narrative that legitimated the work done at the school.

* * * * *

When Zitkala-Sa published her autobiographical essays in the *Atlantic Monthly,* she cut right to the heart of Pratt's project by speaking to his most important and indispensable audience—the White moneylenders and Indian education supporters. Zitkala-Sa offers her own Indian perspective to this critical readership as she asks them to engage in a side of the Indian educational debate with which they were not familiar:

> Perhaps my Indian nature is the moaning which stirs [the memories] now for their present record. But, however tempestuous this is within me, it comes out as the low voice of a curiously colored seashell, which is only for those ears that are bent with compassion to hear it. (1900c, 190)

By providing an Indian vantage point from which her "compassionate" readers could view White educational practices, Zitkala-Sa challenges Carlisle's educational strategy by countering three of the prevailing narratives that underpinned the school's objectives: the first, that the atmosphere at Carlisle can save the Indian child from the darkness and chaos of the reservation; the second, that Carlisle offers the student a better and more prosperous future; and the third, that Carlisle can transform its students from "savage" to "civilized." Her ultimate goal throughout her essays is to prove to her White readership that Indian people possess a worthy and valuable culture, even though it is different from that of the White world, and that Carlisle's form of cultural erasure extinguishes Indian cultural practices and social codes that are just as significant as those that Carlisle attempts to impose on its students.

The first educational narrative that Zitkala-Sa addresses is one that degrades Indian life by inscribing Carlisle as the hero that would rescue the Indian child from the "dark" and "barbarous" reservation. Carlisle's papers reflect this objective by continually advertising that it was the off-reservation school that provided the "ATMOSPHERE" that the Indian needs:

> The reservation is the cellar and the Indian boys and girls are the plants who are DYING for want of light. Carlisle says, carry the plant OUT into the light and ATMOSPHERE which breed English, industry and incentive. Carry it OUT where it will grow and gain strength and amount to something; where it will soon be able to hold its own head up and care for itself. (*Indian Helper,* August 30, 1895)

Carlisle uses this extended metaphor to create an ostensibly logical argument. Because the reservation is supposedly a place of darkness, chaos, and desolation, Indian children must be saved and put in a place where they will be able to "grow and gain strength, and amount to something." Such an appeal works to convince readers that the actions of the school are based on common sense: of course the Indian should be taken from the tribe; of course the Indian should be civilized. Thus, Carlisle uses what Terry Eagleton (1991) calls an "ideology of common sense"—an ideology which naturalizes certain practices by "creating as tight a fit as possible between itself [the common sense proposition] and social reality, thereby closing the gap into which the leverage of critique can be inserted" (58). Through its narratives, Carlisle creates an (almost) impermeable hegemonic notion of common sense that assumes that all Indians should leave their tribes and reservations to travel to the paradise known as Carlisle.

But as Zitkala-Sa's autobiographical essays show, Carlisle's schooling system was a far cry from what its narratives promised. Zitkala-Sa's private letters and public writings indicate that she was at odds with the most basic component of Carlisle's plan: that Indians should leave the reservation. She writes to Montezuma that she doesn't "exactly agree with Col. Pratt about the great superiority of non-reservation schools" because she believes that "[t]he *old folks* have a claim on us. It is selfish and cruel to abandon them entirely" (February 20, 1901). Here, Zitkala-Sa rejects White assimilationist plans to distance young Indians from their families and their heritage and implicitly argues for the preservation of Indian culture.

As Zitkala-Sa inscribes her own educational journey, on the pages of the *Atlantic Monthly,* she provides a counterargument to Carlisle's conviction that Indian children should be taken from their homes on the reservation. Zitkala-Sa's educational trajectory was not one from darkness into light, as Carlisle promises. Instead, she moved from a peaceful childhood filled with "bright clear days" where "the cool morning breezes swept freely through [her] dwelling, now and then wafting the perfume of sweet grasses from newly burnt prairie" (1900b, 40) to the chaotic atmosphere of the school, where the breakfast bell went "crashing through the belfry" in a "loud metallic voice" (1900c, 186). It was the "constant clash of harsh noises" and the "undercurrent of many voices murmuring an unknown tongue" which made the school "a bedlam within which [she] was securely tied" (186).

Zitkala-Sa's counternarratives speak to and disrupt her readers' ideological conceptions of both White and Indian culture. Her essays work through a particular problematic that Native-American scholar Gloria Bird addresses in her essay "Autobiography as Spectacle: An Act of Liberation or the Illusion of Liberation" (2000). Bird writes that "the difficulty of communicating is not so much a question of speaking across cultures so much as it is a problem of speaking across realities that are culture bound" (68). Zitkala-Sa deals with this "difficulty" by enabling her readers to realize the material effects of imposing one culture's values, specifically its educational values, on another. To move from speaking across cultures to speaking across culturally bound realities, Zitkala-Sa exposes her readers to the reality she experienced as an Indian student, and troubles dominant educational storylines that define what is good and right for Indian children.

After countering the idea that Indians should leave the reservation, Zitkala-Sa contests the narratives that declare that the off-reservation school provides the Indian with a better future than the one on the reservation. The conventional Carlisle success story found in the *Indian Helper* and the *Red Man* usually followed the general formula of this letter from a former Carlisle student:

> I am now working at a large store as bookkeeper and Assistant-Postmaster [. . .]. That is what a chap like me can do when he tries. I have been working here ever since my return from Carlisle. [. . .] I can thank Carlisle for what it has done for me, because it has done worlds of good to me. (*Indian Helper,* 26 June 1895)

Before Zitkala Sa published her essays, she too was one of Carlisle's success stories. Like it did for the student above, the *Indian Helper* celebrated the success of Zitkala-Sa, who was known by those at Carlisle as "Miss Simmons," writing that she "was of our corps of teachers a year ago and has since been taking a course of violin instruction at the Boston Conservatory. She is a fine violinist. If her interesting articles get into such papers as the Atlantic Monthly her reputation is along literary lines. [. . .] Thus the Indian is entering into the highest and best places. We are not content to be mediocre" (*Indian Helper,* November 3, 1899). Through narratives such as this, Carlisle proved that off-reservation schooling was the only sure way for the Indian to find a future of success.

Zitkala-Sa counters this claim by writing that although this was the only narrative that White readers and educators wanted to acknowledge, it was not the only one available for Indian students. In her second essay, "The School Days of an Indian Girl," Zitkala-Sa recounts the life her Indian education had provided for her:

> After my first three years of school, I roamed again in the Western country through four strange summers. During this time I seemed to hang in the heart of chaos, beyond the touch or voice of human aid. My brother, being almost ten years my senior, did not quite understand my feelings. My mother had never gone inside of a schoolhouse, and so she was not capable of comforting her daughter who could read and write. Even nature seemed to have no place for me. I was neither a wee girl nor a tall one; neither a wild Indian nor a tame one. This deplorable situation was the effect of my brief course in the East, and the unsatisfactory "teenth" in a girl's years. (1900c, 190–91)

Here, Zitkala-Sa writes of an education that did not give her entry or access to anything. Instead it distanced her from her tribe and made it impossible for her to live among her own people. A future of exile and displacement is all to which she looks forward.

Dorothea Susag (1993) seconds this assessment in her essay "Zitkala Sa (Gertrude Simmons Bonnin) A Power(full) Literary Voice," stating that because of her education Zitkala-Sa occupied a liminal space between the White and the Indian worlds:

> As a child of the nineteenth-century reservation system, she couldn't claim the freedom of a traditional Yankton landscape. As a child removed from her family and transplanted in a boarding school for three years, she couldn't claim the presence of her childhood home or family. As a mixed-blood studying and later working in the East, she couldn't claim the emotional or even the intellectual security of a home in the "White Man's ways." (6)

Susag's assessment here rings true. Zitkala-Sa's autobiographical essays tell of the tension she felt and the middle space that she occupied between Indian and White worlds. Zitkala-Sa's off-reservation education transformed her Indian home into a "deplorable situation," a foreign place to which she no longer belonged. Because of her education, she had "no place in nature" and existed in a comfortless space between "neither's" and "nor's," located somewhere on the borders of Whiteness and Indianness.

Finally, Zitkala-Sa challenges Carlisle's narrative that inscribed Indian savagery. Carlisle writes that "Indian heathenism is a poisonous and disgraceful element of our American home life, and whatever soils and corrupts the purity and integrity of our American home life ought to be either destroyed or put outside" (*Indian Helper,* March 1, 1895). To Carlisle, the off-reservation school was the only way for Indian children to learn what civilization and culture were. Accordingly, Carlisle taught its students "civilized" practices through the "Do's and Don'ts" sections of their newspapers. "Do we know that we should not do these things?" Carlisle asked. "It may be that we are awkward in our manners at table simply because we do not know any better. [. . .] Don't gurgle or draw in your breath with a spoonful of soup! Don't eat with your knife! Never put your knife in your mouth!" (*Indian Helper,* April 5, 1895). Carlisle, it would seem, was the Emily Post for Indian students, preparing them to enter civilly into White society.

In this part of the narrative, Carlisle sets up a simple dichotomy between White and Indian cultures. Carlisle "others" Indian culture by choosing particular cultural traits of Indian life and then transforming those traits into sites of "contestation, abuse, insult and discrimination" (Bhabba 1999, 16). Carlisle defines Indian life as bad, ignorant, and savage and situates White life and culture on the opposite side of the spectrum, (re)producing the idea that White is good, individual, and civilized. This dichotomy perpetuates the asymmetrical power relationship between Whites and Indians by reinforcing and reproducing beliefs about good, White heritage and, at the same time, degrading and devaluing Indian cultural narratives. With this dichotomy in tact, Carlisle composes a narrative guided by the story line of "noblesse oblige." It is Carlisle's social and moral obligation to fulfill its "duty" as an

American institution, to take pity on the Indian community, and to cleanse Indians of their "badness," "ignorance," and "savagery," raising this "degraded" class to what is "good," "civilized," and, of course, White. Indians are thus seen as the "pathology of the healthy society" that must be cured by the medicine of Carlisle's education before they can enter into the White world (Freire 1998, 55). Anything good that comes from an Indian, Carlisle implicitly argues, must have come from education and exposure to White society.

But Zitkala-Sa responds to this narrative by reversing the White = civilized, Indian = savage script. Zitkala-Sa asserts that her Indian home life was marked by art, etiquette, and social code—a cultural world Carlisle's narrative chose to ignore. At home as a child, Zitkala-Sa did not "run wild," as Carlisle would promote. Erasing the image of the Indian savage, Zitkala-Sa inscribes her mother as a skilled artist who gave Zitkala-Sa "lessons in the art of beadwork" and "spread upon a mat beside her bunches of colored beads just as an artist arranges the paints upon his palette" (1900a, 40). And just as Carlisle has its "Do's and Don'ts" for White culture; so too, Zitkala-Sa argues, does Indian tribal life. Zitkala-Sa writes of her home traditions, recalling the daily practices in which her mother would cordially invite the neighboring old men and women to eat supper after which would come the "time when old legends were told" (1900a, 38). Zitkala-Sa informs her readers that there was a particular etiquette to asking: "My mother used to say to me, [. . .]: 'Wait a moment before you invite any one. If other plans are being discussed, do not interfere, but go elsewhere'" (39). Here, Zitkala-Sa relays to her readers that Indian culture mandated particular social rules concerning any conversation, interruption, and invitation.

In these instances, Zitkala-Sa's essays resist the dominant discourses that presumed everything Indian is savage. Her personal experiences reveal and then break down the false dichotomies that produce and reproduce asymmetrical power relations that legitimate White control of Indian lives. By setting these contradictory narratives against Carlisle's expected and accepted narrative, Zitkala-Sa calls her *Atlantic Monthly* readers to reconsider their view of Indian life and their support of Indian education.

* * * * *

In her first two essays, Zitkala-Sa uses the stories of her life to challenge Carlisle's narratives. It is not until her final essay, though, that Zitkala-Sa reaches her ultimate goal and asks her readers to reflect on and change their own practices. In "An Indian Teacher Among Indians," Zitkala-Sa writes, "I remember how, from morning till evening, many specimens of civilized peoples visited the Indian school" (1900b, 386). These visitors "boast[ed] of their charity to the North American Indian" and were "well satisfied: they were educating the children of the red man!" (388). Speaking directly to an audience that may have done such boasting, Zitkala-Sa poignantly asks her readers to reflect on her autobiographical accounts and then "[pause] to question whether real life or long-lasting death lies beneath this semblance of civilization" (388). Nowhere in her writings is Zitkala-Sa more clear and direct than in these final words. Here, she defines what seems to be the enlightened and invaluable process of Indian education as a mere "semblance of civilization" and asks her readers to consider exactly what it is that White education is offering Indian students: real life or long-lasting death. After reading Zitkala-Sa's sketches, her readers could only answer that Indian education offers nothing but the latter.

Not surprisingly, Carlisle responded strategically to Zitkala-Sa's work, dedicating space in at least three issues of the *Indian Helper* and the *Red Man* to silence and contain Zitkala-Sa's words. All of Carlisle's responses sounded much like the following critique:

> All that Zitkalasa has in the way of literary ability and culture she owes to the good people, who, from time to time, have taken her into their homes and hearts and given her aid. Yet not a word of gratitude or allusion to such kindness on the part of her friends has ever escaped her in any line of anything she has written for the public. By this course she injures herself and harms the educational work in progress from which she sprang. In a list of educated Indians we have in mind, some of whom have reached higher altitudes in literary and professional lines than Zitkalasa, we know of no other case of such pronounced morbidness. (*Red Man*, April 12, 1901)

Such overt attempts to delegitimate her essays prove that Zitkala-Sa had intervened in and disrupted Carlisle's educational narrative. These writings were not the end to Zitkala-Sa's resistance though; she had just begun her life's work as a political activist.[8]

Through these initial autobiographical essays, Zitkala-Sa found an outlet which enabled her to enter a public space not regulated by Carlisle and speak out against the injustices she saw in Indian education. Zitkala-Sa used her life's events to persuade the White community to discontinue its support of off-reservation schooling by showing how this educational program discards a valuable and worthy Indian culture. Not only did Zitkala-Sa disrupt the seemingly seamless narrative that Carlisle constructed, but she also enacted an instance of rhetorical sovereignty by using her autobiographical essays to argue for the right of Indians to control their own schooling. If, as Victor Villanueva states (1993, 21), rhetoric is both how hegemonies are maintained and how they are countered, then Zitkala-Sa counters Carlisle's hegemonic rhetoric through her own rhetoric of resistance that both claims and legitimates Indian culture, civilization, and life.

Acknowledging that Zitkala-Sa's essays are acts of resistance is imperative for educators and students discussing her work today. Zitkala-Sa's simple presence in today's anthologies cannot be enough because, as Vine Deloria

(1970) argues, educators cannot feel "they have done justice to the group concerned" by simply "emphasizing that Black is beautiful or that Indians have contributed the names and rivers to the road map" (38). Instead of simply throwing down the multiculturalism card and embracing differences in race, ethnicity, class, gender, sexual preference, religion, age, and physical ability, educators need to work toward what Keith Gilyard (1997) calls a transcultural education in which they ask themselves and their students to engage these differences in more meaningful ways (325). By taking up this transcultural pedagogical vision, educators would make Zitkala-Sa's work *matter* by pronouncing, rather than ignoring, the ways she reconfigured the terms of the educational debate and made space for narratives of her own that refuted the common-sense claims about Indian life. Through such a stance, educators and students would be called to question what it means when Zitkala-Sa's work is placed next to that of other "great" American writers like James, Frost, and Crane without discussing the systematic silencing that accompanied Zitkala-Sa's literary and political endeavor. Finally, both educators and students would make connections between Zitkala-Sa's educational battles and the educational battles waged by Indian teachers and students today by interrogating the semblances of civilization that attempted (and attempt) to erase Indian life and culture both then and now.

Notes

1. An expanded version of this chapter appeared in the November 2002 issue of *College English*.

2. Zitkala-Sa was known for most of her life as Gertrude Simmons. When she began her literary career, she took on the Indian name she chose for herself: Zitkala-Sa, which translates into "Red Bird." She later returned to Gertrude Simmons and then took her husband's name, becoming Gertrude Simmons Bonnin.

3. My use of "Carlisle" in this essay signifies the forces that drove the educational imperatives at the Carlisle Indian School, the most influential of these forces being Carlisle's founder, Colonel Richard Pratt.

4. For comprehensive biographies on Zitkala-Sa's life, see Doreen Rappaport, *The Flight of Red Bird* (New York: Puffin, 1999); P. Jane Hafen, Introduction (*Dreams and Thunder: Stories, Poems and The Sun Dance Opera*. By Zitkala-Sa. Ed. P. Jane Hafen. Lincoln: University of Nebraska Press, 2001) and "Gertrude Simmons Bonnin: For the Indian Cause" (*Sifters: Native American Women's Lives:* Ed. Theda Perdue. New York: Oxford University Press, 2001); Dexter Fisher, Foreword (*American Indian Stories*. By Zitkala-Sa. Lincoln: University of Nebraska Press, 1985).

5. Zitkala-Sa and Montezuma were engaged, but they never married. Their letters indicate that Zitkala-Sa broke the engagement because she wanted to live on the Indian reservation, whereas Montezuma chose to live and practice medicine in Chicago. Reasons for their split are evidenced in this March 1901 letter to Montezuma: "I do not want to demoralize you! I had no thoughts of limiting your

ambition. Perhaps the Indians are not human enough for you to waste your skill upon! Stay in Chicago. Do!" They did not break their engagement, though, until 1902.

6. These papers were both printed on site at Carlisle. O. B. Super writes in his 1895 article, "Indian Education at Carlisle" that "A characteristic of the school is the printing-office, which has always been regarded as one of the most valuable departments of the school. Under the editorial supervision of a woman, the pupils publish two papers, the *Red Man,* an eight-page quarto, with a monthly circulation of about two thousand copies, and the *Indian Helper,* a small four-page weekly, with a circulation of over ten thousand copies" (230).

7. I have received permission to quote from the *Indian Helper* and the *Red Man* from the Cumberland County Historical Society in Carlisle, Pennsylvania.

8. Zitkala-Sa spent the rest of her life lecturing and campaigning across the country discussing such issues as Indian education and citizenship, employment of Indians in the Bureau of Indian Affairs, equitable settlement of the tribal land claims, and stabilization of laws relating to Indians (Fisher 1985, xv). In 1916, she was elected to the Society of the American Indian, an organization that "sought redress for the multitudes of inequities they had suffered" (xv) and edited the *American Indian Magazine* from 1918 to 1919. She also founded her own political organization, the National Council of American Indians, in 1926, serving as president until her death in 1938.

Works Cited

Adams, David Wallace. 1995. *Education for Extinction: American Indians and the Boarding School Experience 1875–1928.* Lawrence: University of Kansas Press.

Bhabba, Homi. 1999. Interview. "Staging the Politics of Difference: Homi Bhabba's Critical Literacy." In *Race, Rhetoric and the Postcolonial,* edited by Lynn Worsham and Gary Olson, 3–39. Albany: State University of New York Press.

Bird, Gloria. 2000. "Autobiography as Spectacle: An Act of Liberation or the Illusion of Liberation." In *Here First,* edited by Arnold Krupat and Brian Swann, 63–74. New York: Modern Library.

Deloria, Vine. 1970. *We Talk, You Listen: New Tribes, New Turf.* New York: MacMillan.

Eagleton, Terry. 1991. *Ideology: An Introduction.* London: Verso.

Fisher, Dexter. 1985. Foreword. *American Indian Stories.* By Zitkala-Sa, v–xx. Lincoln: University of Nebraska Press.

Freire, Paulo. 1998. *Pedagogy of the Oppressed.* New Revised 20th Anniversary Edition. Trans. Myra Bergamn Ramos. New York: Continuum.

Gilyard, Keith. 1997. "Cross-Talk: Toward Transcultural Writing Classrooms." In *Writing in Multicultural Settings,* edited by Carol Serverino, Juan C. Guerra, and Johnella E. Butler, 325–31. New York: Modern Language Association.

Herzog, Kristin. 1998. Foreword. "Gertrude Simmons Bonnin (Zitkala-Sa)." *Heath Anthology of American Literature.* 3rd ed. Vol. 2, edited by Paul Lauter. Boston: Houghton Mifflin.

Indian Helper. March 4, 1898.

———. March 1, 1895.

———. April 5, 1895.

———. April 12, 1895.

———. August 30, 1895.

———. June 26, 1985.

———. November 3, 1899.

Krupat, Arnold. 2001. "Review: Red Matters." *College English* 63 (5): 655–61.

Lyons, Scott Richard. 2000. "Rhetorical Sovereignty: What Do American Indians Want from Writing?" *College Composition and Communication* 51 (3): 447–67.

Powell, J. W. 1895. "Proper Training and the Future of the Indians." *Forum* (February): 622–52.

Super, O. B. 1895. "Indian Education at Carlisle." *New England Magazine* 18 (April): 224–39.

Susag, Dorothea M. 1993. "Zitkala-Sa (Gertrude Simmons Bonnin): A Power(full) Literary Voice." *Studies in American Indian Literature* 5: 3–24.

The Red Man. February 1900.

Villanueva, Victor. 1993. *Bootstraps: From an American Academic of Color*. Urbana, IL: National Council of Teachers of English.

Zitkala-Sa. 1900a. "Impressions of an Indian Childhood." *Atlantic Monthly* (January): 37–47.

———. 1900b. "An Indian Teacher Among Indians." *Atlantic Monthly* (March): 381–86.

———. 1900c. "The Schooldays of an Indian Girl." *Atlantic Monthly* (February): 185–94.

———. Letter to Carlos Montezuma. March 5, 1901. The Papers of Carlos Montezuma. Wilmington, DE: Scholarly Resources, 1983.

———. Letter to Carlos Montezuma. Summer 1901. The Papers of Carlos Montezuma. Wilmington, DE: Scholarly Resources, 1983.

4

Extending the Hand of Empire: American Indians and the Indian Reform Movement, a Beginning

Malea Powell

This essay is a part of an ever-growing project on Indians and Reform in the late nineteenth century in which I look both at Euro-American reform discourse and at the responses to and negotiations of that discourse offered by Sarah Winnemucca Hopkins, Charles Alexander Eastman, Susan LaFlesche Picotte, and Andrew Blackbird, all prominent Native people who had extended interactions with Eastern reformers. What follows is less an extended rhetorical analysis than a brief tour through some of the historical materials which connect two of the sites from my larger project—the Women's National Indian Association and Susan LaFlesche Picotte. The result of this tour is, I think, a beginning—a basic investigation of the rhetorical relationship between these reformers and this Indian which hints at a broader understanding of the more complicated relationships produced in the interactions between reformers and Indians in the late nineteenth century; and, the first inklings of a theory about how the indigenous peoples of North America survived the extended hand of empire proffered by these reformers, the "friends of the Indian."

This is a story.

In *The Rhetoric of Empire*, postcolonial studies scholar David Spurr (1996) claims that there are "particular languages" that belong to "the historical process of colonization" and that such languages—both generative and enabling—"are known collectively as colonial discourse" (1). For me and many other postcolonial critics, studying "colonial discourse" is an essential component in any study of resistance to that colonization. The focus point for much of that discursive energy during the last half of the nineteenth century in the United States was commonly referred to as "the Indian problem" or "the Indian question," and was a problem/question intimately related to a vision of America as abundant and bountiful, ripe for the enactment of the desires of those settlers and colonists who would constitute the new nation. This vision depended on settlers having access to as much land as they desired. The "problem," then, became the material contradiction of the indigenous peoples of North America who already lived on the land that had been ideologically declared empty and available.

This "problem" has its rhetorical beginnings in the beliefs of the seventeenth-century colonists, in what Roy Harvey Pearce (1988) calls "the Ideas, Symbols, and Images of Savagism and Civilization" that were imposed by Europeans and, later, Euro-Americans as a way to make sense out of the seeming chaos of the "new World" (xviii, 3). He writes:

> The colonial concern with the savage Indian was a product of the tradition of Anglo-French primitivistic thinking—an attempt to see the savage, the ignoble savage, as a European manqué. When, by the 1770's, the attempt had obviously failed, Americans were coming to understand the Indian as one *radically different* from their proper selves. . . . [so they] worked out a theory of the savage which depended on an idea of a new order in which the Indian could have no part. (4, emphasis mine)

Pearce (1988) emphasizes that this new "American" came to "know who and what he was and where he was going, to evaluate the special society in which he lived and to know its past and its future" most effectively through comparison with "the Indian who, as a savage, had all past and no future" (135). "The Indian," then, became a figure against which "the American" could be rendered from the raw materials of "the Euro-colonist," and rendered most effectively by making "the Indian" a thing of America's past. Pearce claims that pity and censure were the result of such Euroamerican renderings—pity at the Indian's passing; censure at his manifestly destined inability to be civilized.

The translation of pity and censure into policy can be seen in President Ulysses S. Grant's Peace Policy (1870). Although it is impossible within the scope of this essay to even begin to explain the breadth of U.S.–Indian policy in the nineteenth century, the general movement was from a strategy of extermination and/or removal to one of assimilation. Under the "peace policy," the attempt was made to force all Indian nations, even those exempt from removal by treaty agreement, onto reservations for their own "protection" and allowed religious groups (Quakers, Methodists, Presbyterians, etc.) control of appointments to both the Bureau (Office) of Indian Affairs (BIA) and the

Board of Indian Commissioners. This protectionism was justified as a humanitarian attempt to disrupt the unfair policies which had been visited on tribal communities by corrupt BIA officials (the Indian ring). These new Christian agents were also to provide the proper "example" of piety, private property, and agrarian work ethic necessary to convince Native peoples to "choose" civilization over "savagery." Like the scores of missionaries who preceded them, the reformers of the late nineteenth century most certainly believed that Christianity would lead the tribes to civilization, but prior to the peace policy, reform efforts "lacked the direction and leadership to implement Indian reform policies" (Mathes 1990, 6). In 1879, the visibility of Indian reform grew dramatically with the intense public interest in the Ponca tour.

The Ponca tour marks an important rhetorical moment for the discourse of Indian reform. In 1868, the federal government had created the Great Sioux Reservation and, in doing so, inadvertently included land previously reserved for the Poncas. The Poncas were then forced away from these lands and moved to Indian Territory (Oklahoma, 1877) where there was little food or housing. During the winter of 1879, Standing Bear, a Ponca leader, and thirty other Poncas tried to return to Nebraska, only to be stopped by federal troops and returned to Indian Territory where they were put on trial. The former abolitionist, Thomas Tibbles, heard about Standing Bear and quickly publicized his predicament in the Eastern press. By August of 1879, Tibbles had arranged an East coast lecture tour for Standing Bear and his "Indian Princess" advocate, Susette (Bright Eyes) LaFlesche (soon-to-be Tibbles), an Omaha/Ponca mixed-blood. The Ponca episode is doubly significant. First, it marks the entrance of "the Indian" into the public arena of Indian reform. Like the slave testimonies of the abolition movement, "real" Indian voices lent credence and urgency to reformist arguments and put a human face, one that could thus be made the object of pity and censure, on governmental policy decisions. No longer was the Indian simply "imagined" by the audiences of Eastern reformers; the Indian was present, a presence that signified the absence of thousands of others who had been removed from the arena of daily American life. Second, the Ponca tour prompted the formation of new reform groups like the Boston Indian Citizenship Committee (BICC), the Philadelphia-based Women's National Indian Association (WNIA), the Indian Rights Association (IRA), and the Lake Mohonk Friends of the Indian conference. It would be these new organizations, formed with a different rhetorical and material relationship to the presence of Indians in the reform community, who would participate in creating a series of reform polices that aggressively sought to break up tribal structures in order to draw Indians into the very bosom of the republic through private property, education, and Christian conversion.

An influential writer who had previously been uninterested in Indian affairs, Helen Hunt Jackson, was outraged over the treatment of the Poncas and became "a veritable one-person reform movement" (Prucha 1984, 627). Well-educated and outspoken, Jackson had close ties to the literati and publishers in Boston and New York. She heard Standing Bear speak while in Boston for the celebration of Dr. Oliver Wendell Holmes' seventieth birthday. Immediately inspired, she confessed to her good friend Thomas Wentworth Higginson that "I think I feel as you must have felt in the old abolition days. I cannot think of anything else from morning to night" (qtd. in Mathes 1990, 21). Jackson immediately began to pester her influential friends to hear Standing Bear and to support the Ponca cause. She also began a long-running feud with then Secretary of the Interior Carl Schurz, carried out mostly in newspaper editorials published in the *Tribune* and the *Boston Daily Advertiser*. Soon, Jackson's outrage extended to treatment of the Utes, the Cheyenne, and the Arapaho. She confessed to Charles Dudley Warner, co-proprietor and co-editor of the *Hartford Courant,* that she wanted to write "simply and curtly a Record of our Broken Treaties—& call it 'A Century of Dishonor' " (qtd. in Mathes 33). She claims that she "never so much as dreamed what we had been guilty of" in dealings with Indian nations and that she wanted "to awaken the conscience of America to the flagrant wrongs that had been perpetrated upon the Indians" (qtd. in Mathes 33; Prucha 1984, 627). She wrote *A Century of Dishonor* (1881) in seven months and spent two additional months gathering materials for the appendix. Jackson received a "wet copy" of *Century* in January of 1881 and distributed special copies of it to every congressman.

Century is a collection of narratives about past injustices, and Jackson herself claims that it is "only a sketch, and not a history," a sketch that will "show our causes for national shame in the matter of our treatment of the Indians" (7). It is also a nearly perfect example of the sentimental outrage and persuasive style which characterizes this period of reform writings. Native people are throughout portrayed as the "helpless" objects of the "dishonorable conduct" of the United States government (18, 27). Jackson introduces her study with a long argument about the "right of occupancy" of Indian peoples to the lands that contain the United States. Marshaling a host of "expert" opinions on such matters such as Peters' "United States Statutes at Large" (vii), Vattel, Hobbes, Grotius and others, and citing copiously from actual treaties and Supreme Court cases, Jackson uses the language of jurisprudence mixed with that of Christian morality to explain, in detail, "the shame of breaking national compacts, and the wickedness of the nations that dare to do it" (23). Her conclusion is, of course, that "[t]he history of the United States Government's repeated violations of faith with the Indians thus convicts us, as a nation, not only of having outraged the principles of justice, which are the basis of international law; and of having laid ourselves open to the accusation of both cruelty and perfidy; but also of having made ourselves liable to all punishments which follow upon such sins" (29). In other words, our national honor was at stake in how we dealt with a problem that was, according to Jackson, of our own making.

Jackson offers the ten historical sketches and lengthy appendix as proof of the "evil-doing" enacted by the Government on the "weak and helpless"

Indians. There is only one solution to this state of affairs for Jackson. She writes, "[t]he only thing that can stay this is a mighty outspoken sentiment and purpose of the great body of the people" (30), and thus presents "the record of the history of the Indians; every page and every year has its dark stain" (337) as an opportunity for the Congress to "cover itself with a lustre of glory, as the first to cut short our nation's record of cruelties and perjuries!" (31). Indians are to be given citizenship, education, and property (340–41)—the triumvirate solution of the reform movement—though she warns that this will not be enough, that statesmanship, philanthropy, and Christianity will have to work tirelessly to ensure these solutions are carried out in a way that is honorable and just (342). After the publication of *Century,* Jackson went to work on behalf of the Mission Indians of Southern California, continued to use her well-placed friends and associates to publicize her cause, and actually worked for the Indian Bureau gathering information about the situation of the Mission Indians. Her early death in 1885 made her a martyr to groups like the Women's National Indian Association.

The organization that would become the Women's National Indian Association (WNIA) was formed in 1879 in Philadelphia. The WNIA began as the Indian committee of the Women's Home Mission Society of the First Baptist Church, organized by Amelia Quinton and Mary Bonney. They, too, were outraged at the Ponca affair and "hoped to stir up the god-fearing people of the United States" by "reviving the old abolitionist tactic of presenting petitions to Congress" as a way to demand reforms in the Indian Bureau (Prucha 1984, 612; Hoxie 1984, 11). In June 1881, they changed their name to the Indian Treaty-keeping and Protective Association and in October of 1883 to the Women's National Indian Association. By 1883, this women's association had eighty-three national branches and a large contributions pool. Their actions consisted of presenting petitions, circulating educational literature, holding public meetings, and establishing missions with tribal groups across the country. In her essay "Care of the Indian" (1891), Amelia Quinton writes that the "first impulse" of the WNIA "was an impulse of protection for the Indians and their lands from the robberies and horrors of enforced removals" and a plea for "treaty-keeping and the honest observance of all compacts with the Indians" (386). She attributes these desires to "a common humanity," which recognized "the manhood and womanhood of Indians" (386). Quinton cites, again and again, the ways in which Indians are at the mercy of the government and the military and it is this fact of their utter victimhood which "thunders out appeals to Christian consciences" (386). Quinton neatly joins the already common trope of Christian parenting—the federal government was called the Great White Father—with the seemingly progressive notion that Indians are full human beings and, as such, are candidates for all the rights and privileges of citizenship. Although this seems reminiscent of Pearce's claims regarding seventeenth-century understandings of Indians as less advanced Europeans, its twist is in the desired outcome—persuading

Euro-Americans AND Natives to see Native land as private property, not as communally held territory.

The WNIA's first petition, sent to the President and to Congress in 1880, condemned the invasion of Indian lands by White settlers and contained thirteen thousand signatures. In 1883, a committee of the whole delivered to the President a four-pronged petition, signed by one hundred thousand people, which was also read by Senator Henry Dawes to the Senate. Their demands were straightforward: that the government maintain all treaties "with scrupulous fidelity"; that it make provision for reservation schools "sufficient for the education of every child of every tribe"; that it allot 160 acres of land in severalty (fee simple, inalienable for twenty years) to every Indian who desired it; and, that it grant Indians full rights under the laws of the United States, including those that grant religious liberty, while implementing programs that would encourage Indians in industry and trade (Quinton 1891, n382). Although some western senators (Preston Plumb of Kansas and Henry Teller of Colorado) criticized the petition and its accompanying letter for being overly sentimental and naive, the movement gained ground.

The WNIA distributed copies of their annual reports as well as hundreds of leaflets on Indian rights. They pushed for wider circulation of books that agreed with their position on the Indian question and put together press kits for reporters and newspapers as well as created a presence in regional religious and secular papers. At public meetings, organized by branch groups and local churches across the East and Midwest, they spoke to interested citizens about their "national duty to the Indians" as missionaries and Christians (Prucha 1984, 614). In its own descriptive pamphlet entitled "Our Work. How? What? Why?" (Jan. 1893), the WNIA states its work as twofold:

> It is the work of informing the public regarding the needs, capabilities and progress of our native Indians, and also, by direct appeals, it is the work of moving the Government to render just help to them. It also points out how Indians may wisely be helped industrially, educationally, morally and religiously, and it seeks to win such help for them. Second, it is the work of sending helpers to reside among Indians to labor for their instruction and elevation, to assist them in home building, in special and professional education, by hospital work, and in all other practical and practicable ways. (2)

As historian Valerie Mathes (1990) writes, the women of the WNIA believed if they could pressure the government to adopt policies of "equity and justice to Indian affairs," this would "gradually lead to the abolition of the reservation system and give all Indians the same laws, education, and citizenship enjoyed by all other races" (16) Through their "educational and missionary work, they hoped to hasten the civilization, Christianization, and enfranchisement" of Native peoples (17).

This mission is apparent to some degree in the life and writings of one of their most successful enfranchisees, Susan LaFlesche Picotte. Born around 1865 in the Omaha Nation (now Nebraska), Susan LaFlesche was the daughter of then-principal chief Joseph (Iron Eyes) LaFlesche and Mary Gale, and was the sister of activist and "Indian Princess" Susette LaFlesche. Of mixed Plains ancestry—Omaha, Oto, Iowa, Ponca, French Canadian, and Euro-American—LaFlesche was enrolled as an Omaha, was a fluent speaker of Umohan, and devoted her life to improving living and health conditions for the people of the Omaha Nation. A graduate of the Women's Medical College in Philadelphia (1889), LaFlesche became the first female Indian M.D. in the country. She immediately applied for a government position at the Omaha agency and became physician to the government boarding school. By the end of that year she had been appointed the BIA physician for the entire Agency. Ill throughout her adult life, LaFlesche died of bone cancer in September of 1916. In the twenty-seven years she spent working among the Omahas, she not only practiced medicine and advocated preventive strategies for maintaining the good health of the tribe but was also an aggressive temperance advocate, the official Presbyterian Church missionary to the Omahas, a land-and-deed-rights advocate, and a member of the state medical society. She founded the Thurston County Medical Society and was the chair of the state health committee of the Nebraska Federation of Women's Clubs. She married Henry Picotte (in 1894) and with him raised two sons, cared for her elderly mother, owned her own home and several rental properties, and in 1913 built (with the help of her various missionary friends) a hospital on the Omaha reservation that is today the Susan LaFlesche Picotte Community Center.

In one of the pamphlets she wrote for the WNIA, "Report of Susan LaFlesche, M.D., Medical Missionary of the WNIA Among the Omaha Indians" (1891), LaFlesche clearly responds to the interests of the organization, reporting on the progress of her own medical work—"it has been two years since I returned from the East to engage in medical work among my people" (4), the building of her medical office—"it is exceedingly nice and well furnished" and is "being used just as much by the tribe as by my children here" (6), the disposition of government annuity payments among the Omahas—"they made splendid use of the money. Over fifty houses were built . . . they bought machinery of all kinds . . . almost all are having wells dug" (6), and the fate of the supplies sent by the WNIA—"All scrapbooks and picture papers which were sent me I have used" (7). LaFlesche concludes her report with thanks—"I thank you so much for all you have done for me and my people" (8). Significant in my early readings of this document is that LaFlesche clearly sees her goals as similar to the WNIA's but also sees herself as an Omaha, an Indian, and as part of her home community. She writes "I am enjoying my work exceedingly, and feel more interest in, and more attached to my people than ever before" (7). So, though her work is part of the mission of the WNIA, it is also part of LaFlesche's own call, formulated while still a young woman, that educated Indians should "keep on living and working for our people" (qtd. in Tong 1999, 86). After all, LaFlesche's work as a temperance advocate had been based on her belief that drinking and drunkenness destroyed trust in the community, and in her letters to the BIA concerning allotment problems, deed ownership, and land rights, she had cited the detrimental effects of greedy and dishonest outsiders to the Omahas' efforts to "care for themselves" and become citizens of the republic. At nearly every rhetorical turn in the text of her life, LaFlesche presents us with a complicated intertwining of reform agendas and desires and the need to heal and build the community in which she lived. Even the peyote church, which she first pronounced as a "great evil," eventually came to be, in her mind, merely an Omaha variant of Protestant Christianity and the method through which Omahas could "make a change for the better" (qtd. in Tong 1999, 130).

Henry Dawes credited the women of the WNIA with laying the groundwork for what would later become the General Allotment Act, or the Dawes Act. Policywise, the Dawes Act marks the ideological erasure of tribal nations. The Dawes Act was designed to allot a quarter section of 160 acres to the head of each Indian family; orphans and unmarried Indians over the age of eighteen would be issued half that amount of land. Indians who refused or failed to select an allotment would have one selected for them by the Secretary of the Interior. The new land "owner" would not, however, receive a patent for the land until it had been held in trust for twenty-five years by the Office of the Secretary of the Interior; the land could not be sold or its title encumbered by its "owner." All reservation lands left over after the initial allotment would be purchased by the government, and the moneys from that purchase would be held in trust "for the education and civilization of the former tribe members" (Berkhofer 174). Before the Dawes Act, Indians "held" 138 million acres. Sixty percent of that land was lost through sale of "surplus" lands, twenty percent was lost through "disposal of allotments," plus an unknown amount was leased in perpetuity (Berkhofer 175).

The education and ideological groundwork laid during the early days of the WNIA combined with the symbolic cultural capital of Jackson's *A Century of Dishonor* to give the American public a language in which to rearticulate "the Indian problem," a language of Christian parenting and civic morality. It is a language that had immense consequences for its historical moment. Historian Frederick Hoxie (1984) urges us to remember that moment, to remember that "while Standing Bear was inciting the merchants of Boston, Southern redeemers were busily rebuilding their White supremacist state governments with the tacit approval of federal authorities. Westerners, assisted by Congress, succeeded in placing a ban on all Chinese immigration. And anti-Catholicism was a regular feature of life in most major cities" (33). If the goal were "Anglo conformity," then Indians could, and would, serve as a powerful litmus test of the possibility of incorporating "others" into the Euro-American whole. The "Friends of the Indians," were, as Pearce (1988) has pointed out, creating an understanding of what it meant to be American and were still using their ideas about "the Indian" as a test case for that larger national identity. Though the reformers failed to imagine real resistance and the equitable but probably "Un-American" survival of Native communities and cultures, what we get when we begin to look at the lives and writings of folks like Susan LaFlesche Picotte, Sarah Winnemucca Hopkins, Charles Alexander Eastman, and Andrew Blackbird is the possibility of such survivance, clues to how some Native people used reform to strengthen their communities, to build pan-Indian awareness, and, of course, to survive . . . and to resist that extended hand of empire.

Works Cited

Berkhofer, Jr., Robert. 1978. *The White Man's Indian: Images of the American Indian from Columbus to the Present.* New York: Knopf.

Etnier, Ruth Shaffner. n.d. "Training Indian Girls." Philadelphia: Women's National Indian Association.

Hoxie, Frederick E. 1984. *A Final Promise: The Campaign to Assimilate the Indians, 1880–1920.* Lincoln: University of Nebraska Press.

Jackson, Helen Hunt. 1881. *A Century of Dishonor: A Sketch of the United States Government's Dealings with Some of the Indian Tribes.* New York: Harper.

Mathes, Valerie Sherer. 1990. *Helen Hunt Jackson and Her Indian Reform Legacy.* Austin: University of Texas Press.

"Our Work—What? How? Why?" August 30, 1893. Philadelphia: Women's National Indian Association.

Pearce, Roy Harvey. 1988. *Savagism and Civilization: A Study of the Indian and the American Mind.* Rev. ed. of *The Savages of America,* 1953. Berkeley: University of California Press.

Picotte, Susan LaFlesche. October 24, 1891. "Report of Susan LaFlesche. M.D., Medical Missionary of the Women's National Indian Association Among the Omaha Indians." Philadelphia: Women's National Indian Association.

Prucha, Francis Paul. 1984. *The Great Father: The United States Government and the American Indians, vols. 1 and 2.* Lincoln: University of Nebraska Press.

Quinton, Amelia Stone. 1891. "Care of the Indian." In *Woman's Work in America,* New York: Henry Holt, 373–91.

Spurr, David. 1996. *The Rhetoric of Empire: Colonial Discourse in Journalism, Travel Writing, and Imperial Administration.* Durham, NC: Duke University Press.

Tong, Benson. 1999. *Susan La Flesche Picotte, M.D.: Omaha Indian Leader and Reformer.* Norman: University of Oklahoma Press.

5

Uniqueness or Borderlands?: The Making of Asian-American Rhetorics

LuMing Mao

The tendency to define a particular, emergent discipline in terms of its uniqueness always exists both for ideological and for disciplinary reasons. The making of ethnic rhetorics is no exception. It becomes not uncommon, then, to see scholars in our field trying to articulate a core set of discursive features for ethnic rhetorics—because every ethnic rhetoric, in order for it to be visible as well as viable, needs to be unique. For example, Asian-American rhetorics, whatever disciplinary characteristics they may end up embracing, must be Asian-American enough so as to be different from any other ethnic rhetoric. On the other hand, it seems that its own rhetorical uniqueness and visibility will not become completely accepted unless it has been compared to, if not adjudicated against, Western rhetorical traditions.

Renato Rosaldo (1989) criticizes the tacit methodological norms in ethnographical studies that conflate the notion of culture with the idea of differences. Following these norms, he suggests, the term "cultural difference" becomes just as redundant as that of "cultural order" (201). As a result, to study a culture now amounts to no more than seeking out its differences and showing how such a culture makes sense on its own terms (201). This critique can almost be applied to the making of ethnic rhetorics. We have seen increasing efforts being made to associate the making of ethnic rhetorics with the idea of uncovering and articulating rhetorical differences, on their own terms, from Western rhetorical traditions. And we have also seen ethnic rhetorics becoming more oriented toward activism politics as ethnic rhetoricians try to transform their own invisible practices into visible, viable ones—though often in a setting that pits them against those who are in a position to define what counts as visible and viable.[1]

But to claim rhetorical uniqueness, like claiming cultural uniqueness, may not be quite tenable anymore because, to quote Rosaldo again, "our everyday lives are crisscrossed by border zones, pockets, and eruptions of all kinds" (207). And for Gloria Anzaldúa (1999b), there is no pure other because "we are all implicated in each other's lives" (243). As a result, the effort to strive for rhetorical uniqueness may turn out to be what Rosaldo calls a "revealing distortion" (217)—to the extent that it betrays a nagging anxiety, however distorted, to overvalidate the existence of ethnic rhetorics, and still to cling to the Western ideology of autonomy.[2]

On the other hand, it is at these border zones that ethnic rhetorics can become most visible and viable—not necessarily only in relation to Western rhetorical traditions. It is at these spaces that individuals can perform acts of signification, creativity, as well as ambiguity to reconstitute and reshape their identities and their relationships. Insofar as these spaces provide liberating possibilities, invite different voices, or create new energies, these border zones become what I call "rhetorical borderlands."

Anzaldúa has characterized borderlands as "vague and undetermined," as places that are "in a constant state of transition" (1999a, 25). The rhetorical borderlands I am going to investigate here are no exception. They are vague and undetermined because there is always an excess of meaning involved, and because identity reconstitution is always an open-ended process. At the same time, these rhetorical borderlands can neutralize the kinds of power relationship that often accommodate, if not reduce, our analysis of ethnic rhetorics to the terms of the other, the more powerful. After all, it has always been the more powerful who make pronouncements in the realm of truth and differences. Rhetorical borderlands can enable their inhabitants to enter an entirely different kind of relationship, one that takes the other's perspectives as seriously as one takes her own (cf. Rosaldo 1989, 207)—however contradictory, ambiguous, or vague these perspectives may be.

To illustrate my move from claiming rhetorical uniqueness to opening up rhetorical borderlands, I will focus, for the rest of this essay, on how Chinese rhetorical traditions influence, and contribute to, the formation of Asian-American rhetorics through rhetorical borderlands. I have chosen two sites here: writing classrooms, where the concept of Chinese face is brought back to the foreground; and cultural spaces, where patterns of indirection meet head on with patterns of directness. These two sites are both visible and invisible, and they are both safe and unsafe. It is their contradiction, ambivalence, as well as their creativity that make them compelling candidates for rhetorical borderlands; in turn, they help shape and constitute the making of Asian-American rhetorics.

Writing classrooms are visible sites. As Asian-American teachers, we are quite visible, too. But our rhetorics, our ways of communication, may not be equally visible especially when we want to meet the needs of our North American students. To play safe and to avoid tension, we even downplay or hide away these visible characteristics. We try hard to fit in—even though we are presumably in control. The question then becomes this: How can we—Asian-American teachers—once again make our writing classrooms productively visible and pedagogically viable? Both teachers and students alike can then participate in contextual engagement whereby one party's perspectives are taken as seriously as the other party takes its own.

For that purpose, I use the concept of *face* to tap the productive tension embedded in our classrooms and to illustrate how the making of Asian-American rhetorics can actually emerge out of this process. Face is a regularly invoked concept in the Chinese rhetorical repertoire. Its visibility has caught the attention of Western rhetoricians and linguists, but ironically, their attention has only made it become less visible. For example, sociolinguists Brown and Levinson (1987) have characterized face, which they openly acknowledge is originated from Chinese, as a *public-self* image that we all want to claim for ourselves (emphasis added). It consists of two related aspects: which they dub "negative face" and "positive face." They define "negative face" as the basic claim to freedom of action and freedom from imposition, and they characterize "positive face" as the desire for appreciation and approval (61–62).

Such characterization, however appropriate or relevant to the communicative dynamics of White, middle-class Anglo-Americans, has removed from the concept of Chinese face its emphasis on the public, its otherwise visible feature. In other words, in spite of the continuing circulation in public of such popular expressions as "save face" or "lose face" on this side of the Pacific, the significance of the public underpinning the original concept becomes increasingly diminished as face becomes more of a personal property. Herein lies a revealing irony: It is the visible characteristic of Chinese face that has captured the attention of those who are in the business of drawing upon one set of familiar concepts (North American face) to make use of and assimilate the other (Chinese face). As they succeed in accommodating Chinese face to North American face, they have also obscured or neutralized the Chineseness that is central to the concept of Chinese face.

In my own writing classroom, I have been trying to deal with this irony, this contradiction, by making Chinese face more visible again. I broadly define face as a public image that the self likes to claim for him/herself in a communicative event—an image that ideally allows for a "balanced" expression or positioning of the self and the public/the tradition. In an influential essay titled "The Chinese Concepts of 'Face'," the cultural anthropologist Hsien Chin Hu (1944) proposed that Chinese face is constituted by two specific concepts; they are *lian* and *mianzi*. According to her, lian refers to "the respect of the group for a man (sic) with a good moral reputation;" it embodies "the confidence of society in the integrity of ego's moral character," and it is "both a social sanction for enforcing moral standards and an internalized sanction" (45). In this sense, the concept of lian conveys a strong moral connotation by incorporating the self into the public. This is also a public that is, in traditional Chinese context, hierarchical, and that usually seeks the past for guidance and inspiration. On the other hand, Professor Hu suggests that mianzi stands for prestige or reputation, which is achieved either through getting on in life or ascribed by members of one's own community (45). Mianzi in this sense becomes a property obtained and owned in a public arena with a self-component. The internal dynamics between "lian and mianzi can be characterized, in the words of Goffman (1967), as "face-work."

For example, there is a lot of lian at stake when we give our presentations at our professional conferences. In order for me to earn my Chinese lian, I need to conform to all the necessary conventions and protocols associated with such practices. Should I decide, on the other hand, to be unnecessarily boastful, it would cost me a great deal of lian. Similarly, if I could wear a nice suit and a tie in delivering this paper, I would be able to earn some mianzi. By contrast, if I were to give the same paper while wearing a disheveled face, I would temporarily lose some mianzi—the consequence of such loss may put unwanted pressure on my otherwise safe lian.

Chinese discourse patterns can realize these dynamics, too—that is, the never-ending tussle between lian and mianzi. For example, in writing personal statements writers can use the strategy to provide a detailed chronological past to establish their credentials and credibility. And they can further project both their present and their future back into the past by suggesting what they have done in the past has already shaped and determined what they are doing now and what they will be doing in the future. Such a strategy helps construct a self that is squarely positioned in the past, and that values the communal over the individual. The self, as a result, becomes more lian oriented, and a good lian is bound to give credit and respectability to one's mianzi.

I certainly would like to restore the visibility due to Chinese face by highlighting its emphasis on the public, on the communal—though not under the shadow of Western rhetorical traditions. But this is not the only reason for me to engage in this discussion. As I have argued earlier, the claim for rhetorical uniqueness, however rhetorically useful it may be at the time, could eventually become problematic simply because it is empirically nonverifiable. For example, the emphasis on the public evidenced in Chinese face may very well be found in other "faces" (or any other such nomenclatures) belonging to other cultures and communities—even though we have yet to "discover" these "faces." And since "our everyday lives are crisscrossed by border zones, pockets, and eruptions of all kinds" (Rosaldo 1989, 207), Chinese face will have to face other discursive concepts, other rhetorical tropes with similar emphasis or orientation. We all are, in short,

implicated in each other's faces. Therefore, I am more interested in exploring the question of what transpires when Chinese face meets, face to face,
Anglo-American face. I intend to suggest that when these two kinds of face
begin to interact with each other, a new set of associations may begin to
solidify—associations that are the stuff of which Asian-American rhetorics
can be made.

Put side by side, these two concepts of face obviously conflict with each
other. More specifically, Anglo-American face focuses on the self, and on the
ideology of the individual, whereas Chinese face puts emphasis on the public,
and on the ever-expanding circle of the communal. Conflict embeds the
potential for confrontation, for creating an unsafe environment. But as each
gets displayed on its own terms, it can begin to reflect on itself in relation
to the other; in the process it can come to a better understanding of its own
dynamics, its own ideologies, and its own histories. This encounter is perhaps an example of what Scott Lyons (1998) refers to as "contact heteroglossia"—where, as he develops a mixed-blood pedagogy of conflict and
contact, his Indian students produce their own narratives "against, within, and
in tandem with the grand narratives of contemporary American life and culture: race and racism, intelligence and learning, literacy and orality, success
and failure, them and us" (88–89).

There is more than meets the eye, of course, when Chinese face looks
North American face in the eye. This reflective encounter between them
yields a third possibility, a third face, as it were. This third face is not just
a mere hybrid of the two that tries to assimilate central features from both
into a coherent whole. After all, there is no coherent whole in this kind of
encounter. Otherwise stated, this third face makes no effort to minimize the
contradictions, to disambiguate the ambiguities. Instead, it unabashedly
embraces the differences by articulating them through their own evolving
contexts. Such a face embodies a critical awareness that allows its owners to
be flexible, tolerant, and always mindful of the conflicts and the tensions.
And it gives rise to a correspondingly complex identity that is always relational and always expanding. It is this kind of identity that can move more
nimbly and more inclusively between conflicts, and can help break down traditional dichotomies or divides. I want to call this kind of encounter "creative heteroglossia"—which constitutes the making of Asian American
rhetorics.

Now, let me move to my second site—where different rhetorical practices are being singled out for comparison and for analysis. Here I will focus
on the comparison between indirection and directness. For some time now,
Chinese indirection has curiously been compared to the indirect style of
communication among Anglo-American women—with the direct style of
communication among Anglo-American men as an implicit norm. For
example, many Chinese are said to be reluctant to make their requests right
away at the beginning of their discourse. Instead, they prefer to establish a

shared, sometimes elaborate, context where their requests can be judged. As a result, their requests can be seen as "expressions of a regretted inability" (Young 1994, 39). This need to be indirect, to nurture a sense of sharedness or bonds, according to Young, "bears a striking similarity to some of the goals pursued by American women when conversing with American men" (59). Drawing upon work by Gilligan (1982), and Maltz and Borker (1982), Young tells us that when American women ask questions in a conversation with American men, they are often doing so just to keep the conversation going (59)—an example of indirection. Such a comparison, however intriguing, clearly runs the risk of over-generalizing each communicative style and of shortchanging their distinctive characteristics. Further, this kind of sweeping narrative has also transformed, perhaps inadvertently, the visible— Chinese indirection—into the less visible. For now the Chinese talk *just* like American women.

Chinese discourse style with its many variations has often been cited (or sighted) as examples of indirection, and this style has been attributed, in varying degrees of directness, to a lack of public debate and argumentation through Chinese history—a characterization that is more of a myth than a reality (Lu 1998, 29–33). For example, Becker (1986) suggests that such a style tends to value standardization over individuality and to favor classical quotation and ritual phrases over individual expression (77). Similarly, according to Jensen (1987), eloquence and argumentation are generally deprecated in China, as they are indicative of "shallowness, superficiality, untrustworthy cleverness, pretentiousness, pride, hypocrisy, and flattery" (221).

The indirect style of communication among Anglo-American women, popularized by feminist linguists such as Robin Lakoff (1975), Jennifer Coates and Deborah Cameron (1989), and Deborah Tannen (1990), to name a few, is associated with being nonassertive, and being intent on establishing rapport over relationships. It seems clear that by undertaking such a comparison, one inevitably ends up privileging one particular analytical paradigm over the other. Here, as Garrett (1999) has argued, it is the Western public address paradigm that is being invoked to evaluate the Chinese communicative style (as well as that of Anglo-American women) (57–58).

We are only performing, at best, a disservice if an understanding of Chinese indirection becomes divorced from its own dynamic context. Namely, to understand Chinese indirection more completely, we have to understand its relation to correlative thinking that underpins much of Chinese ways of thinking and speaking. According to Hall and Ames:

> Correlative thinking is a nonlogical procedure in the sense that it is not based upon natural kinds, part-whole relations, an implicit or explicit theory of types, or upon causal implications or entailments or anything like the sort one finds in Aristotelian or modern Western logics. Correlative thinking employs analogical associations. (1995, 124)

In contrast to the rational mode of thinking, correlative thinking "involves the association of elements into image clusters which guarantee to its constituents richly vague significance" (Hall and Ames, 124).

So, Chinese indirection takes on a new set of meanings when it is viewed in the context of correlative thinking. That is, Chinese indirection becomes an example of different semantic associations, and these associations reflect into one another and provide richly vague significations. For example, it has often been pointed out that in traditional Chinese prose one is bound to encounter many quotations, literary allusions, and celebrated sayings, many of which may not include their sources. And Western readers have often been quoted as being frustrated in sorting out Chinese writers' own claims and warrants, which are said to be embedded amid other people's, albeit well-known, statements and arguments.

For example, Matalene, in her influential essay (1985) on the study of Chinese rhetoric, suggests that Chinese rhetors (or her Chinese composition students) like to appeal to authority and tradition rather than to Western logic (800). They also like to accumulate a series of parallel or complementary images instead of developing an argument from a synthetic or analytic perspective (789). Similarly, Gregg (1986) identifies four major characteristics that she claims are associated with Chinese expository writing style. The first has to do with its descriptive and syncretic, rather than individually innovative, approach to topics; and the second refers to its frequent appeal to authorities by continual quotation and/or by unacknowledged reproduction of their key thoughts (356). She ties these characteristics to the fact that the individual's expressive needs within the Chinese value system are subordinated in order to promote the welfare of the community (355–56).

However, informed by correlative thinking, different forms of Chinese indirection—be they clusters of unacknowledged quotations, series of parallel statements, or repeated appeals to tradition or authority—actually can serve as a discursive move to invite the audience to make necessary associations, to recognize the interdependence of texts, and to participate in this meaning-making process. They do not necessarily have anything to do with the alleged Chinese desire to promote the harmony of the community. Of course, audience participation in meaning-making is never not ambiguous, and it is never not incomplete, because there is always a surplus of meaning in communication. Chinese indirection makes no effort to control that surplus, and in fact it thrives on this kind of meaning surplus. Therefore, to simply dub Chinese indirection as an example of a lack, or worse still, of "Chinese inscrutability," is to miss the point altogether.

Once again, as I have suggested earlier, it is not my intention here to engage exclusively in this kind of comparative critique. Rather, I want to use this critique to begin articulating what discursive consequences may occur when Chinese indirection encounters Anglo-American directness. For me at least, the meeting of one with the other helps nurture a critical awareness—one that foregrounds those underlying forces shaping their content and their direction. This kind of critical awareness thus helps us "discover in our search for the multiple selves in that consciousness we refer to routinely as 'I' " (Eoyang 1994, 111). And this kind of awareness is not attainable without this reflective encounter, without what I call "creative heteroglossia."

But reflective encounter offers more. To perform Chinese indirection in the face of North American directness could further generate meaningful outcomes, and these kinds of outcomes can go a long way toward the making of Asian-American rhetorics. Namely, such performance of Chinese indirection creates both tension and energy. Its own discursive visibility, as well as our own individual efforts not to do anything about this visibility, generates such tension, such contradictions. At the same time, out of this process comes productive energy that, to quote Anzaldúa, "keeps breaking down the unitary aspect of each new paradigm" in spite of being "a source of intense pain" (1999a, 102).

Because this kind of energy emanates from a more comprehensive understanding of each other's discursive characteristics, I envision a different kind of discursive style born out of this encounter. This new style not only embraces their differences but also, more importantly, engages them by stepping outside of its own boundaries, its own spatial–temporal conditions. This is a style that allows for semantic associations, imagery clustering, and it is capable of generating its own contexts, and its own meanings. Such a discursive style is more than the sum total of the two being put together. Therefore, it is not easy to tease out from this style the strands of Chinese indirection from the strands of Anglo-American directness. Further, this kind of style commands its own context, and it breeds and nurtures a new identity, one that is not afraid of differences, and one that is more interested in localized significance and efficacy—even though the process of arriving at that can be indeterminate as well as ambiguous.

Throughout this essay, I have argued, as directly as I can, and with the minimum risk of damaging my own lian, that the making of Asian-American rhetorics lies in uncovering and articulating these kinds of reflective encounters and these kinds of border crossings. In the process, these encounters give birth to Asian-American rhetorics with both identity and visibility, and they help produce and promote new forms of understanding and representation for practitioners of Asian-American rhetorics. To the extent that I have accomplished my objective, I have then projected and enhanced my new "face." Such a face is quite mindful of Chinese face (lian and mianzi) and Anglo-American face (positive and negative face). And in my efforts to put Chinese indirection in direct dialogue with Anglo-American directness, I have not been afraid of confronting and tolerating their contradictions; in the process, I have made my fair share of direct allusions and indirect pronouncements. To the extent that I have succeeded in doing so, I have then contributed to the making of this third discursive style—a style that forever shapes and promotes an evolving identify for its practitioners in rhetorical borderlands where creative heteroglossia becomes the norm.

Notes

1. Here I am not arguing against the ongoing, quite meaningful undertaking to uncover and articulate different ethnic rhetorical traditions on their own terms. What I am trying to do is to call our attention to how we have arrived at these differences; to what prices this kind of undertaking may have exacted; and to what actions we are going to take with these differences.

2. Clifford Geertz (1983) aptly describes this ideology of autonomy as conceiving of an individual "as a bounded, distinctive, and independent whole, which is set both against other such wholes and against its own social and cultural background" (59).

Works Cited

Anzaldúa, Gloria. 1999a. *Borderlands/La Frontera: The New Mestiza.* 2nd ed. San Francisco: Aunt Lute Books.

———. 1999b. "Interview with Gloria Anzaldúa." By Karin Ikas, 227–46. *Borderlands/ La Frontera: The New Mestiza.* 2nd ed. San Francisco: Aunt Lute Books.

Becker, Carl B. 1986. "Reasons for the Lack of Argumentation and Debate in the Far East." *International Journal of Intercultural Relations* 10: 75–92.

Brown, Penelope, and Stephen Levinson. 1987. *Politeness: Some Universals in Language Usage.* Cambridge: Cambridge University Press.

Coates, Jennifer, and Deborah Cameron, eds. 1989. *Women in Their Speech Communities: New Perspectives on Language and Sex.* London: Longman.

Eoyang, Eugene. 1994. "Seeing with Another I: Our Search for Other Worlds." In *An Other Tongue: Nation and Ethnicity in the Linguistic Borderlands,* edited by Alfred Arteaga. Durham: Duke University Press.

Garrett, Mary M. 1999. "Some Elementary Methodological Reflections on the Study of the Chinese Rhetorical Tradition." *International and Intercultural Communication Annual* 22: 53–63.

Geertz, Clifford. 1983. " 'From the Native's Point of View': On the Nature of Anthropological Understanding." In *Local Knowledge: Further Essays in Interpretive Anthropology,* 51–70. New York: Basic Books.

Gilligan, Carol. 1982. *In a Different Voice: Psychological Theory and Women's Development.* Cambridge, MA: Harvard University Press.

Goffman, Erving. 1967. *Interaction Ritual: Essays in Face-to-Face Behavior.* New York: Pantheon.

Gregg, Joan. 1986. "Comments on Bernard A. Mohan and Winnie Au-Yeung Lo's 'Academic Writing and Chinese Students: Transfer and Developmental Factors.' " *TESOL Quarterly* 20: 354–58.

Hall, David L., and Roger T. Ames. 1995. *Anticipating China: Thinking Through the Narratives of Chinese and Western Culture.* Albany: State University of New York Press.

Hu, Hsien Chin. 1944. On the Concept of Chinese Face." *American Journal of Sociology* 81: 867–84.

Jensen, Vernon. 1987. "Rhetorical Emphasis of Taoism." *Rhetorica* 5: 219–32.

Lakoff, Robin. 1975. *Language and Women's Place.* New York: Harper.

Lu, Xing. 1998. *Rhetoric in Ancient China, Fifth to Third Century B.C.E.: A Comparison with Classical Greek Rhetoric.* Columbia: University of South Carolina Press.

Lyons, Scott. 1998. "A Captivity Narrative: Indians, Mixedbloods, and 'White' Academe." In *Outbursts in Academe: Multiculturalism and Other Sources of Conflict,* edited by Kathleen Dixon, 87–108. Portsmouth, NH: Boynton/Cook.

Maltz, Danny N., and Ruth A. Borker. 1982. "A Cultural Approach to Male-Female Miscommunication." In *Language and Social Identity,* edited by John J. Gumperz. Cambridge, MA: Cambridge University Press.

Matalene, Carolyn. 1985. "Contrastive Rhetoric: An American Writing Teacher in China." *College English* 47: 789–808.

Rosaldo, Renato. 1989. *Culture and Truth: The Remaking of Social Analysis.* Boston: Beacon.

Tannen, Deborah. 1990. *You Just Don't Understand: Women and Men in Conversation.* New York: Morrow.

Young, Linda W. L. 1994. *Crosstalk and Culture in Sino-American Communication.* Cambridge, MA: Cambridge University Press.

6

Contrastive U.S. and South American Rhetorics

Barry Thatcher

This essay explores how very broad cultural values of the United States and South America manifest themselves in distinct rhetorical patterns. To demonstrate this distinctiveness, I use two English translations of an Ecuadorian/U.S. writing situation. Letter O (Figure 6-1: Original version) is a close English translation of an actual letter (Luque) that was published in Guayaquil, Ecuador's daily newspaper, *El Universo*. Letter R (Figure 6-2: Rhetorical revision) is my rhetorical reworking of Letter O to make it more appropriate for U.S. audiences (based on my knowledge as a U.S.-born professor of professional communication). The letter addressed the difficulties in car registration and taxation in Ecuador. As a pilot project for my research in U.S./South American professional communication (*Orality*), I surveyed two hundred South Americans and two hundred U.S.-Americans about their rhetorical preferences, asking them which letter they preferred and why.

I present these letters here not to essentialize or reify South American or U.S.-American writing patterns but to demonstrate the broad rhetorical differences between the two cultures. Although U.S. researchers might not be surprised to learn that all 200 U.S.-Americans preferred Letter R, they might be surprised that 67 percent of South Americans preferred Letter O, 21 percent were undecided, and 12 percent preferred Letter R. Such a striking difference in the rhetorical approaches of these two letters prompt two central questions for rhetorical scholars: Why are rhetorics such as these so different, and what happens when they interact in professional contexts? This essay examines the cultural and rhetorical history of U.S. and South American populations as a means to understand the rhetorical differences in the two letters.

Figure 6–1
Original Ecuadorian letter (my translation).

TRANSIT COMMISSION
OF THE GUAYAS PROVINCE

[O]

TO THE PUBLIC

In response to the publication made by the Bureau of Industrial Development on April 15, 1993, the Transit Commission of the Guayas Province unanimously resolved to publish a clarification and/or answer through the means of communication about the assessments and negotiations that this body adopted against the methods of **REGISTRATION** and **TAXATION** of new and imported cars. That in a terse and clear way it was determined that this Directorate which began to function since August of 1992 has been against those procedures that have been utilized for more than twenty years and began to carry out negotiations so that this system did not continue, as is evident in the deliberative nature of the resolution adopted by this organization in an ordinary session on February 15, 1993, in which it was unanimously resolved to solicit the most distinguished Constitutional President of the Republic, Sixto Durán-Ballén to reform by executive decree, according to the Art. 78, Letter A) of the Constitution, the Art. 14 of the General Rule of Tax Law of Motorized Vehicles of Land Transportation, published in the Official Register N. 127 on February 13, 1989, in the sense of which: "The owners of new vehicles will pay the tax within 30 days from the date of acquisition, according to that which is established in the Art. 8 Law 004 and the Art. 52 of the political constitution of the state, that is, paying the annual portion determined from the first day of the month following the month of acquisition of the new vehicle, until the 31 of December of that year, or giving up ownership of the vehicle, this last applicable in the case of residents or naturalized persons that are not dedicated to the selling of automotive vehicles."

What is needed is to respect the proportionality that the constitution mandates without having an answer for the moment to the legal requirements from the Ministry of Finances that was sent in a correspondence dated February 9, 1993. In light of that we are doing the respective consultations to the Attorney General and Inspector General of the government to avoid possible future clarifications, since the civil servants of this Ministry in multiple occasions have verbally indicated to our civil servants to levy taxes for the complete year, notwithstanding the date in which the vehicle was registered.

Clarifying that the Transit Commission of the Guayas Province does not receive not even five percent (5%) of the total value that the owner of the vehicle pays.

The problem first presented itself to our institution from the moment we were converted to an agency for withholding monies which corresponds to the Treasurer and we hope the Finance Ministry will receive tax payments through the province administrators and that as requirement for registering the vehicle, the owner will have to present the receipt for having fulfilled the payment of this obligation to the Treasurer.

José Plaza Luque
President
TRANSIT COMMISSION
OF THE GUAYAS PROVINCE

Figure 6–2
Rhetorical revision of original letter.

TRANSIT COMMISSION
OF THE GUAYAS PROVINCE
[R]

TO THE PUBLIC

The Transit Commission of the Guayas Province proposes to reform the terms and administration of new car registration and taxation.

The terms of taxation are unfair. The Attorney and Inspector General insist that taxes are to be levied for the whole year, notwithstanding the date the car was registered. As a result, one car owner pays the same tax for a car acquired on December 31 that another owner pays for the same vehicle that he acquired on January 1st of the same year. Because of this inequity, we resolved to solicit President Durán-Ballén to reform the terms of taxation by executive decree.

To be more fair to the owners, we suggest changing the terms to a monthly basis, or as follows: "The owners of new vehicles will pay the tax within 30 days from the date of acquisition, according to that which is established in the Art. 8 Law 004 and the Art. 52 of the political constitution of the state, that is, paying the annual portion determined from the first day of the month following the month of acquisition of the new vehicle, until the 31 of December of that year, or giving up ownership of the vehicle, this last applicable in the case of residents or naturalized persons that are not dedicated to the selling of automotive vehicles."

In addition to these terms, the methods of charging and withholding taxes need clarification. Although the Attorney and Inspector General want our Commission to administer the transaction, they have not given us the legal guidelines. Thus, we suggest for the time being that the Finance Ministry receive tax payments through the provincial administrators.

José Plaza Luque
President
TRANSIT COMMISSION
OF THE GUAYAS PROVINCE

Major Cultural and Rhetorical Differences

To discuss the major rhetorical and cultural patterns in the United States and South America, I have chosen an historical narrative, which provides a broad, holistic view of possible rhetorical differences. The countries of Latin America and what would become the United States were settled at about the same time: The fall of Cuzco (Peru) occurred in 1532; Tenochtitlán (central valley of Mexico), in 1521; and Jamestown was founded in 1607. Although both areas attracted new colonizers, the motivations for colonialization and the ensuing social and cultural orders that evolved "could not be more different" (La Rosa and Mora 1999, 1).

The Spanish colonizers were motivated by economic and religious purposes, and they constructed their societies based on "Iberian institutions and priorities" (La Rosa and Mora 1999, 1). The most important cultural and social mechanism of this institution was the encomienda, or labor grant. A Spanish soldier or colonist was granted a certain track of land or village together with its native inhabitants. The Spaniards routinely set up a strict hierarchy over the land and its inhabitants, effectively creating an intricate caste system. An important part of this intricate caste system was intermarrying between races and social classes, effectively creating innumerable levels of social hierarchy. The encomienda also allowed for the establishment of the Catholic Church, which tended to dominate education and social life. Many of the Spaniards amassed great fortunes and were able to return to Spain as nobleman (La Rosa and Mora 1999).

The United States had a remarkably different historical formation and corresponding social, cultural, and political organization. Many of the original colonies were settled by Dutch and English religious dissidents. They were escaping the religious persecution in Europe and had little desire to return there. Unlike the situation in Latin America, these religious dissidents were automatically skeptical of authority, especially traditional religious authority mixed with state government. They tended to set up small, highly independent communities of "like-minded individuals" (La Rosa and Mora 1999, 2). Significantly, the U.S. colonizers did not intermarry with the indigenous populations; they just exterminated them or forced them onto reservations. The U.S. colonizers had much weaker ties to their mother countries than did their Latin American counterparts; U.S. independence was much shorter and easier to carry out; and breaking with the cultural, religious, and social order of the mother countries was relatively easy and abrupt.

In distinction, the Latin American journey to independence was much more ambiguous and complex, and most importantly, the independence gained by the Latin American countries did little to change the cultural, religious, and social order that existed in the pre-independence society. Latin American independence has been characterized as "same mule, different rider" (La Rosa and Mora 1999, 3).

As most intercultural theorists have argued, these two different foundations eventually yielded strikingly contrastive cultural and rhetorical patterns. In Latin America, the result of the encomienda foundation is a collective, yet highly stratified culture. Collective means that personal identity, seeing the world, and dealing with the world are based on the person's kinship or social group. Hofstede (1994), an important intercultural theorist, argues that four of the top ten noncommunist "collective cultures" in the world are Chile, Colombia, Peru, and Venezuela. Trompenaars (1994) similarly argues that many South American countries are highly collective. Osland, de Franco, and Osland (1999) argue that the high collectivity in this region is different from the horizontal, often harmonious, collectivity common in other parts of the world such as Japan. Latin American collectivity is very hierarchical, creating strict observance of in-groups and out-groups.

Two critical patterns result from this collective-hierarchy: One is inequality and the other is particularism. Many scholars maintain that in Latin America the societal norm is *inequality:* "there should be an order of inequality in this world in which everyone has his or her rightful place; high and low are protected by this order" (Hofstede 1994, 94; see also Jorge Castañeda 1995). This high collective-hierarchy corresponds to particularism, meaning that laws, policies, and procedures are applied differently to everyone, depending on that person's social standing. Both Hofstede (1984) and Trompenaars (1994) argue that Latin American countries are consistently the most particular cultures in the world. This particularism creates in Latin America what legal and social scholars label a "dual morality" (Eder 1950; Rosenn 1988). This dual morality created different expectations about the application of law between the familiar group and the public as a whole.

On the other hand, most intercultural scholars argue that individualism is a very strong value in the United States (Castañeda 1995; Dealy 1992; Hofstede 1994; Kras 1989; Stewart and Bennett 1991; Trompenaars 1994). Individualism means an acknowledged reliance on the self as the source of one's identity, one's way of viewing the world, and one's way of dealing with the world. In the United States, the individual tends to be the basic unit and reference point for society (Stewart and Bennett). And to ensure appropriate self-actualization, the United States tends to emphasize universalist thinking patterns. In direct distinction to particularism, universalism essentially means that all people should be treated equally under the law or policy, despite that person's social standing. From Hofstede's (1984) and Trompenaars's (1994) research, the United States consistently ranks as one of the top two or three most universalist countries on earth. As Trompenaars argues, however, this universalism is the ideal, not the practical norm. Stewart and Bennett (1991) further define this as an equality of opportunity, not of achievement. As a result, Dealy (1992) argues that in the United States there has been historically a fusion of the public and private realms into one moral system that is ideally applicable to all—though the equality of this application can be debated, especially among minority groups. This emphasis of applicability stresses due process, adherence to standards, and impersonal routinization of policies, procedures, and standards of conduct.

These different rhetorical and cultural heritages also imply different values in organizational behavior. According to many theorists, management in South America valorizes dependency, hierarchy, and close overseeing of subordinates' activities; whereas management in the United States tends to emphasize more independence and equality, leaving a reasoned amount of problem solving to the subordinates (Adelaar 1997; Hofstede 1994; Kras 1989). Closely related to this distinction is the concept of *power distance,* which measures the ability of two people with different power and authority to influence the other (Hofstede). South America has some of the highest power distance scores, which means that the subordinate has very little influence on the superior, but the superior significantly influences the subordinate. The United States generally has much lower scores, indicating more mutual influence. Thus, both manager and subordinate in South America prefer that the superior closely oversee the work of the subordinate, whereas the U.S. style is more consultative. The communication patterns associated with high-power distance cultures are usually one-way, exact, and to be followed literally. In Latin America, these patterns reflect authoritative relationships that are often set up in the home, church, and school and then carried to the workplace (Kras). Communication in lower-power distance cultures is often more consultative and less literal, involving more feedback, creativity, and flexibility in interpretation and application.

Letters O and R exemplify many of the historical and cultural patterns of collectivism/individualism and power distance. First, the level of formality and careful articulation of relationships in Letter O reflect the collective and high-power-distance values in Ecuadorian society. Thus, whereas a uninformed U.S. scholar would characterize the rhetoric as flowery and pretentious, Ecuadorian collective and ascriptive values encourage such sensitivity to social structures and position. It is also interesting that the argumentative strategy for Letter O is based on articulating the particular relationships among the groups involved. Essentially, Letter O states that the Import Law is unfair because it places all of these groups in very uncomfortable relationships.

Letter R draws on typical U.S.-American approaches to argumentation. First, it focuses on the individual, placing the individual as a reference point for all laws by arguing that the law is unfair because "one" owner might pay more than his or her fair share. Second, and more importantly, Letter R uses universal strategies of fairness: The law is unfair because it is particular and treats people differently based on their particular situations. Letter R is very individualistic and universalist oriented, whereas Letter O is very group and particularistic oriented. Letter R also allows much more voice for the author, one in which the author is not afraid to disagree with a superior, a rhetorical characteristic of more low-power-distance cultures.

These two different social and historical foundations also exemplify different approaches to law, which might explain again the distinct rhetorical patterns. The civil law is the basic legal system in all the countries in Latin America, although some are developing some tenets of common law (Alcalde 1991). The civil law tradition in Latin America is based on a long tradition that dates back at least until the Roman Empire when Justinian developed a remarkable set of codes (Eder 1950; Rosenn, 1988). On the other hand, the United States developed its legal tradition from the common law of England, which began as an unwritten assumption about appropriate conventions and behaviors.

In the civil law tradition, the legislature is responsible for creating deductive legal frameworks or comprehensive codes that are to be applied by judges to each case at hand, independent of previous cases. The system is also designed to be judge-proof. "Latin America inherited from Spain a lack of confidence in the judiciary. It is for that reason that its hands are tied . . . by the rigid formalism of the Codes of Procedure" (Eder 1950, 145). Thus, judges in Latin America have historically been subordinated to the legislature in creating laws (Rosenn 1988). On the other hand, the common law tradition is an inductive system based on case or common law precedence. Legal interpretations were based on previous cases of similar situations or what was commonly accepted as proper or legal conduct. Judges tend to have significant creative power in linking the case at hand with previous precedences, thereby continuously extending and refining the law, case by case.

These different legal approaches imply different expectations about certainty and ambiguity, especially as they relate to written communications. One principal purpose of the civil law is to obtain certainty in judicial decisions. Merryman (1969) explains that "there is a great emphasis in the literature of the civil law tradition on the importance of certainty in the law . . . it has come to be a kind of supreme value, an unquestioned dogma, a fundamental goal" (50). In this search for certainty, then, the codes or legal frameworks developed for judges have become exceedingly complex and ostensibly comprehensive, trying to cover as many contingencies as possible (Alcalde 1991; Rosenn 1991). They are also unwieldy and difficult to adapt to new situations. The U.S. legal tradition is best characterized as a loose framework of principles and guidelines (Alcalde). Ambiguity can be good because it can invite effective interpretation and application of laws. The U.S. legal system, however, can be described as just as unwieldy because it has fostered a very litigious culture (Alcalde).

Letters O and R seem to represent some of these different assumptions about law. First, Letter O very precisely cites the law, placing great value to where the law is cited. On the other hand, Letter R has a precedence-setting logic to its arguments: What happens to one car owner should set the precedence for everyone that follows. To U.S. readers, this difference might seem minimal, but to many Latin American readers, the difference is great. Most Latin Americans who commented on the differences in these two letters argued that the letters actually contain different content. Letter O more competently states where the law resides and how it can be applied deductively.

In addition to the legal systems, the different values assigned to writing and orality are key historical and cultural distinctions. The Latin American preference for orality and ambivalence to writing have historically been important cultural values. The Peruvian scholar, Antonio Cornejo-Polar (1994) argues that this paradigm actually started in 1532 at Cajamarca, Peru, when the Archbishop of Cuzco, Vicente Valverde, and the Incan leader, Atahualpa, met to discuss the fate of the two nations and cultures. These two leaders failed to reach an agreement because, among a variety of reasons, their assumptions about orality and writing corresponded to mutually unintelligible communication patterns. After Atahualpa refused to pay homage to the King of Spain, Valverde brought him the Bible and asked him to pay homage to Christ. After turning a few pages, Atahualpa "became disillusioned with the book and angry at the strangeness of what Valverde was saying, certainly foreign, unintelligible, and heretical for his consciousness" (Cornejo-Polar 1994, 37). Coming from a completely oral cultural, Atahualpa exclaimed that because he couldn't "listen to the book," or "the book didn't speak to him," he threw it down (38). As Cornejo-Polar argues, this critical incident at Cajamarca eventually became a cultural and rhetorical paradigm for many Latin Americans, both natives and mestizos, who developed their own oral dramatizations of it to continue to resist Spanish religious and governmental domination. Five hundred years later, many researchers still argue that orality predominates in this Andean region of South America (see, for example, Adelaar 1997; Harvey 1997; Howard-Malverde 1997; Lienhard 1997; Lund 1997; Mignolo 1994).

These assumptions about writing that are exemplified in the incident at Cajamarca contrast remarkably with the U.S. tradition of writing, such as the signing of the U.S. Declaration of Independence. According to many comparative legal scholars (Alcalde 1991; Rosenn 1991), the signers of the Declaration of Independence and the U.S. Constitution were able to rely on a cultural and rhetorical context that enabled such a use of written communication. Further, orality and ambivalence to writing reflect and reinforce Latin American collective-hierarchical social organizations and particular thinking patterns. On the other hand, writing seems to correspond closely to U.S. cultural values of individualism, universalism, and the common law heritage.

It is important to point out, however, that these oral–written differences are based on preferences for each medium and for the rhetorics implicit in each medium. David Kaufer and Kathleen Carley (1993) argue that almost all cultures speak and write, but one medium usually is preferred because a variety of social, economic, and technological contexts correspond more closely to the rhetoric of that medium. There is indeed a great history of written literacy in Latin America, and written literacy is widespread; but importantly, many researchers contend that in addition to the preference for orality, oral-like, dramatistic narratives are extremely important in Latin American written discourse (Cornejo-Polar 1994; González 1993; González-Echeverría 1991).

Letter O did originally appear in written form as a letter to the public, but it does feature many elements of an oral rhetoric. As Ong (1987) explains, oral cultures learn through immersion into the context, using step-by-step procedures, guided by an expert, listening to and repeating formulas, and developing a "cooperative memory" (18). Letter O is highly contextualized with names, dates, people, and events. Further it is formulaic in its titles, phrases, and relationships. And finally, Letter O seems to read like an affirmation of a cooperative memory about the car tax situation. This oral approach is different from written cultures that use writing to explicitly abstract out contextual details and analytically order and organize the experience. Letter R is more analytical in its organization, breaking the topics into related parts; it's more linear, abstract, and "organized." As one Ecuadorian friend of mine, Aníbal Cueva, mentioned, Letter R is "más trabajado," which means "more worked over," not as spontaneous and oral-like as Letter O. This predominance of orality *as well as* oral-like writing corresponds closely to South American values of collectivism, particularism, and high-power-distance leadership. On the other hand, writing and written-like orality seemed to correspond closely to U.S. cultural values of individualism, universalism, and more consultative leadership styles.

The oral and written rhetorics also imply different uses of context in communications. Just as a drama or play relies on the stage props, costumes, actors' interactions, and background to add meaning to the spoken words, so do communications in Latin America tend to rely on the context—the stage of the communication—to make the point. Thus, based on the oral and dramatistic traditions, written communications in Ecuador tend to invoke the contextual information right into the text. Letter O is full of stage-like markers: dates, people involved, circumstances, prior dialog, and issues. This strategy is what some researchers have argued as *high-context* communications (Hall 1976). This high-context strategy is probably what made Letter O difficult for U.S. readers to understand. Notice how indirectly the point is stated: Politeness strategies in high-context cultures such as Ecuador tend to be based on articulating the main point by articulating the relations among people, issues, and the stage in which they happen. U.S. communicators tend to be lower context; that is, the U.S. writer should make the meaning literally clear in the text itself without relying too much on the context. Writing for U.S. authors and audiences is less like writing a script for a play and more like developing policies like the constitution that are supposed to be mostly stageless—understood and applied regardless of context. Letter R reduces many of the contextual markers that seem to be stumbling blocks for U.S. readers.

However, one difficult adjustment for U.S. writers working in higher-context cultures is that when both author and audience know the stage or context, the communication can be very indirect and subtle, yet powerful and precise. On the other hand, when the context is uncertain, the communication tends to be loaded with contextual markers. Thus, in high-context cultures, the degree of contextual detail needed in the communication, based on prior knowledge, varies much more than in lower-context cultures such as the United States. It is not surprising that Letter O was loaded with contextual markers because it was published in a daily newspaper, a context that was so general that the author could not assume the audience understood much about the stage. From my research, I have argued that U.S. writers have a more homogenized sense of audience and context—They seem to envision a real basic scenario that can be applied to many other scenarios (Thatcher 1999). Latino writers, on the other hand, seem much more sensitive to place and the audience and to how much information in that place the audience will need.

Other important differences between U.S. and Latin American cultures seem to be rooted in perceptions of problem solving and time. Many inter-cultural researchers argue that the predominant logic of the United States is "null logic," or thinking that is structured to avoid future problems (Stewart and Bennett 1999). The argument is that many U.S.-Americans tend to see life as a problem to be solved. Thus, they structure their existence around avoiding future problems, and, in so doing, they miss out on a lot of the positive experiences of the present. As Stewart and Bennett argue, many other cultures emphasize the attainment of positive characteristics instead of seeing life as a problem to be solved.

U.S. and Latin American cultures also seem to have different perceptions of time. Some researchers have argued that Latin American time frames are often polychronic, that is, characterized by flux; simultaneity; multiple tasks managed simultaneously; and apparent disorganization, focusing on the importance of place and involvement of people rather than on adherence to present schedules. On the other hand, U.S. time frames are characterized as monochronic: linked linear structures of cause and effect with an organized flow of events (Condon 1985; Hall 1976). This monochronic time "seals off one or two people from the group and intensifies relationships with one other person, or at most, two or three people . . . [and] it alienates people from the context and experience of social relations" (Hall 1976, 19–20).

When analyzing Letters O and R, it's easy to note the differences in the problem solving and time frames. Letter O has a complex, polychronic time frame, one in which relationships, people, and events are orchestrated in complex ways. In fact, it's usually the simultaneity of issues that makes Letter O difficult for U.S. readers. Letter O is also more positive and its tone is not nearly as harsh. Letter R tends to be monochronic with an organized, linear flow. Additionally, Letter R tends to have a more negative tone; a problem really exists, it needs to be solved, and the letter can solve it. Additionally, the letters tend to invoke different feelings about the future. Letter O seems rooted in a tangible, existential present, whereas Letter R is quite future oriented.

This difference in time and problem solving corresponds to differences in agency and cause and effect. The Spanish equivalent of *I dropped the ball* is *Se me cayó la pelota,* which, literally translated, means *the ball fell from me myself.* The Spanish-language syntax tends to mask the agency behind the cause of something, whereas the structure of English tends to highlight the person or thing responsible, making it an agented language (Stewart and Bennet 1991). This difference also reinforces the polychronic and mono-chronic time frames. Many scholars have argued that understanding cause and effect is perhaps the greatest difficulty for U.S. personnel working in Latin America (Albert 1996). Castañeda (1995), a Mexican theorist, argues that cause and effect in Mexico is so complex and so deeply rooted in social and historical frames that North Americans rarely can grasp it. Albert (1996) explains that even when U.S. personnel have years of experience working in Latin America, they should still consult local Latin Americans when understanding cause and effect. Most Latin Americans who have compared Letters O and R argue that Letter R feels foreign in Spanish because Spanish syntax does not correspond well to such an agented, linear, and direct approach. Further, some Latin Americans who are bilingual have commented that Letter O feels foreign in English because English does not correspond well to the polychronic, complex agency, and contextualized rhetoric.

In addition to the historical, legal, and organizational differences, many second-language researchers argue that Latin American and U.S.-American academic compositions have distinct textual patterns. Montaño-Harmon (1991), Santana-Seda (1974), Reid (1992), and Reppen and Grabe (1993) all conclude that in Spanish compositions, flexible organization is possible, even desirable; paragraph development is not abrupt, but circumlocutory. Spanish sentences tend to be longer and with more subordination, use more synonyms and more repetition. Spanish compositions were organized via additive relationships with more conscious deviations, digressions, and run-on sentences. Letters O and R seem to perfectly resemble many of the distinctions these second-language scholars have made.

Conclusion

This essay briefly introduces some of the major rhetorical differences between the United States and South America. Obviously, such a brief and generalized approach cannot cover many other cultural variables such as gender, race, ethnicity, education, religion, economics, politics, and interpersonal relations. In addition, such a brief essay cannot articulate local differences—in the countries of Latin American and regions of the United States. Thus, the brevity of the discussion should not imply deterministic or overly generalized approaches to the rhetorical traditions of the two populations. For some scholars, this grouping of all Latin American countries or the whole U.S. population into a single category is infuriating and fictitious because every country in Latin America is "different" and the United States is culturally and rhetorically complex. Obviously, these criticisms are correct. However, the "difference" lens to intercultural relations should not blind us to the fact that at some level, the cultural, linguistic, and historical heritages of the two populations have created distinct rhetorical traditions in the United States and the countries in Latin America, despite the regional and local differences. Understanding these basic rhetorical differences critically highlights how the two populations might interact rhetorically, but more importantly for U.S. scholars, this comparison denaturalizes the individualistic, universal, common law, low-context, and agented rhetoric that is commonly assumed to be the benchmark for "clear" writing.

Further research also needs to address how increased cultural and economic interactions between the two populations are changing the rhetorical traditions. For example, in my area of the country—the border region between New Mexico and Chihuahua, Mexico—the two rhetorical traditions have been interacting since the colonialization. Indeed there is a "border rhetoric," which draws on both rhetorical traditions, but key questions focus on the rhetorical patterns that remain or are strengthened in light of intercultural interactions and those rhetorical patterns that are lost or hybridized. Other important questions address issues of technology and global economies: How are the Internet, email, and other international communications affecting these basic cultural and rhetorical traditions? How is the interdependent nature of the global economy influencing these two great rhetorical traditions?

Works Cited

Adelaar, Willem F. 1997. "Spatial Reference and Speaker Orientation in Early Colonial Quechua." In *Creating Context in Andean Cultures,* edited by Rosaleen Howard-Malverde, 135–48. New York: Oxford University Press.

Albert, R. D. 1996. "A Framework and Model for Understanding Latin American and Latino/Hispanic Cultural Patterns." In *Handbook of Intercultural Training,* 2nd. ed. Edited by Dan Landis & Rabi S. Bhagat, 327–48. Thousand Oaks, CA: Sage Publications.

Alcalde, Javier. 1991. "Differential Impact of American Political and Economic Institutions on Latin America." In *The U.S. Constitution and the Constitutions of Latin America,* edited by Kenneth W. Thompson, 97–123. Lanham, MD: University Press of America.

Castañeda, J. G. 1995. *The Mexican Shock: Its Meaning for the U.S.* New York: The New Press.

Condon, J. C. 1985. *Communicating with the Mexicans.* Yarmouth, ME: Intercultural Press.

Cornejo-Polar, Antonio. 1994. *Escribir en el Aire: Ensayo Sobre la Heterogeneidad Socio-Cultural en las Literaturas Andinas [Writing in the Air: Essay about the*

68   Rhetoric and Ethnicity

Socio-Cultural Heterogeneity in the Andean Literatures]. Lima, Peru: Editorial Horizonte.

Dealy, Glen C. 1992. *The Latin Americans: Spirit and Ethos*. Boulder, CO: Westview Press.

Eder, Phanor J. 1950. *A Comparative Survey of Anglo-American and Latin-American Law*. New York: New York University Press.

González, Aníbal. 1993. *Journalism and the Development of Spanish American Narrative*. Cambridge, MA: Cambridge University Press.

González Echevarría, Roberto. 1990. *Myth and Archive: A Theory of Latin American Narrative*. Cambridge, MA: Cambridge University Press.

Hall, E. T. 1976. *Beyond Culture*. New York: Doubleday.

Harvey, Penelope. 1997. "Peruvian Independence Day: Ritual, Memory, and the Erasure of Narrrative." In *Creating Context in Andean Cultures,* edited by Rosaleen Howard-Malverde, 21–44. New York: Oxford University Press.

Hofstede, Geert. 1984. *Culture's Consequences: International Differences in Work-related Values*. Newbury Park: Sage.

Howard-Malverde, Rosaleen. 1997. "Between Text and Context in the Evocation of Culture." In *Creating Context in Andean Cultures,* edited by Rosaleen Howard-Malverde, 1–18. New York: Oxford University Press.

Kaufer, David and Kathleen Carley. 1993. *Communication at a Distance: The Influence of Print on Sociocultural Organization and Change*. Hillsdale, NJ: Lawrence Erlbaum Associates.

Kras, Eva. 1989. *Management in Two Cultures*. Yarmouth, ME: Intercultural Press.

LaRosa, Michael, and Frank Mora. 1999. "Introduction: Contentious Friends in the Western Hemisphere." In *Neighborly Adversaries: Reading in U.S.-Latin American Relations,* edited by Michael Rosa and Frank Mora, 2–18. Lanham, Maryland: Rowman & Littlefield.

Lienhard, Martin. 1997. "Writing from Within: Indigenous Epistolary Practices in the Colonial Period." In *Creating Context in Andean Cultures,* edited by Rosaleen Howard-Malverde, 171–85. New York: Oxford University Press.

Lund, Sarah. 1997. "On the Margin: Letter Exchange among Andean Non-literates." In *Creating Context in Andean Cultures,* edited by Rosaleen Howard-Malverde, 185–95. New York: Oxford University Press.

Merryman, John Henry. 1969. *The Civil Law Tradition: An Introduction to the Legal Systems of Western Europe and Latin America*. Stanford: Stanford University Press.

Mignolo, Walter D. 1994. "Signs and Their Transmission: The Question of the Book in the New World." In *Writing Without Words: Alternative Literacies in Mesoamerica and the Andes,* edited by Elizabeth Boone and Walter Mignolo, 220–70. Durham, NC: Duke University Press.

Montaño-Harmon, María Rosario. 1991. "Discourse Features of Written Mexican Spanish: Current Research in Contrastive Rhetoric and Its Implications." *Hispania* 74: 417–25.

Ong, Walter. 1987. *Oralidad y Escritura: Tecnologías de la Palabra* [Orality and Writing: Technologies of the Word.] Trans. Angélica Sherp. Mexico City: Fonda de la cultura Económica.

Osland, Joyce, Silvio de Franco, and Asbjorn Osland. 1999. "Organizational Implications of Latin American Culture: Lessons for the Expatriate Manager." *Journal of Management Inquiry* 8 (2): 219–34.

Reid, J. 1992. "A Computer Text Analysis of Four Cohesion Devices in English Discourse by Native and Nonnative Writers." *Journal of Second Language Writing* 1 (2): 79–107.

Reppen, Randi, and William Grabe. 1993. "Spanish Transfer Effects in the English Writings of Elementary School Children. *Lenguas Modernas* 20: 113–28.

Rosenn, Keith. 1988. "A Comparison of Latin American and North American Legal Traditions." In *Multinational Managers and Host Government Interactions,* edited by Lee Tavis, 127–52. South Bend, IN: University of Notre Dame Press.

———. 1991. "The Success of Constitutionalism in the United States and its Failure in Latin America." In *The U.S. Constitution and the Constitutions of Latin America,* edited by Kenneth Thompson, 53–96. Lanham, MD: University Press of America.

Santana-Seda, Olga. 1974. "A Contrastive Study in Rhetoric: An Analysis of the Organization of English and Spanish Paragraphs Written by Native Speakers of Each." *Dissertation Abstract International*, 35, 6681A. (University Microfilms No. 75-08562).

Stewart, Edward, and Milton Bennett. 1991. *American Cultural Patterns: A Cross-cultural Perspective*. Rev. ed. Yarmouth, ME: Intercultural Press.

Thatcher, Barry L. 1999. "Cultural and Rhetorical Adaptations for South American Audiences." *Technical Communication* 46 (2): 177–195.

———. 2000. "L2 Professional Writing in a U.S. and South American Context." *Journal of Second Language Writing* 9 (1): 41–69.

Trompenaars, Fons. 1994. *Riding the Waves of Culture: Understanding Diversity in Global Business*. New York: McGraw-Hill.

7

They Could Be Giants: Gregorio Cortez, Carmen Lomas Garza's Familias, and *Spy Kids*

Jaime Armin Mejía

In the seemingly new area of Ethnic American Rhetorics, it is important to remember that Mexican Americans, as a large and culturally varied group, hold a unique place within the history of the United States. Mexican Americans have had to rely on forms of rhetoric that have changed dramatically over time as a result of political and cultural conflicts. Having had an ancestral presence in the Southwest long before Anglo Americans, Mexican Americans have many times had to alter their means of persuasion because of the colonial imposition of English and everything signified through this language. It is certainly true that indigenous peoples in Mexico and the Southwest underwent another colonial imposition when Spanish colonizers imposed Spanish as well as Catholicism on them. But unlike the Spanish Mexican Empire's distant colonial rule, the similarly enforced imposition of English by Anglo Americans has had a more dramatic effect that persists today, even as it is resisted. This resistance to the dominant Anglo-American group culture arises in part from the political nature of the conflict of languages. Each language, its variations, and what it signifies culturally and politically, that is, rhetorically, has marked everyone engaging in interpersonal communication within this contact zone, resulting in a continually evolving rhetorical dynamic.

Several years ago, for instance, while returning from a conference of the National Association of Chicano and Chicana Studies, held in Hermosillo, Sonora, México, a group of Texas-Mexican students and I stopped just across the U.S.–Mexico border in Nogales, Arizona, to appease my students' appetites. On this Saturday night and much to my surprise, we ran across a very busy Shakey's Pizza establishment, which on this evening featured a live conjunto band entertaining a packed house of Mexican-origin families. The commercialized ragtime theme for this particular Shakey's Pizza establishment had somehow been altered at this bordertown by the conjunto's norteño music. In some ways, finding this type of live performance seemed almost ironic, because we'd just returned from a Chicano/a studies conference which had been held in Mexico instead of in Arizona because Arizona had yet to adopt the Martin Luther King, Jr. holiday. The pizzeria establishment, Shakey's, traditionally based on ragtime music, and the holiday honoring the heroic efforts of the African American Martin Luther King, Jr. had thus been caught in the middle of cultural forces which were at odds with each other at this time in Arizona.

However, these conflicts over the cultural and political hegemony of the U.S. Southwest have a long history, and I shall explore subjects that I believe shed light on how the rhetorical dynamic has changed as a result of these conflicts. First I will consider an historical figure, Gregorio Cortez, about whom corridos (ballads) were composed and performed by conjuntos a century ago. I shall then look at the artistic depiction and reception of Mexican-American families by the Chicana artist, Carmen Lomas Garza. Finally, I shall move to a recently released mainstream movie, *Spy Kids* (2001), which has the central theme of "family," and not coincidentally includes a main character named Gregorio Cortez. I shall be arguing that the tropes found in these works have played an almost archetypal influence on the rhetorical power of such subjects in Mexican-American culture. But their power has changed as they've met with changed ideological conditions caused by the changing audiences receiving them.

Rhetorically, these three subjects in different ways articulate the tropes of heroic struggle and resistance against the dominant group. Additionally, the ideal of the family often contributes a necessary cohesion and stability for the maintenance of the culture. Because these tropes are often strongly held, they've had a significant impact on how most Mexican Americans have constructed their cultural and political identities in the twentieth century. When (re)viewed together, they reveal a progression of how these tropes have evolved with the changes many Mexican Americans have had to endure as members of the United States citizenry.

Gregorio Cortez, whose exploits have been recorded in several corridos, composed shortly after his infamous escapades with the Texas Rangers and hundreds of members of several vigilante groups one hundred years ago, received critical prominence in Américo Paredes' landmark study, *With His Pistol in His Hand: A Border Ballad and Its Hero* (1958). Paredes' study describes the dominant culture's racialized politics against which Gregorio Cortez had to defend both himself and his family. As the story goes, the

Mexican-born Cortez and his brother Romaldo had rented some farmland and were sitting on their front porch with their respective wives and mothers and Gregorio's family when approached by a local sheriff and his two deputies. The latter were seeking some horse thieves and stopped to ask about a horse Gregorio had recently traded. Because the sheriff and his men didn't know Spanish well and Cortez and his brother's English was limited, a misunderstanding ensued, causing the sheriff to shoot and wound Cortez's brother, which in turn caused Gregorio to kill the sheriff in self-defense. Caught by surprise, the deputies ran away to seek help, while Cortez chose to escape because he was sure he would be pursued and killed by agents of the local Texas Anglo authorities. According to Paredes, in Texas at this time the rule of law for Mexicans and Blacks meant Texas Anglos would shoot first and ask questions later.

When this incident occurred, Cortez had a wife and four children, and his fallen brother also had a wife. The women and children sought shelter with some nearby relatives, but were soon caught and jailed. Meanwhile, Cortez made his getaway by fleeing first north and then south, thereby eluding literally hundreds of Texas Rangers and other vigilante posses. At one point, he found himself at the home of a Texas-Mexican friend, and while he was there another sheriff and posse surrounded the house and began shooting. In self-defense, Cortez shot and also killed this sheriff, and once again managed to escape. He eventually reached just north of Laredo, where he learned of the fate of his jailed family and decided to turn himself in rather than have his family suffer any more. His concern over his family's well-being caused him to quit his retreat to Mexico, but in Central Texas, numerous Mexicans were getting lynched or shot to death by Texas Anglos because they were suspected of being part of Cortez's gang of desperadoes. These killings probably also caused him to turn himself in.

Cortez was repeatedly tried and convicted of killing the two sheriffs, all but one of these trials' verdicts being overturned by the Texas Court of Appeals because his attorneys successfully argued he had killed the sheriffs in self-defense. When Cortez was ultimately convicted, he was sentenced to life in prison at the state penitentiary where he served eleven years before the governor of Texas pardoned him in 1913. After his pardon, he went to Nuevo Laredo where he fought in the Mexican Revolution, was wounded after being suspected as a spy, and returned to Texas to convalesce. He eventually made his way to West Texas, where he died in Anson, Texas, in 1916.

In Gregorio Cortez, we have a legendary figure whose escapades against greater Texas Anglo odds made him a hero to many Texas Mexicans and Mexicans, one with whom they identified, largely because of their own treatment at the hands of the dominant culture. Because Cortez defended himself and his family from injustices routinely endured by most Texas Mexicans, his actions were viewed as courageous and honorable. But whereas he may have eventually escaped the long arm of the racist Texas law, he ironically was not able to escape from several women who sought him out in jail and married him after his previous wives left him. While in jail, his first wife, who'd also been jailed, left him after other women began showing up. While in jail, he married a woman named Garza before being pardoned and released. But another woman, writing the Governor on his behalf and seeking his pardon, claimed to have been engaged to him when the killings of the sheriffs occurred, and planned on marrying him after his release. Paredes found no mention of their marrying after his pardon, and after returning to Texas from the Mexican Revolution, Cortez quite mysteriously died on his wedding day, after purportedly being poisoned.

Paredes seems quite puzzled by Cortez's romantic escapades because they are not mentioned in any of the versions of the corridos that raised Cortez's stature and were the starting point for Paredes' landmark study. Most of the scholarly interest in this man revolves around his heroic stature as narrated in the corridos and not in who he actually was. Rhetorically, then, Paredes's decision to focus on Cortez's heroics against the dominant group completely overshadows what might have proven to be an even richer treatment had gender been part of Paredes' analysis. When Paredes does mention Cortez's interests in women he sets his discussion off by the ironic section title "Through thick and thin," thereby impugning their lack of fidelity and not Cortez's. Thus, as central as the trope of "family" is within Mexican-American culture, earlier analyses of family, like Paredes's, simply never accorded women a significant place, especially when compared to masculine heroic resistance against the dominant group.

Twenty years after Paredes published his study, Carmen Lomas Garza began depicting Mexican-American family life from a Chicana point of view. Currently on exhibit at the San Antonio Museum of Art, her art works can also be found in three children's picture books recently published by her, which include the artist's short two-language narratives. Garza's images largely feature her own extended family in a variety of domestic settings, with women typically playing central roles. Many consider her depictions of family as traditional, conventional, and safe. In fact, when the first major exhibition of Chicano and Chicana art toured the country in the early 1990s, it featured two of Garza's art works. But when this exhibition, called *Chicano Art, Resistance Art,* or *CARA* for short, had its stay at the Smithsonian in Washington, D.C., the Smithsonian curators refused to use the exhibition's chosen logo. They instead selected Garza's now famous *Cama para sueños (Bed for Dreams)* to advertise and thereby water down this politically charged touring exhibition of Chicano and Chicana art. When approached about this substitution, Garza voiced her concern that her art piece did not entirely represent *CARA's* intended mission, which was to disrupt the mainstream's utterly myopic and elitist conception of American art. In the end, her *Bed for Dreams* was not only used as the exhibition's logo at the Smithsonian, but was one of three Chicano and Chicana art works the Smithsonian acquired for its permanent collection of American art.

The Chicana critic Alicia Gaspar de Alba (1998) considers Garza's art to be modernist, which may be one of the reasons the Smithsonian chose her *Bed for Dreams* as *CARA's* logo, thereby seeking to diffuse the more radical postmodern and conflictive messages sent by the *CARA* exhibition. But Garza's strategy may have also served purposes the Smithsonian curators failed to grasp and arguably helped *CARA* artists infiltrate hallowed halls of art previously closed to Chicanos and Chicanas. That is, Garza's modernist strategy ironically raises the cultural status of the Mexican-American family by using monitos, or stylized, almost cartoonish static figures, modeled after similar figures found in classical works of Mesoamerican art. Such figures, for instance, can be seen in Guaman Poma's *The First New Chronicle and Good Government,* which Mary Louise Pratt utilizes to illustrate autoethnographic texts arising from a contact zone. In Garza's case, though, she uses premodern figures in a modernist medium to send a postmodern message illustrating the cultural autonomy of the Chicano and Chicana community.

Although Garza's technique replicates what high modernists did to raise the status of their art and literature by basing their works on classical art from the ancient Western world, Garza's rhetorical maneuver represents a transcultural shift. Her artistic strategy not only raises the status of a contemporary minority culture but also raises the status of classical indigenous art from Mesoamerica. From a Chicano ideological perspective, her artistic maneuver connects the ancient world of indigenous peoples of Mexico, Central America, and South America with Chicano and Chicana culture. In this idealized epic world Garza has created, time stands still, with the nefarious consequences of racial discrimination from without and gender discrimination from within Mexican-American culture all but absent. Canonized as her art is now within the U.S. art world, Garza's works continue to stand alone in their depictions of an idealized and self-contained Chicano and Chicana world of family.

Garza's strategy of resistance to the dominant group is therefore quite different because it rides against the more male-centered approach typically found in works by Chicanos. Acts of defiance from a Chicano's perspective often represent lone males taking on seemingly insurmountable odds without making use of the support found within their cultural group. When such support is sought, it is often from other males, with women usually holding peripheral roles at best. More recent Chicana writers and artists adopt a similar strategy by having their protagonists seek support only from other females in order to fight not only Latino males but also forces from the dominant group, thereby raising their protagonists' heroic statures even higher. These male- or female-centered rhetorical strategies, however, make Garza's artistic approach impressive because she embraces members from the entire community.

Exactly one hundred years after Gregorio Cortez shot his first sheriff, Chicano director Robert Rodriguez produced *Spy Kids* for mass consumption, with McDonald's even selling toys modeled after the gizmos used by the film's characters. One of the most interesting aspects of this movie is that Rodriguez named the father of this spy family "Gregorio Cortez." And as we're pointedly told at the movie's end by the main characters, the toughest mission spies can undertake is keeping the family together, which for this contemporary interethnic Latino family means using high technology. The summary of the movie distributed by Dimension Films states:

> Gregorio and Ingrid are the two greatest secret agents the world has ever known: masters of disguise, mavens of invention, able to stop wars before they even start. Working for separate countries, they are sent to eliminate their most dangerous enemy . . . each other. But in an exotic corner of the world when they finally come face to face, they fall in love instead and embark on the most dangerous mission they have ever faced: raising a family. Now, nine years later, after their retirement, having exchanged the adventure of espionage for parenthood, Gregorio and Ingrid Cortez are called back into action. When their former colleagues . . . start disappearing one by one, the Cortez's are forced to take on techno-wizard Fegan Floop and his evil, egg-headed sidekick, Minion. But when the unthinkable happens and they too disappear, there are only two people in the world who can rescue them . . . their kids. Armed with a bag of high tech gadgets and out-of-this world transportation, Carmen and Juni . . . save their parents . . . and maybe even the world. Sometimes the biggest heroes are the smallest ones.[1]

As disguised by techno-wizardry and espionage drama as this movie is, it is clearly a Latino film, even though it is intended for a mainstream audience. To infiltrate this venue, Rodriguez strips the film of geographical specificity, refusing to place the film and its characters in any specific locale. He also keeps the film from attracting too many cultural codes restricting it from attracting just a Latino/a audience, despite the music's distinct Latin flavor, with Los Lobos playing a part. And athough he disguises these cultural codes, he still incorporates the two tropes of family and resistance to a dominant group, although reversing the plot by having kids as heroes.

So if we can say that the corridos of Gregorio Cortez's escapades were intended for a male Texas-Mexican audience and Garza's family pictures appeal to the entire family of Mexican Americans, Robert Rodriguez's *Spy Kids* crosses over from the self-contained world of Garza's Chicano and Chicana families and enters the mainstream of popular culture. But when Latinos and Latinas attempt crossing over into the mainstream, the rhetorical dynamics of this maneuver still come with the price of disguising our cultural identity. This price nevertheless signifies a rhetorical progression suggesting how our future lies not just with prior figureheads, but ironically with our kids and their use of technology. Rhetorically, it's therefore my view that our technologically savvy children might actually be the giants who save us from the rhetorical oversights of our past, or at least that's what I see coming out of the Chicano and Chicana artist community.

Note

1. Summary of *Spy Kids* from http://movietimes.go.com/cgi/movielistings/request.dll? MOVIESPECIFIC

Works Cited

Gaspar de Alba, Alicia. 1998. *Chicano Art Inside/Outside the Master's House: Cultural Politics and the CARA Exhibition*. Austin: University of Texas Press.

Garza, Carmen Lomas. 1990. *Family Pictures/Cuadros de familia*. San Francisco: Children's Book Press.

Paredes, Américo. 1958. *With His Pistol in His Hand: A Border Ballad and Its Hero*. Austin: University of Texas Press.

Spy Kids. 2001. Directed by Robert Rodriguez. Dimension Films.

8

Police Violence
and Denials of Race

Richard Marback

In April 1992, several neighborhoods in the city of Los Angeles were torn apart by violent reactions to the not guilty verdict in the trial of police officers charged with beating Rodney King. Americans watched with dismay and contempt and anger and sadness as the national media characterized the events as a riot and the participants as largely African Americans either outraged at the verdict or opportunistically taking advantage of a chaotic situation. As Rodney King said during the violence, "We're all stuck here for awhile" (qtd. in Gooding-Williams 1993, 3). We are all stuck. Stuck not only in places torn by violence and circumstances beyond our control, but stuck as well in attitudes and accounts that hinder our capacities to change our situations.

Analyses that keep us stuck in current conditions do so by abstracting political, economic, and cultural conditions to the point of explaining away the potential people have to choose their responses to unjust acts. Cornel West (1994) provides an example of just such an analysis, "What happened in Los Angeles in April of 1992 was neither a race riot nor a class rebellion. Rather, this monumental upheaval was a multi-racial, trans-class, and largely male display of justified social rage. For all its ugly, xenophobic resentment, its air of adolescent carnival, and its downright barbaric behavior, it signified the sense of powerlessness in American society" (3–4). Not only do people feel powerless and stuck, according to West, but also they—we—become trapped by the abstract hegemonic powers of social forces beyond our control.

Analyses that reduce violent events to the actions of specific human agents also fail to get us unstuck, explaining away the power that political, economic, and cultural legacies exert over our choices. Such a too-specific analysis is that of Floyd, a regular in a Detroit bar, responding to the beating death of another African-American motorist, Malice Green. Less than six months after the televised violence in Los Angeles, on the night of November 5, 1992, Detroit police stopped Malice Green in front of a suspected crack house. When he refused to open his hand to show police the vial of cocaine that he was holding, they beat him on the head with their flashlights. He died soon after. With the events in Los Angeles still fresh in everyone's minds, city officials moved swiftly to avoid property damage and further loss of life—immediately suspending the officers, initiating investigation into the incident, and encouraging calm. Many Detroit residents anticipated little disruption. And there was none. Less than a year after the incident, two Detroit police officers, Larry Nevers and Walter Budzyn, were convicted of manslaughter. As Floyd put it, race had little if anything to do with Green's death, because Nevers would beat everyone with equal vigor and without discrimination, "Well, if they didn't take you in, they'd beat the shit out of you right then and there. . . . That was how they did it" (qtd. in Hartigan 1999, 5).

West's analysis and Floyd's explanation keep us stuck because they misjudge the relationship between conditions of law and lawlessness and the discretion of individual police officers to utilize state-sanctioned violence. As legal scholar Robert Cover (1992) has explained, the work of state agents such as police officers is fundamentally an exercise of violence. It is "a practical activity, designed to generate credible threats and actual deeds of violence, in an effective way" (214). This does not mean that the violence of state agents such as Nevers is always legitimate. "Sheer force is not law" (Ross 1996, 7). What we count as law and as legitimate use of state-sanctioned violence is justified through rhetorics that express our situatedness, and so betray our indiscretions and prejudices. Thomas Ross explains it this way, "State's law is a product of the mix of rules and narratives which together yield meaning, coupled with the state's commitment [to bring the specter and reality of force and violence that is the state's] to that meaning" (1996, 8). In the person of the police officer, the law he or she will enforce, the violence she or he will bring to bear in order to assert and establish at that moment a given meaning for the law is a product of rules of conduct and narratives—personal narratives of fear and pride, collective narratives of decay and disorder, and even institutional narratives of legality and proceduralism. It is in the particularity of these narratives that we legitimate (or not) violent acts and experiences of violence. All these narratives are racialized as the partiality of our experiences are racialized. As Michael Omi and Howard Winant (1994) argue, racial identity formation is a "sociohistorical process by which racial categories are created, inhabited, transformed, and destroyed" (55). Getting ourselves unstuck from unjust police violence requires that we see racial formation as a process by which we enact racialized structures and racialized representations, as "simultaneously an interpretation, representation, or explanation of racial dynamics, and an effort to reorganize and redistribute resources along particular racial lines. Racial projects connect what race means in a particular discursive practice and the ways in which both social structures and everyday experiences are racially organized, based upon that meaning" (Omi and Winant 1994, 56). Discussing the tangled narratives that organize the social structures and everyday experiences which assign meaning to the beating death of Malice Green, I ask just how easy it is to get ourselves unstuck by disentangling the cultural, economic, and political narratives used by specific agents to explain (or explain away) their actions.

Although the use of force by police officers has racializing consequences, the experiences of violence among police organize racialization into more personal terms. Soon after Malice Green's death, Detroit Police Chief Stanley Knox repeated at several police roll calls the view that media coverage had "engendered false and unnecessary apprehension on the part of some members of the department." That view was repeated by several officers who said, like officer Steve Dolunt, that their enthusiasm for their work had been crushed by news reports critical of the Detroit Police Department. As Officer Morris Joseph put it, "The kind of police work we used to do was aggressive police work . . . [But now] if we make a stop, I'm worried about what if I do hassle with some guy. I have to second-guess myself and I might get killed" ("Cops Say," *Detroit Free Press,* November 29, 1992). Police officers make sense of the violence of law in personal terms that for better or worse bolster their capacity to use lethal force. As Joseph suggests, aggression is not thought to be willful as much as it is thought to be a defense. They are only violent when they have to be. According to Fred Walker, an attorney who specializes in representing police officers, "I've represented police in maybe 50 shootings in the past five years, and what I see is a lot of restraint on their part. . . . They have to deal with an unbelievable level of violence" ("Police Lawsuit," *Detroit Free Press,* January 22, 1993).

Such narratives are echoed among citizens who accept the need for police to violently enact the order of law. Years after Green's death, as the conviction of Larry Nevers was upheld in a Federal Appeals Court, letters to the editor of the *Detroit Free Press* supported the discretion of police officers to use violence to give meaning to the law. George Sevald wrote, "Your paper always gives the lawbreaker the benefit of the doubt. . . . It must be nice to possess such knowledge. The testimony was that Green resisted arrest and sought to grab officer Nevers' gun. In a law-abiding society, that is justification for severe retaliation" ("From Our Readers," May 22, 2000). In the same issue, Tom Ferguson wrote, "News pages are laden these days, locally and nationally, with stories about edgy, frightened cops who go unpunished after shooting innocent civilians. If Nevers had shot every citizen who refused orders to take his hands out of his pockets . . . the bodies would form a line from here to Toledo." Not all reactions were similarly supportive of police violence. Dale Weathers, for example, had a different view, "Nevers can cry all he wants. . . . The bottom line is he was found guilty of manslaughter, and he has to do his time. No one, not even the police, are above the law. Nevers may believe in his heart that he is innocent, but he will never convince me or thousands of others that those head injuries Green received were from his head hitting the ground. Why didn't Nevers just shoot him if he thought he was in so much danger? I could understand that more than cracking someone's head wide open" ("From Our Readers," May 22, 2000). Weathers does not seem to deny the sanction of police violence, but he does distinguish that violence from brutality. The complaint about Detroit police is not that they use violence but that they are brutal.

Brutality and violence coalesce and become inscribed with longtime narratives of race, violence, and law. Of the two Detroit police officers convicted in the death of Malice Green, one, Larry Nevers, had been a member of an undercover police unit called STRESS—Stop the Robberies, Enjoy Safe Streets. Nevers was a member of the unit for eleven months in the early 1970s. STRESS had a reputation for brutality and was involved in the deaths of twenty people, seventeen of them Black. Coleman Young, first Black mayor of Detroit, was initially voted into office on a campaign against police violence in the city in general and among STRESS unit officers in particular. Young disbanded the unit in 1974. After Green's death in 1992, Nevers was suspended without pay. Former members of STRESS collected funds for him. As one former member of the unit explained, "It was felt by us that we should really gather up the troops, if you will, and just very simply do something for him from us" ("Ex-Stress Members Aid Charged Officer," *Detroit Free Press,* December 15, 1992).

In Detroit, bureaucratic responses to racialized police brutality blurred discrimination into other economic and political realities. The same year that Coleman Young disbanded the STRESS unit, a five-member Board of Police Commissioners was created to aggressively monitor a police department that Young had characterized as a predominantly White paramilitary organization that often brutalized city residents. Since 1974, however, the commission had languished, failing to demand accountability from police executives, in part because of limited financial resources, the racial integration of the police department, and the fact that members of the board were mayoral appointees unaccountable to anyone else. Sharon Bernard, a commissioner in 1979–1984, said city officials and commissioners mistakenly believed that once the department was integrated, brutality "would take care of itself." In response to Green's death, Bernard remarked, "We're seeing now that's not necessarily so. I just don't think they've been as involved as they were in the old days. Maybe it's a function of the commission's makeup or just a comfort level with the department." Another former commissioner characterized the ineffectiveness of the oversight commission as a consequence of Coleman Young's influence over all aspects of city government, "This mayor, who came into office so critical of the police department, ought to encourage an independent voice. But he's really discouraged it" ("Detroit Police Board Faulted," *Detroit Free Press,* November 21, 1992).

The record of the STRESS unit demonstrates that the physical realities of police violence have very real racial consequences and, at least initially, racist causes. But in an integrated department with an ineffectual oversight commission, appeals to race do not, by themselves, fully explain or completely resolve excesses of police violence. Race matters, yes. But it makes itself felt through the structures of rules and narratives that we make use of everyday to organize our institutions and make sense of our lives. It is not simply that we take up these rules and narratives to make sense of our lives: They take us up, propelling our experiences into structures of meaning that then become accessible to others. At the trial of Officer Nevers, Officer James Kijek, who witnessed the beating of Green, testified that Green was "kicking and squirming a lot, and he was very strong" ("Nevers Witness Says Green Was Raging," *Detroit Free Press,* April 7, 2000). Nevers testified on his own behalf that hitting Green on the head with his flashlight constituted appropriate force because Green was so violent ("Nevers Is Firm in Defense," *Detroit Free Press,* April 13, 2000).

Whether a jury, or anyone else, would be persuaded that Green was violent and a threat to the officers again depends on the structures of meaning we draw on to make sense of state-sanctioned violence in general and in this instance. An EMS worker who also responded to the scene of Green's beating testified that Nevers said, "Yes, I hit him and I'll hit him again" ("Nevers is Firm in Defense"). Robert Fox, an attorney who had defended Green, said that Green "would always give police a hard time, because he was not going to buckle under to authority. . . . Taking the worst-case scenario, he pissed off the police officers. . . . So he's flaunting authority, he's telling them to 'go away and stop bothering me.' Why did they stop him at all? Because he was in the vicinity of a drug house? But that's it."

In Ann Arbor, thirty miles west of Detroit, soon after the death of Malice Green, former Los Angeles police chief Darryl Gates criticized Detroit officials who condemned the officers in the beating death of Green. As he put it, the officials were only doing "what they thought was politically correct . . . but I thought it was wrong." Gates went on to invoke Malcolm X, saying that "you take rage and you use it to get control of your life and take responsibility for your life" ("Cops Struck Trying to Subdue Man at Crime Scene," *Detroit Free Press,* November 20, 1992). We can only guess to whom Gates was referring, whether he meant to say that the officers were justified in their violence, using their rage to enact legal order. We can be more certain that Gates was quoting Malcolm X to deflect the claim that Green's death was the result of racism.

Gates' reference to Malcolm X may sound mean spirited, but it was well-timed. Spike Lee's movie on the life of Malcolm X opened in Detroit twelve days after Green was murdered. The movie became a catalyst that further confounded race rhetoric in Detroit. On the day the movie opened, the Michigan branch of the National Association for the Advancement of White People distributed flyers in Detroit-area theaters (there are no movie theaters in Detroit), that read, "Let's put an end to Spike's, violent 'hate whitey' movies, at least in our good neighborhoods." The Michigan director of the group distributing the flyers told reporters that he and his members became concerned about increased racial tensions after the beating death of Malice Green, "You can just imagine our fears that there might be violence against white people" (Gilchrist 1992).

Other people in Detroit reacted in other ways to the film. Reverend Milton Henry, who knew Malcolm X, characterized the movie as "a theological piece." Constance Cumbey, an attorney fighting the Malcolm X Academy (a charter school in the city of Detroit designed to enhance self-esteem in African-American males through an Afrocentric curriculum), saw the movie as anti-Christian, anti-Semitic, and potentially inflammatory. Inner-city youth worker Bernard Spragner said the movie sends a needed message to Black communities desensitized to Black self-destruction. Keana Wright, a Black high school student, said her hero was still Martin Luther King; whereas Steve Mitzel, a White college student, said Malcolm X's message of social and economic equality is a message for all (Wilson 1992).

In a eulogy delivered at Green's funeral, the day Spike Lee's movie opened, Reverend Charles Adams invoked Malcolm X, as well as other Black leaders, and explained that racism killed Malice Green. "America's malignant racism killed Malice Green, and unless that disease is eradicated, everyone is threatened. . . . The blood of Malice Green also says that the root of the problem that killed him is the uncured sickness of racism that plagues this society. . . . And if racism is not destroyed, nobody in America can be safe. For if they got him at night, they'll get you in the morning!" Adams went on to connect Malice Green with a long line of African-American politicians, Black nationalists, civil rights workers, and South African leaders, "They crushed W. E. B. DuBois, they exiled Marcus Garvey, they compromised Booker T. Washington, they excoriated Malcolm X, they murdered Medgar Evers, they persecuted Paul Robeson, they expelled Adam Clayton Powell Jr., they slandered Harold Washington, they smeared George Crockett, they slew Martin Luther King Jr., they excommunicated Father Stallings, they discredited Marion Barry, they incarcerated Nelson Mandela, they killed Steve Biko, they bludgeoned Rodney King, and they killed Malice Green!" (qtd. in Chesley 1992).

One way to understand the eulogy given by Adams is to recognize that it appeals for justice by drawing attention to a global history of discrimination and fundamental injustice. Such appeals have the force of emotion: They sensitize us to the historical trajectory of racial prejudice, but in doing so they make possible counterclaims about prejudice of a different kind. In 1997, U.S. District Judge Lawrence Zatkoff overturned the conviction of

Larry Nevers, ruling that jurors in the original trial were prejudiced by their awareness that the city was bracing for riots if a not guilty verdict was returned and because they saw the movie *Malcolm X* during a break in deliberations. According to the judge, the movie's subplot of police violence prejudiced jurors. Dominant and prevalent narratives of police violence, such as those articulated by Detroit police officers and in the letters to the *Detroit Free Press,* did not have the same prejudicial influence, in part because they are so much a part of our narrative order that they are rarely seen as different.

Rather than legal narratives, we must look elsewhere for challenges to the racialization of state-sanctioned violence by which we order our lives. In the Detroit neighborhood where Malice Green was beaten and died, people invoke spiritual narratives of Green's death, mobilizing these to make sense of violence that orders human bodies and structures the legitimacy and meaning of state law. Residents of the neighborhood joined together after Green's death, forming citizen patrols and maintaining public areas. As one woman put it, "It angered me that [Green] had to die, but I knew it would bring about some change. It's like he was sacrificed" ("In Troubled Neighborhood," *Detroit Free Press,* November 29, 1992). The notion that Green was somehow sacrificed for racial justice has been made real by Bennie White Ethiopia, an artist who painted a portrait of Green on the façade of the building in front of which he was beaten. Because it rained soon after Ethiopia painted the portrait, streaks of paint run down the face from the eyes, making it appear as though Green is crying. In addition to the painting, flowers and mementos have been propped up against the building, left as a memorial. Through the portrait and the memorial, residents of the neighborhood have minimally reclaimed the area from criminalization and police violence. But they have not been able to lift their community out of racialization. The night after Nevers was released from prison in 1998, the Green portrait was defaced with a swastika and the words, "Nevers Rules." After Ethiopia restored the painting, community activist Malik Shabazz encouraged local residents not to lose hope, "Don't let the devil steal the joy from your heart. We're going to win in the end" ("Green Memorial Portrait Restored," *Detroit Free Press,* January 8, 1998).

Whether we win in the end, whether we can get ourselves unstuck from circumstances and dispositions that enable police officers to disproportionately use violence on African-American males depends in part on how well we can disentangle narratives of justice, race, and violence. Appeals to justice can demonstrate the arbitrariness and partiality of excesses of violence. But justice by itself does not guide our insight into the racialization of our lives. Appeals to race can expose the excessive uses of force that maintain economic and political structures dividing people and shaping their lives. But appeals to race are not enough to end the brutality when violence is built into our social structure, is the foundation of law, and is a fundamental dimension of our experience. Ending the brutality means nothing short of shifting our experiences, reclaiming our fear and our hope for the institutional reorganization of our legal order. This is a daunting task. According to Thomas Ross, whom I quoted at the beginning of this essay, our legal order has meaning to the extent that it is embodied by the actions of state agents such as police officers. But the law is more than state agents exercising authority and power. The law gathers meaning because ordinary citizens interact with state agents, accumulating experiences and developing dispositions. Movies such as Spike Lee's biography of Malcolm X challenge the structures of police interactions with African-American males. For the murder case against Officer Nevers, the movie was too incisive, cutting too close to the racism of police violence and too far from the racialized violence of one police officer. Challenges that become more effective describe state agents so that we increasingly see them and they see themselves as bringing institutions into being rather than as brought into being by institutions. Acts as simple as Bennie White Ethiopia painting a portrait do exactly that. The portrait did not change everyone's mind about Green's violent death or the justice of Nevers's verdict. But it did make area residents aware that people can be more than victims and victimizers in a legal order where much of their lives is beyond their control.

Works Cited

Chesley, Roger. "'Racism Killed . . . Green. If It's Not Destroyed, No One Is Safe,' Pastor Tells Mourners." *Detroit Free Press.* November 13, 1992.

Cover, Robert. 1992. *Narrative, Violence, and the Law: The Essays of Robert Cover,* edited by Martha Minow, Michael Ryan, and Austin Sarat. Ann Arbor: University of Michigan Press.

Gilchrist, Brenda J. "White Group to Protest Lee Film." *Detroit Free Press.* November 17, 1992.

Gooding-Williams, Robert, ed. 1993. *Reading Rodney King Reading Urban Uprising.* New York: Routledge.

Hartigan, Richard. 1999. *Racial Situations: Class Predicaments of Whiteness in Detroit.* Princeton: Princeton University Press.

Omi, Michael, and Howard Winant. 1994. *Racial Formation in the United States: From the 1960s to the 1990s.* New York: Routledge.

Ross, Thomas. 1996. *Just Stories: How the Law Embodies Racism and Bias.* Boston: Beacon.

West, Cornel. 1994. *Race Matters.* New York: Vintage Books.

Wilson, Amy. "The Messages of 'Malcolm X' Detroiters Weigh in on Movie, Man." *Detroit Free Press.* November 18, 1992.

Part II

Identity and Pedagogy

9

Nonessentialist Identity and the National Discourse

Marilyn M. Cooper

"We have room for but one language here, and that is the English language."

Theodore Roosevelt

"We choose worlds with our words."

Linda Brodkey

With the goal of rethinking the fundamental premises of literacy education in response to the increasing salience of cultural and linguistic diversity and of multiple communication channels, the New London Group argues that a primary change in assumptions about language is needed: "Clearly the main element of this change [is] that there [is] no singular, canonical English that either could or should be taught any more." They propose instead a pedagogy of multiliteracies, "one in which language and other modes of meaning are dynamic representational resources, constantly being remade by their users as they work to achieve their various cultural purposes" (Cope and Kalantzis 2000, 5). Here I want to suggest that a pedagogy of multiliteracies also requires us to rethink the notion of identity, how it is enacted in language use, and also what teachers of college writing tell students about choosing correct or appropriate languages.

Language and identity are, of course, inextricably linked, but they also have been addressed in strikingly similar ways. Just as language has sometimes been assumed to be a necessary and historically effective unifying force in a society (English in the United States), crucial to forming a strong and stable national identity, so too a stable, unified identity has often been

assumed to be necessary for the effective functioning of an individual. Multicultural communication, both virtual and real (through immigration patterns), has shaken the foundations of these assumptions. Though the United
States has never been a monolingual country, individuals are increasingly
likely to be bilingual and/or bidialectal (or tri or more), to live in multicultural communities and/or families, to interact in their neighborhoods or in
their work environments with speakers of many different dialects and languages. In these circumstances, both languages and identities mix and blur
boundaries, as individuals try on and use different languages and roles as the
need arises. And the result has not been chaos; instead, both language
and identity are understood to be simply more complex, more flexible, less
threatened by difference.

> *Identities are boring. Nation-states are boring. Languages are interesting.*
> *Language itself, modeling and refining language from inside out, is most*
> *interesting. In a world of more than one language, there is language in*
> *abundance. There is stimulation in abundance to literally change my mind.*
> *Given the chance to change one's style, the habitual way of thinking, the*
> *grammatical structure, I take the opportunity to change my writing and*
> *therefore my nature. Verena Stefan* (in Ogulnick 2000, 29)

Many of the arguments about what language or languages to teach in
classrooms center on the need to allow, preserve, or create individual and
national identity, and these two goals often seem to be at odds: Is our goal
to enable students to write in their own voices or to instill in them common
cultural values? In her "challenge to identity-disclosing pedagogies,"
Michelle Baillif (1997) argues that interest in identity is a symptom of the
discipline's clinging to a notion of a foundational self:

> Jacqueline Jones Royster, speaking of her poly-vocal subjectivity, says that
> "all my voices are authentic," acknowledging that her "voices" make her sub-
> jectivity possible. Royster could have said "all my voices are false"—or rather
> "all my voices are neither authentic or false." But that Royster said all her
> voices are "authentic" once again underscores how invested we are in the
> notion of "Truth," and in the notion that rhetorical/speaking Being has some
> essential relation to Truth, or should have such a relation. Richard Lanham
> argues that the discipline of composition studies maintains, "a common-sense
> positivism that finds a real world out there, a sincere soul inside all of us, and
> a prose style that opens a transparent window between the two." (1997, 86–87)

Baillif's choice of Royster as an example of our discipline's allegiance to
ideas of an authentic self makes sense; who better to quote than a past Chair
of CCCC? But as I read this passage from Royster's address, she is not really
saying that her voices make her subjectivity possible nor buying into a
common-sense positivism that invests in a real world, sincere self, and
language as a transparent window. Earlier, she made the point more "gently,"

in words her friend did not understand: "Yes, I do have a range of voices, and I take quite a bit of pleasure actually in being able to use any of them at will" (Royster 1996). Thus, if I were to rephrase her words, I would suggest "all my voices are mine," an assertion of identity that escapes—or doesn't recognize—the problem that has transfixed Baillif here.

> *In the otherworldly accents of Spanish, Japanese, French, and now Chinese, I thought I heard echoes of a Platonic me, the self that cast shadows on the cave wall of my mundane existence. I seemed to discover a more authentic self as I used other languages to examine, twist, test, transform what I had learned growing up in the dreary swamplands of Louisiana, in the yellow dust West Texas caliche, in the Arizona desert where saguaro cactuses open their hands in prickly greeting and point always to the sky. Doug Millison* (in Ogulnick 2000, 149)

Contrasting what Doug Millison says about his feelings in learning new languages with what Royster says and what Verena Stefan says in the passage quoted earlier makes clear how the search for a foundational self problematizes the notion of identity for many North American (and Western European) Anglo thinkers. Millison sees in language a chance to discover "a more authentic self," or as Baillif quotes Lanham as saying, "a sincere soul," whereas instead Royster sees "a range of voices" that allow her to "affirm differences, variety" and Stefan sees a chance to "change my mind . . . style . . . habitual way of thinking . . . change . . . my nature." While Royster and Stefan translate themselves into new voices, new languages, welcoming change and the opportunities new ways of thinking offer them, Millison seeks in other languages an escape from "mundane existence," a way to seize the freedom to recreate his own true self. For Millison, an identity shaped by the languages of his mundane existence is not authentic, not true; for Royster and Stefan, languages are a mode of identities; they might say, all my voices, all my identities, are authentic because I live in them all.

Baillif, earlier in her article, critiques positional theories of identity like those of Nancy Hartsock, Adrienne Rich, and Linda Alcoff, because they offer no escape from the trap of identity:

> this positioning in no way *liberates* the subject from the process of subjectification, the process of becoming subject, or coming to know, to be, and to have an "identity." This scenario of production is symptomatic of the metaphysics of presence and representation whereby the real—what Is (which always has some relation to the notion of Truth)—is constantly forced to materialize. People, subjects, identities, must be produced and thus positioned at all times—politically and "correctly" so. Therefore, emancipatory pedagogies, espousing liberation and redemption, far from liberating the students, are "hailing" the students as responsible subjects. Such a "liberation" propagates slaves—guilty slaves—to serve the Master: the State. (1997, 83)

The foundational self needs a guarantee (a foundation), but the foundation—essential nature or social construction (in opposition to and thus in thrall to the Other)—imprisons the self in determination, denies its freedom. Thus, because the notion of identity fails to liberate the individual from her "subjectification" to her language, her culture, her community, her society, any attempt at identity politics or affirmation of identity as empowering is seen as delusional.

> *Every path I/i take is edged with thorns. On the one hand, i play into the Savior's hands by concentrating on authenticity, for my attention is numbed by it and diverted from other, important issues; on the other hand, i do feel the necessity to return to my so-called roots, since they are the fount of my strength, the guiding arrow to which i constantly refer before heading for a new direction. Trinh T. Minh-ha (1989)*

But there are good reasons to hold onto the notion of identity, to remember the intimate connections of the self to its experiences and material reality. Keith Gilyard in his CCCC Chair's address explains:

> It's useful at times to complicate notions of identity, but primary identities operate powerfully in the world and have to be productively engaged. I think King had it right, for example, when he dreamed of Black kids and White kids holding hands. There are whole realities attached to those Black hands and White hands that have been insufficiently dealt with to date and won't be if we insist on prematurely converting King's dream to one of hybridity kids holding hands with junior border crossers. When we engage in discussions about fluidity, we ought to keep in mind the question of who can afford to be anchored to a focus on the indeterminate. (2000, 270–71)

Primary identities are formed by the experiences of living in particular places and particular times, and dealing with those whole realities attached to Black hands and White hands is a better route to a democratic politics than are attempts to empower individuals through enabling them to "escape" their subjectivity.

> *Although the linguistic truths about me are fraught with many political complexities, I usually offer this short and somewhat ingenuous answer: "I was born in Montréal." What I do not usually add, however, is that although I cannot produce a grandmother from St-Pie-de-Bagot, a grandfather from Glasgow, or even a parent from a stetl in Galecia, I am nonetheless a Québécoise. I have learned French and Québec culture through inclination, not legislation. Moreover, while I resent the fact that this "otherness" has been imposed on me by the imperialistic ambitions of warring groups of anti-Semitic elite European men centuries ago, I prefer my "otherness" to identifying with them. Ultimately, I celebrate the richness and diversity otherness has brought me, along with the opportunity for solidarity with other "others" in the world. Tant pis; j'y suis et j'y reste (Too bad; I'm here and I'm staying!). Greta Hoffman Nemiroff (in Ogulnick 2000, 19)*

Addressing the connection of identity politics with essentialism directly, bell hooks argues forcefully for the value of incorporating personal experience in classroom discussions along with other ways of knowing:

> I want to have a phrase that affirms the specialness of those ways of knowing rooted in experience. . . . To me this privileged standpoint does not emerge from the "authority of experience" but rather from the passion of experience, the passion of remembrance.
>
> . . . When I use the phrase "passion of experience," it encompasses many feelings but particularly suffering, for there is a particular knowledge that comes from suffering. It is a way of knowing that is often expressed through the body, what it knows, what has been deeply inscribed on it through experience. This complexity of experience can rarely be voiced and named from a distance. It is a privileged location, even as it is not the only or even always the most important location from which one can know. (90–91)

It is the value of recognizing the complexity of experience, of each individual's experience, that makes the concept of identity worth saving, or releasing, from the problems that beset it in Western systems of thought. And it is identity in this sense that is so inextricably tied up with each individual's languages.

A nonessentialist notion of identity—often referred to as a postmodern identity or self—has been developing in academic discussions in recent years. It's a tricky notion, and Gilyard is right to be wary of fluidity, hybridity, and indeterminate definitions of identity, as they often are deployed to erase identities (and differences). In the nonessentialist notion of identity I wish to define, the self is fluid and in process, but determinate at any particular moment; it is not necessarily hybrid but always complex, determined by its experiences to a certain extent but still also constructed or chosen with varying degrees of awareness; and it defines itself not in opposition to others or to its community but in relation to others. A nonessentialist identity (self) is (to reverse the order) relational, complex, and in process.

All three of these characteristics are problematic for Western thinkers, but especially the notion of the self as relational. The most influential thinker to have proposed a relational notion of self is Emanuel Levinas (1985), who asserts that the self is constructed not in opposition to the other, as in the Hegelian master–slave dialectic, but rather is grounded in responsibility for the other: "Responsibility is what is incumbent upon me exclusively, and what *humanly,* I cannot refuse. This charge is the supreme dignity of the unique. I am I in the sole measure that I am responsible, a non-interchangeable I" (101). Identity is founded in this originary sociality, the response to the face of the other. I am I not because I am not you (the Hegelian binary identity) but because I respond to you, am responsible to you, in a way that no one else does, or can. And as Levinas makes clear, this responsibility is not a matter of control or of omniscience; instead, the responsibility is ongoing, for I can never know if I have done the right thing or done enough.

This is a difficult conception of the self (perhaps especially difficult in the United States with its cultural myths of the solitary, self-reliant frontiersman and the lonely rebel against the system), as it requires an understanding of one's obligations to others not as a restriction on the individual but as the ground of individuality. And responsibility may seem a very shaky ground if one is used to thinking of oneself as grounded in unitary self-consciousness. But the idea that the self can be relational, that individuality can be grounded in a strong sense of community, is not difficult for many other cultures.

In particular, the practices and beliefs of traditional Native-American culture show how, as in Levinas' thought, individual identity can rest on relatedness and responsibility. First among the first principles of the *Sacred Tree,* a book that came out of a conference of elders from various Native communities in North America, is the principle of wholeness: "All things are interrelated. Everything in the universe is part of a single whole. Everything is connected in some way to everything else" (Bopp, Brown, and Lane, Jr., 1989, 26). In his work as a crown attorney with the Ojibwe in Canada, Rupert Ross (1996) observed that a preferred method of treating wrongdoers is temporary banishment:

> The assumption is that this is the most effective way to teach "lost" people that everything in Creation, including them, survives primarily because of mutually supportive relationships with everything else. Once that is understood, it is a short step to understanding that each being has a responsibility to contribute to the health of all those relationships, rather than just taking away as they please. (95)

The responsibility for the health of relationships, for recognizing and responding to the wholeness of Creation, is an individual one, a responsibility that must be, as in Levinas's thought, undertaken by each person in their own way. Ross explains that at first he misunderstood the "noninterference approach to raising children" he observed in Indian communities, "with its understanding that it is improper to tell children what to say, do, watch, build, read, listen to, and so forth. To me that seemed like a recipe for chaos in today's world" (1996, 83). Eventually he came to understand that the approach was grounded in the teaching of wholeness:

> It taught first that life was a matter of responsibilities that all people have to bear at all times. Second, it taught children how to develop the personal qualities they would need to be able to carry out those responsibilities. What people actually did in fulfilment of their duties, however, was largely a matter of free choice. (84)

Free choice as a determinant of identity, figured in Western thought as freedom from responsibility to others, here appears as a necessary aspect of being responsible to others, of being a responsible member of a community.

In Baillif's description of the problem with identity, it is the fear of determination by social structures, the structural response to the loss of the ground
of essentialism, that is seen as the fatal flaw in identity politics. Identity is
seen as a process of control, of interpellation into the predetermined roles of
the society (Althusser). Jane Flax (1993) argues that the modern self was intimately tied up with the notion of control, of the rational mind controlling the
irrational body, of rational Western man controlling the irrational Others. If
identities are not conceived as a mode of controlling individuals, but as built
up through relations with others, identities become more complex. Maria
Lugones (1994), developing a notion of identities as "impure," curdled like
improperly mixed mayonnaise, sees the complexity of nonessential identities
as resisting control:

> I think of the attempt at control exercised by those who possess both power
> and the categorical eye and who attempt to split everything impure, break-
> ing it down into pure elements (as an egg white and egg yolk) for the pur-
> poses of control. Control over creativity. And I think of something in the
> middle or either/or, something impure, something or someone mestizo, as
> both separated, curdled, and resisting in its curdled state. Mestizaje defies
> control through simultaneously asserting the impure, curdled multiple state
> and rejecting fragmentation into pure parts. In this play of assertion and
> rejection, the mestiza is unclassifiable, unmanageable. She has no pure parts
> to be "had," controlled. (460)

This process of rejection of pure identity is what Michelle Fine (1994) refers
to as "working the hyphen." Her description of the case of her nineteen-year-
old niece, adopted from Columbia into a middle-class Jewish family and now
a single mother, giving a deposition in a suit against a department store security officer who sexually assaulted her when she was sixteen exemplifies the
complexity of the performance of nonessential identities:

> Jackie mingled her autobiography with our surveilled borders on her Self
> and the raced and gendered legal interpretations of her Other by which she
> was surrounded. She braided them into her story, her deposition, which
> moved among "hot spots" and "safe spots." She slid from victim to sur-
> vivor, from naïve to coy, from deeply experienced young woman to child.
> In her deposition she dismantled the very categories I so worried we had
> constructed as sedimented pillars around her, and she wandered among
> them, pivoting her identity, her self-representations, and, therefore, her audi-
> ences. She became neither the Other nor the Same. Not even zippered. Her
> mobile positioning of contradictions could too easily be written off to the
> inconsistencies of adolescence. Maybe that's why she ultimately won the
> settlement for damages. But she would be better viewed as an honest
> narrator of multiple poststructural selves speaking among themselves, in
> front of an audience searching relentlessly for pigeonholes. (71)

As evident too in this account, we can also see identities, at least in part, as consciously chosen. Stuart Hall sees identity formation as taking place as we reflect on our constructions of positions in language:

> we . . . occupy our identities very retrospectively: having produced them, we then know who we are. We say, "Oh, that's where I am in relation to this argument and for these reasons." So, it's exactly the reverse of what I think is the common sense way of understanding it, which is that we already know our "self" and then put it out there. Rather, having put it into play in language, we *then* discover what we are. I think that only then do we make an investment in it, saying, "Yes, I like that position, I am that sort of person, I'm willing to occupy that position." (qtd. in Drew 1998, 173)

The idea of identity as an ongoing process of self-construction, adumbrated by Hall here, obviates the modernist fear of the fragmentation of the self while at the same time resisting the ideas that identities are pure and rationally constructed.

That the postmodern self is not fragmented but multiple is also the argument of Jane Flax, who points out that the postmodern self is not just the reverse mirror image of the modern self:

> Often theorists posit an apparently dichotomous choice between two ideas of subjectivity. Subjectivity is depicted either as a coherent entity or as formerly solid ones that have (or should) now splinter into fragments. These ideas are actually mirror images of and dependent on each other. We can develop more adequate accounts of subjectivity if it is conceived as heterogeneous and incomplete processes. (1993, 93)

Flax emphasizes subjectivity as an array of ongoing processes, never completed, and she sees these processes as heterogeneous, involving the body as well as the mind, and as not amenable to control. Contrasting the postmodern self to the Cartesian schizoid self that splits the mind from the body and centers the self in the rational mind, Flax comments: "we never encounter a person without a body or discursive practices without embodied practitioners. Embodiment is simultaneously somatic, psychic, and discursive" (98). She concludes:

> Subjectivity is not an illusion, but the subject *is* a shifting and always changing intersection of complex, contradictory, and unfinished processes. Total access to and control over these processes *is* an illusion, for (among other reasons) the outer world will not provide the resources for us to discover all of them or the space to express them. (108)

> I grew up in a house of shy and broken languages, *I wrote at the beginning of this text, and I already no longer know how to translate this sentence into German. I would have to write it entirely differently in German to begin with, and right now I wouldn't know how. It has slipped my mind, yielding to something to come. Verena Stefan* (in Ogulnick 2000, 29)

Just as a stable, singular identity is often seen to be essential to the integrity of an individual, linked with and dependent on one's own authentic voice, so too a stable, singular cultural identity, linked with and dependent on a single common, standard language is often seen to be essential to the integrity of a nation or a culture. The integrity of the nation-state and cultural unity are often equated in arguments for the importance of a common or standard language, perhaps because threats to the nation inspire a more immediate reaction than threats to cultural unity. For example, former Secretary of Education William Bennett argues:

> Each of us is justly proud of his own ethnic heritage. But we share this pride, in common, as Americans, as American citizens. To be a citizen is to share in something common—common principles, common memories, and a common language in which to discuss our common affairs. Our common language is, of course, English. And our common task is to ensure that our non-English-speaking children learn this common language. (qtd. in Lippi-Green 1997, 118)

The claim for the importance of a common language to a nation-state is not very compelling, however. Manuel Castells (1997) observes a historic disjuncture between civil society organized by states and national culture organized around identity: He offers as examples the Soviet Union, a plurinational state that failed to create a national identity, and Catalonia, a region that for one thousand years has had a distinct national identity based on shared language and culture but has always been a part of Spain and still has, according to its current president, no secessionist ambitions. There are few nations in the world in which most people speak one standard language. A great number of languages are spoken in China; the citizens of the tiny island nations of the Pacific speak up to a dozen languages; many countries use more than one language in official business.

The claim for the importance of language in creating cultural unity, in contrast, is more compelling. Castells points out that "obviously a common language does not make a nation" (49), but he also argues that language plays a fundamental role in the formation of national identity, that it establishes *"an invisible national boundary less arbitrary than territoriality, and less exclusive than ethnicity"* (italics in original) and that "language, as the direct expression of culture, becomes the trench of cultural resistance, the last bastion of self-control, the refuge of identifiable meaning" (52). The belief that language is the direct expression of culture provides the underpinning for Bennett's assertion that to be American is to share a common language, and that language "of course" is English. Common-sense assumptions like Bennett's represent as settled questions that often are far from settled. Language may express our culture, but the questions of what that language is, how it is to be defined, and what it includes have long been a matter of dispute.

One beeg paht of being Local is da language. Plenny people get dat rigid stereotype equation dat Pidgin=Local and non-Pidgin (Standard English)=non-Local (Haole). I tink nowdays we a little mo' accepting of da different kine varieties of Pidgin. . . . I tink we can say dat jus cuz da guy look haole no mean dat he dunno Pidgin, and conversly, jus cuz da guy look Local no necessarily mean dat his Pidgin is fluent. Cuz I acknowledge da fack not all Local people in Hawai'i talk Pidgin. So Pidgin will nevah be one good identifier characteristic of Localness or non-Localness, but da way I see 'em, I going trow 'em out and I dunno if people going agree or wot, but da way I see 'em is dat to be Local you no haff to speak Pidgin, but you gotta be able to understand Pidgin. . . . Pidgin wuz once tot of as one of da uniting factors during da heyday of Local pride. However, today Pidgin get da potential to be used divisively if attacks are furthered to da extreme. Lee A. Tonouchi (1989)

Consideration of the history of the debate over language in the United States makes clear just what is at stake in defining our common language. In her discussion of the standard ideology, "the belief that there is one and only one correct spoken form of the language, modeled on a correct written form," Lesley Milroy details how the standard ideology is inflected differently in response to the social and political histories of the United States and Great Britain (1999, 174). She argues that in America "the groups which are seen to threaten the social fabric are not an urban proletariat speaking varieties of English rooted in historically established dialects, but immigrants who are speakers of languages other than English" (192). Whereas in Britain standard language ideology focuses on class, in America, the history of slavery, the conquest of indigenous peoples, the annexation of the Spanish-speaking Southwest, and periodic waves of immigration result in a focus on race and ethnicity—although class also plays a role in American versions of the standard ideology as race and ethnicity do in the British version.

Milroy notes that "before the nineteenth century, national multilingualism and personal bilingualism were generally accepted in the United States as a fact of life" (194), and that members of the Continental Congress did not see fitness for citizenship as tied to specific languages. Although there was from the early days of the United States some impetus for establishing English as the official language, Milroy notes that the founders deliberately chose not to restrict the languages used by citizens. Benjamin Franklin was an exception in the Continental Congress in complaining about the large number of "ignorant and stupid" Germans who refuse to learn English; he lamented, "They will soon so outnumber us, that all the advantages we have will not, in My Opinion, be able to preserve our language, and even our government will become precarious" (qtd. in Milroy 1999, 194). The association between undesirable traits and speaking languages other than English that Franklin makes here was unusual at the time, Milroy claims; Franklin adumbrates by one hundred years the development of the English language as an ideological instrument, thinking that is evident also today among those who see bilingualism or bidialectalism not as a pragmatic advantage but as "a social and personal stigma and as a threat to the cohesion of the state" (Milroy 1999, 196).

Dating to pre-Revolutionary times, the stigmatization of African Americans and their languages is the most long-standing and the most complex example of the use of language to enact discrimination. Milroy notes that Black English is not surprisingly the most stigmatized of American dialects because like languages whose threat most inspire the American standard ideology—American-Indian languages and Spanish—African-American-Vernacular English is a marker of race.

> *I carried with me a tremendously empowering repertoire of speaking and listening skills when I shuffled off to public school and continued to expand it once I arrived. Included in my bag of communicative tricks were that prize stragtegem, Black English, a productive (speaking) biloquialism, and a broader receptive (listening) bidialectalism. There was also an adroitness at responding to the perceived need to match each dialect to different sets of social circumstances. All this achievement may appear quite marvelous and, I guess, actually is. But it represents nothing miraculous beyond the basic miracle of existing, nothing special among Black children, nothing that should not be the case if a developing mind is pretty much left alone. Put more succinctly, it really ain't no new news.*
> *Keith Gilyard* (1991)

The shift in attitudes over the history of the country toward American Indian languages and toward Spanish further demonstrates the increasing use of language as a mode of racial discrimination. In the late eighteenth century, Benjamin Rush wrote, "A man who is learned in the dialect of a Mohawk Indian is more fit for a legislator than a man who is ignorant even in the language of the early Greeks" (qtd. in Milroy 1999, 193). But by the end of the nineteenth century, Indian languages were characterized as inimical to civilized behavior; the commissioner for Indian Affairs, J. D. C. Atkins, states, "teaching an Indian youth in his own barbarous dialect is a positive detriment to him. The first step to be taken towards civilisation, toward teaching the Indians the mischief and folly of continuing in their barbarous practices is to teach them the English language" (qtd. in Milroy, 195). And by the end of the twentieth century, the campaign to eradicate Indian languages had succeeded to such an extent that most Indians in the country were not native speakers of their ancestral languages.

> *Lafayette, IN, July 2000: I am in the great room of a lodge overlooking Waapaashiki (the Wabash River) watching an impromptu puppet show performed by a few Miami children. The storyline is imperfect but as we watch*

these kids huddle behind their makeshift puppet-theatre table and struggle to
keep their story afloat, many of us begin to cry. We are watching Miami
children speak the language of our ancestors. We are hearing a new gen-
eration of Native children create themselves as Native people, as Miami, in
the language that named this land long before Europeans made the scene.
Malea Powell (2002)

In 1848, The Treaty of Hidalgo stipulated protection of the language and culture of the seventy-five thousand Spanish-speaking residents of the lands
annexed from Mexico, but in 1878 this protection was rescinded when
California became the first English-Only state. Large-scale immigration at
the end of the nineteenth century provoked a strong reaction that focused on
language, and another strong wave of immigration in the late twentieth
century similarly sparked the current English-Only movement.

. . . the startling event within that event [Vietnam] was when the Japanese
American company commander shouted to us (as we huddled in our bunker)
that we were in the American Army and that we would speak English, even
in private. . . .
  Whatever Captain Yamashita's angry invective, we continued to speak
in Spanish. Look outside the bunker. See if anyone's around. Speak quietly,
nearly in whispers. Speak Spanish. We are Spanish, though not one of us
would deny being American. Victor Villanueva, Jr. (1993)

Theodore Roosevelt's oft-quoted comment—"We have room but for
one language here and that is the English language, for we intend to see
that the crucible turns our people out as Americans, of American nation-
ality, and not as dwellers in a polyglot boarding house" (qtd. in Milroy,
192)—contrasts sharply with the earlier attitude of most of the members
of the Continental Congress, and if it were not for the remarks of Benjamin Franklin, on the one hand, and ongoing countervailing efforts to preserve and validate other languages as important resources, on the other,
one might see the history of language in the United States as one of an
overall decline in tolerance toward diversity. But the fight to define U.S.
national identity through the language or languages used by its citizens is
far from resolved.

In her book *The Language War* (2000), Robin Tolmach Lakoff descries
a new challenge to the standard ideology at the end of the twentieth century. Analyzing a series of news stories that seem on the surface to be
ephemeral and trivial but that receive "undue attention"—the p.c. debate, the
Clarence Thomas hearings, Hillary Clinton's image problem, the OJ trial,
the Ebonics controversy, Bill Clinton's impeachment for moral deficien-
cies—Lakoff argues that such stories "have legs" because they bring into
question the exonimate status of Standard English, the assumption that

Standard English and its users define what is normal for the culture. She says:

> We are currently engaged in a great and not very civil war testing whether the people who always got to make meaning for all of us still have that unilateral right and that capacity. The answer that seems to be winning is NO, but those who want to check the YES box are unaccustomed to not having their choices win by default and are fighting back with the zeal common to lost causes. (20)

For example, in the case of the Clarence Thomas hearings, the "common-sense" or exnominate definition of "sexual harassment" as just joking around and the "natural" narrative of how a woman should respond to instances of sexual harassment—by decisively stopping it through personal or legal action—were put into question, and the slogan that arose out of the whole affair—"you/they just don't get it"—demonstrated women's ability to create the public meaning of an event. Lakoff (2000) notes:

> The slogan itself was about the making of public meaning—and by suggesting that it was women who were the makers of a meaning that men not only didn't create but *couldn't even understand,* it captured the fear that was already surfacing in the p.c. debate. (147)

Her analysis of the verdict of the OJ trial comes to the same conclusion, with the mostly Black jury saying to fearful White Americans, "you just don't get it." What the people who always got to make meaning for the rest of us fear, according to Lakoff, is their loss of invisibility:

> The fact that the official namers are themselves no longer invisible, exnominated, or unnamed means that their linguistic activities are no longer normal or unmarked. Those activities can now be commented on and criticized. They no longer define our cultural frames unilaterally and uncontroversially. (79)

Standard English is no longer "of course" our national language; Lakoff argues that the aim of the war is "equality in the creation of our national discourse" and claims that it is "unifying in intent: . . . we can forge a single language that we can all adopt as our own" (2000, 257).

> Los Chicanos, *how patient we seem, how very patient. There is the quiet of the Indian about us. We know how to survive. When other races have given up their tongue, we've kept ours. We know what it is to live under the hammer blow of the dominant* norteamericano *culture. But more than we count the blows, we count the days the weeks the years the centuries the eons until the white laws and commerce and customs will rot in the deserts they've created, lie bleached. Humildes yet proud, quietos yet wild,* nosotros los mexicanos-Chicanos *will walk by the crumbling ashes as*

we go about our business. Stubborn, perservering, impenetrable as stone,
yet possessing a malleability that renders us unbreakable, we, the mestizas
and mestizos, *will remain. Gloria Anzaldúa* (1987)

I'd like to push Lakoff's notion of the creation of our national discourse
a little further into the realm of multiplicity and indeterminancy than she
wants to take it, and once again, I want to argue that there is something worth
saving in a concept that has seemed so problematic that it must be discarded.
Equating national or cultural identity with a common language, especially
when that language is assumed to be Standard English, would seem to
demand uniformity, the repression of difference and submission to the dominant perspective. But we don't want to forget or ignore the historical and
material realities that connect us and constitute our lives in the United States,
that make up the American culture; we don't want the heterogenous groups
that make up our culture to disengage from one another and stop trying to
make a better society together. It is the assumption once again that identity
is a matter of control that makes the goal of national/cultural identity seem
to be oppressive, to leave us with the equally unsatisfactory options of the
melting pot or the tower of babel: either we completely resolve our differences rationally and agree on the values that ground our actions or we are
incapable of any productive action or interaction. But if instead of looking
to Standard English to control and secure our cultural identity we instead see
cultural identity as the ongoing creation of a national discourse, a dialog or
multilog rather than a monolog, we can reclaim all our histories and all our
voices and begin to see more clearly how we have been interacting and taking
action.

Adapting Flax's comments on subjectivity, I argue that cultural identity
is not an illusion, but the culture *is* a shifting and always changing intersection of complex, contradictory, and unfinished processes. Total access to
and control over these processes *is* an illusion, and an illusion that can no
longer be sustained by the equally elusive and illusionary notion of Standard English.

For the most part, this understanding of language and identity has not
been reflected in the practices of the college writing classroom, which instead
assume (and, according to Bruce Horner and John Trimbur [2002], are based
on a commitment to) monolingual Standard American English as the sole
appropriate mode of academic communication. Similarly, most arguments
about what language(s) should be taught in writing classrooms, including
many that advocate pluralistic approaches to language, assume that all students should make the same decisions about what language(s) to use when.
I suggest instead that the intersection of needs, desires, intentions, history,
and identities in any writing situation is so complex that no one can decide
for another what language is correct, and that what we should be doing in
teaching writing is helping students learn how to choose for themselves what

language(s) or creative mix of languages to use to enact their diverse and multiple (not fragmented) identities and meaning intentions in diverse situations. Like all writers and speakers, individual students will make different choices; our role, I argue, is to help them understand the range of languages that are available and to help make them conscious of and responsible for the choices they are making.

I tell my students: The language is yours. Bend it, twist it, curse if you must, in doing so will take you to the point of familiarity, of ease, where the written language becomes your vehicle, too, your conduit to the expression of your reality. Do it for your own sake. Do it for the world's sake. Elizabeth Nuñez (in Ogulnick 2000, 44)

Works Cited

Anzaldúa, Gloria. 1987. *Borderlands/La Frontera*. San Francisco: Aunt Lute Books.

Baillif, Michelle. 1997. "Seducing Composition: A Challenge to Identity-Disclosing Pedagogies." *Rhetoric Review* 16: 76–91.

Bopp, Judie, Michael Bopp, Lee Brown, and Phil Lane, Jr. 1989. *The Sacred Tree: Reflections on Native American Spirituality*. Twin Lakes, WI: Lotus Light.

Castells, Manuel. 1997. *The Information Age: Economy, Society and Culture. Vol. II: The Power of Identity*. Oxford: Blackwell.

Cope, Bill, and Mary Kalantzis, eds. 2000. *Multiliteracies: Literacy Learning and the Design of Social Futures*. London: Routledge.

Drew, Julie. 1998. "Cultural Composition: Stuart Hall on Ethnicity and the Discursive Turn." *Journal of Advanced Composition* 18 (2): 171–96.

Fine, Michelle. 1994. "Working the Hyphens: Reinventing Self and Other in Qualitative Research." In *Handbook of Qualitative Research*, edited by Norman K. Denzin and Yvonna S. Lincoln, 70–82. Thousand Oaks, CA: Sage.

Flax, Jane. 1993. *Disputed Subjects: Essays on Psychoanalysis, Politics and Philosophy*. New York: Routledge.

Gilyard, Keith. 2000. "Literacy, Identity, Imagination, Flight." *College Composition and Communication* 52: 260–72.

———. 1991. *Voices of the Self: A Study of Language Competence*. Detroit: Wayne State University Press.

Horner, Bruce, and John Trimbur. 2002. "English Only and U.S. College Composition." *College Composition and Communication* 53: 594–630.

Lakoff, Robin Tolmach. 2000. *The Language War*. Berkeley: University of California Press.

Levinas, Emmanuel. 1985. *Ethics and Infinity*. Translated by Richard A. Cohen. Pittsburgh: Duquesne University Press.

Lippi-Green, Rosina. 1997. *English with an Accent: Language, Ideology, and Discrimination in the United States*. New York: Routledge.

Lugones, Maria. 1994. "Purity, Impurity, Separation." *Signs* 19: 458–79.

Milroy, Leslie. 1999. "Standard English and Language Ideology in Britain and the United States." In *Standard English: The Widening Debate*, edited by Tony Bex and Richard J. Watts, 173–206. London: Routledge.

Millison, Doug. 2000. In *Language Crossings: Negotiating the Self in a Multicultural World,* edited by Karen Ogulnick, 143–50. New York: Teachers College Press.

Minh-ha, Trinh T. 1989. *Woman, Native, Other: Writing Postcoloniality and Feminism.* Bloomington, Indiana University Press.

Nemiroff, Greta Hoffman. 2000. In *Language Crossings: Negotiating the Self in a Multicultural World,* edited by Karen Ogulnick, 13–20. New York: Teachers College Press.

Ogulnick, Karen, ed. 2000. *Language Crossings: Negotiating the Self in a Multicultural World.* New York: Teachers College Press.

Nuñez, Elizabeth. 2000. In *Language Crossings: Negotiating the Self in a Multicultural World,* edited by Karen Ogulnick, 40–45. New York: Teachers College Press.

Powell, Malea. 2002. "Listening to Ghosts: An Alternative (Non)argument." In *Alt Dis: Alternative Discourses and the Academy,* edited by Christopher Schroeder, Helen Fox, and Patricia Bizzell, 11–22. Portsmouth, NH: Heinemann–Boynton/Cook.

Ross, Rupert. 1996. *Returning to the Teachings: Exploring Aboriginal Justice.* Toronto: Penguin.

Royster, Jacqueline Jones. 1996. "When the First Voice You Hear Is Not Your Own." *College Composition and Communication* 47: 29–40.

Stefan, Verena. 2000. In *Language Crossings: Negotiating the Self in a Multicultural World,* edited by Karen Ogulnick, 21–29. New York: Teachers College Press.

Tonouchi, Lee A. 1999. "No Laugh Brah, Serious: Pidgin's Association wit Local Comedy. *Hybolics* 1: 22–33.

Villanueva, Jr., Victor. 1993. *Bootstraps: From an American Academic of Color.* Urbana, IL: National Council of Teachers of English.

10

Community, Personal Experience, and Rhetoric of Commitment

Xin Liu Gale

I see us living in an age of "isms": social constructionism, feminism, multi-culturalism, Marxism, political activism and you can add to the list. Accompanying this particular set of isms is an emphasis on community and the community's ideals as goals for people working collectively to reach. In composition and rhetoric, hardly can anyone talk about anything without mentioning some sort of community: interpretive community, discourse community, home community, school community, classroom community, to name just a few. At the beginning, the ubiquity of "isms" and "community" was indeed a culture shock to someone like me who had assumed that this was a country where anyone could become Benjamin Franklin, Ronald Reagan, Toni Morrison, or Michael Jordan as long as he or she was willing to work hard. But soon I realized the folly of my assumption and acquired the terminology rather quickly in my academic discourse.

Deep down inside, however, the puzzlement was not resolved as to why a country founded on individual expression and freedom for its people to pursue personal happiness and fulfillment appears to be so devoted to social "isms" and community. The puzzlement caused a minor crisis after I accepted Keith Gilyard's invitation to speak at the conference on American ethnic rhetorics, for I perceived the title of the conference as asking the political question of identity, belonging, and commitment as well as the rhetorical question of authority and credibility: From what subject position do you speak? To what ethnic community do you pledge loyalty? What gives you the credibility and authority to talk about your community and its rhetoric(s)? If I was to address legitimately the subject of rhetoric, I knew I wouldn't be able to avoid dealing with these questions. For weeks these questions doggedly followed me around driving me crazy. What community do I belong to? What ethnic community do I belong to?

I thought not without envy how easy such questions would be for Keith. He knew the answers even as a child; he always knows where he belongs and he always has a community wherever he is, in New York, in Syracuse, in State College. The whole book *Voices of the Self* (1991) is about his identity and belonging, so when he says that he's committed to the language used in his community and argues for the legitimate status of Ebonics as a language, for a pluralistic view of education that will not marginalize and exclude the African Americans, for a more racially just and fair education system and society, you listen to him attentively and you're readily persuaded. He's all playful and innovative with words and sometimes pokes fun at himself and his people, yet his serious intent and messages are never lost on his audience.

But my case is entirely different. For thirteen years I haven't gone back to my hometown once or written to my friends. I've seldom spoken Chinese and have made very few new friends who came from mainland China. And I haven't written anything about Chinese rhetoric for ten years, not since my article on Chinese persuasion was rejected by a rhetoric journal. I didn't plan all this; it just happened. Now it's too late to try to pick up the old friendships or claim loyalty to my former community if there was one at all or renew my interest in comparative rhetoric. "Lost opportunities," I thought, feeling sad. "I've been working so hard at becoming an American I've lost touch with my Chinese roots. Should I tell Keith I've got nothing to say? At least I won't be wasting other people's precious time."

Then my brother called. He calls once in a long while, mainly to chat. This time he sounded a little breathless. I became concerned. "Have you read Gao Xingjian?"

"No," I said, feeling relieved that the cause of his breathlessness was just his excitement over another Chinese writer, which is not unusual for him. "You know I don't have time for leisure reading. The name rings a bell though. I might've read him a long time ago, in China," I said, keeping the conversation going.

"Ha, you have a good memory. It must be his play, *Bus Stop*. Now you've got to read his *One Man's Bible* and *Soul Mountain!* Masterpieces. Masterpieces. They're not translated into English yet. I'm sending you copies in Chinese."

I didn't want to be a killjoy so I thanked him. His enthusiasm for Chinese literature always sounds threatening to me and I know why. It had been twenty years but I still hadn't found the courage to talk with him about it. This might be a good opportunity.

"Andrew, you're still thinking of becoming a writer?" I ask, tentatively. "You're a programmer but you seem to be thinking about writing more than anything else."

"Oh, it's just a dream," he chuckles. "Perhaps after I retire I'll try to write novels. The guy's brilliant, I mean Gao Xingjian."

"You know I've been thinking all these years how your life would've been different if I hadn't shouted down your idea of becoming a writer." I gaze into the mouthpiece, the corridor to the past, and see the guilty young woman scrubbing away her husband's and son's week's laundry on a washboard in a large wooden basin while her younger brother whispered that he wanted to change his major from English to creative writing in the Chinese department. He said he could do more social good writing about the Cultural Revolution than teaching English. He confided in his elder sister that the urge to write had become so strong that he cried at night when he dreamed that the party secretary in the hospital was throwing all his drafts into a river. His eyes shone and his voice was sonorous. He thought she would drop the laundry and shout in excitement about this great idea of his. He needed only her support. They were very close. She did drop the laundry and shout. But what did she say? "Brother! You must be crazy! Don't you see all those people get into trouble writing, getting their tongues cut off and a bullet in the head? Whatever you write, it's bound to be viewed negatively. With an Episcopalian bishop and a Kuomingtang general for grandfathers, what good would your writing do to society? You're the only son in the family. If anything should happen to you, we'd all be finished. Keep this in mind when you're carried away by your ambition, will you please? Forget it! She's dead and it wasn't your fault or anybody else's." At her vehement reaction his good-natured smile froze and the sparkles dancing in his eyes were gone in an instant. He was enveloped in deep dark shadows. His awkward silence scared her, like the unfathomable ancient well in their grandmother's old courtyard that she never dared to go near. He went to play with his little nephew and she resumed her scrubbing.

They left their conversation at that and that conversation has been her woe ever since she came to America and became a writing teacher. "I've been suffering the guilt for too long and now I've apologized at last," I murmur. There is a long silence on the other end.

"You weren't the only one, Xin," the voice comes back, surprisingly cheerful and light-hearted. "Mother wouldn't even allow me to keep a diary fearing I would end up like Aunt Sheng's brother. Gao Xingjian's different. His mother disappeared at a reform farm and her body was found in a river and nobody knew when or how she died. She was only thirty-eight at the time. Gao's all alone in the world and that's why he can write."

I remember Aunt Sheng's brother. Aunt Sheng was Mother's best friend in college. Her brother, a sophomore majoring in physics, was imprisoned for ten years after his diary, in which he complained about a couple of party members during the Anti-Rightist Movement in 1957, was confiscated. After he served his term he was kept in the coal mine because it was during the Cultural Revolution. Then an accident blew his young body of twenty-nine into pieces. A life wasted. A life that had never been lived. And for what?

For a few words and a few lines and perhaps momentary relief. For these you pay the hefty price of your life, and you wonder if anything's worth it.

"So you don't blame me?" I say, feeling foolish how all these years I've made a big deal of something as necessary as asking Andrew not to write. I've almost forgotten Aunt Sheng's brother. But Andrew obviously hasn't. Now I even feel a little self-congratulatory for the good shouting I gave him twenty years ago. I may have saved his life, who knows? I've almost forgotten how your own words could destroy you in China. Thirteen years in a democratic country will just do that: I'm all courage and voice now, am I not?

"There's no one but myself to blame." His voice becomes a little thick and sentimental in the earpiece. Perhaps I'm reading my own emotions into it. "But we have Gao Xingjian. I know I'd never be able to write like him even if I'd begun to write in 1979. Nobody's ever spoken so well about what it's like to be a Chinese."

Andrew was right. The moment I opened *One Man's Bible* and read the first sentence I was unable to stop. Every word, every sentence, every page, every chapter was sending me in two opposite directions: backward and forward, past and present, and I began to see my thirty-six years of life in China and thirteen in America with such coherence and meaning as I had never before. To give you a sense of what I mean, here is what Gao has the character Daniel say about himself in a play titled *Weekend Quartet*:

> You're a stranger, destined to be a stranger forever, you have no hometown, no country, no attachments, no family, and no burdens except paying your taxes. There is a government in every city, there are officers in every customs station to check passports, and man and wife in every home, you only prowl from city to city, from country to country and from woman to woman. You no longer need to take on any town as your hometown, nor any country as your country, nor any woman as your wife. You have no enemies, and if people want to take you for an enemy to raise their spirits, it's purely their own business. Your only opponent (yourself) has been killed many times; there's no need to look for enemies, to commit suicide, or to do battle in a duel. You have lost all memories, the past has been cut off once and for all. You have no ideals, you've left them behind for other people to think about. (1999, 221–22)

I suspect that Daniel's, or rather Gao Xingjian's, cynicism toward "isms," institutional and human attachments, social and political ideals, and his insistence on an unlimited and unbridled independence may sound naive or even offensive to many in our field. But if you were Chinese and if you had read Gao Xingjian's plays and novels, you would know that such a clean break with politics, communities, and the past is not only necessary but inevitable for the writer. Stories like the one I told you earlier about Aunt Sheng's brother were never in short supply, and a young college student of nineteen being sent to jail for ten years and then to the coal mine to be blown away before he reached thirty was not such a rare and unusual story—and all because he had written in his diary about someone he didn't like. You would never imagine that I would write about Aunt Sheng's brother if I were still in China. For one, I'd have to think about my son's future even if I'd be willing to martyr myself for the advancement of social justice in my country. I'd have to think about my parents' fragile health and advanced age and it would be selfish to force on them the bereavement of their oldest daughter even if I were fearless about my own fate. I'd also have to think about my siblings and their families and children, my good friends, friendly colleagues, nosy but mostly rather nice neighbors, and imagine how they'd all be disgraced only because I wanted to tell some stories that otherwise would not be heard by more than half a dozen people and soon forgotten. Human attachments thus made most of us cowards and confined us to a silent existence that in turn forced silence on others, as I did to my brother. If I hadn't thought that I knew my brother's stories so well, perhaps I wouldn't have smothered the budding writer in him with such determination.

Sometime after Xiao-Xiao had vanished in 1978, right after the scores of the National College Entrance Examinations came out, I had peeked into Andrew's diary and read what he wrote. His writing was almost matter of fact: They had dated for four months. They worked at the same community hospital, he the self-taught physician, she the self-taught nurse. The day he took her home to meet his parents he sensed from Father's taciturnity that the old man didn't approve of his choice. She obviously sensed the elder's displeasure too, for after that she began to talk about going to medical school. She began to apologize for having parents who were not well-known academics like his parents but actors of Beijing opera in the metropolis, their popularity only making her more ashamed of them. He had tried to reassure her that his father could not decide for him whom he wanted to marry, so she was happy when they were together. Then both of them spent all of their time after work preparing for the Entrance Examinations, knowing that this would be the only chance in a lifetime and that millions of others like them were also buckling down for the first opportunity in a decade to compete equally, their eyes fixed on the alluring green light over the college entrance. She was confident and optimistic during their brief talks at work, but he could see that she had black circles under her eyes and that she was losing weight. Her slim body looked skinny like a child's, and he warned her of ruining her health at only age twenty. He had thought that she had a better chance of success, for she had finished high school whereas he had not even had the luck of finishing junior high when the storms of the Cultural Revolution swept him to the bottom of society and turned him into a custodian at the community hospital. Had he foreseen it all he would have married her right after he learned that he was admitted to the university of his first choice whereas her scores were not good enough for a third-tier college. He would've defied Father's anger to save her life. She was so pale and calm and so lovely! But when her farewell letter reached him, her family had already reported her missing to the police department. He had already walked miles and miles in the dark night after night along the Yangtze River looking for her, wishing she would jump out of the dark woods at his calling and weeping and apologize for testing his love in such a cruel manner. He would then forgive her mischief and bring her home. He would then ignore Father's disappointment and marry her. But her farewell letter reached him after he had already attended her funeral, which was held even though her body was never found. The letter ended his walk along the river. "Why would you make such a stupid decision? Why?" he wrote, all his angst, confusion, anger, sorrow, and despair loaded in a question that she would never answer.

I guess this was the diary that Andrew said Mother had asked him to destroy. As an American, a writing teacher, you perhaps wonder what harm could it do to anybody to mourn the death of a girlfriend, a young man's first love. But in a country where everything is interpreted in terms of political intentions, class struggle, and social good, the most innocent story could be construed as a vicious attack on something, either the party policies, the proletarian dictatorship, or someone allegedly responsible for the girl's disappearance. Who could afford to take a chance? Gao Xingjian was among the luckier ones, for even though his plays were banned in China he escaped in one piece. And in France he wrote his *One Man's Bible* and *Soul Mountain* in his mother tongue, his frustration with the ancient language notwithstanding. So who can fault him for wanting "an unlimited and unbridled independence, so that the individual can empty his mind of all the shackles of convention to make the choices best suited to himself"; for being "sceptical of all blind acquiescence to authority, trendiness and ideological detainment"; and for seeking his own personal peace and freedom for "a liberation of the spirit" as a writer and artist (1999, xvii)? After all, he had spent forty-seven years trying to give his talents to a country that neither loves its intellectuals nor wants their thinking, if their thinking is independent and different from the ideology of the party and the "Chinese community." All of his family members had perished and his country is no longer his home, so why would he want to keep the old shackles or inflict new ones upon himself?

I am, of course, not Gao Xingjian, and that's pretty obvious, even though reading him makes me aware that we shared some similar experiences and sentiments. We have substantial differences too, even though both of us are Chinese. Unlike Gao, I've wanted and tried to belong in my adopted country. Over the years my descriptors have undergone a series of changes that indicate my gradual involvement in American life: visiting scholar, international student, TA, writing teacher, Chinese American, Asian American, woman of color, scholar of composition and rhetoric, minority academic, and so forth. And each time these labels, when being first attached to me, would give me such a thrill of acceptance and belonging, of transforming from an escapee, a guest, a foreigner, an outsider, and a Chinese to a participating and contributing American citizen. I was not so concerned about the images these labels might project; I didn't even mind being called "the inscrutable Chinese" or woman of color, two of my least favorite descriptors. I understood everything comes with a price. You want to be an American? Then you have to accept what comes with being an American with a prefix, a Chinese-American, who is often seen in this country as having slanted, wandering eyes, walking with a shuffle, slurping soup noisily, living in a house with walls covered in grease from stir-frying, running a laundry or a restaurant, and speaking English with ugly ching-chong sounds. The silly details were more comical than offensive to me, at least at first, especially those contributed by Chinese-American writers themselves. Who doesn't love a good laugh, even if it's sometimes at your own expense? I don't remember when the comical remarks about Chinese Americans stopped being funny, when the labels began to cause anxiety and the sense of belonging became fleeting and illusory. I cannot pinpoint what caused the subtle changes in me. Nothing in particular, mostly small things too trivial to deserve mentioning, but the cumulative effect of these small things is that I began to see myself differently, and the self I see from others' eyes I know is not the self I am or want to be.

I became interested in stereotyping. In one of my freshman writing classes we read "Black Man and Public Space" by Brent Staples and "Mother Tongue" by Amy Tan. Staples' essay describes his experience of "being ever the suspect" in Chicago and New York, where his innocuous presence often caused women pedestrians to flee and policemen to turn hostile. During the class discussion several students said, "It's all in his head; nobody discriminates against him. He's the problem because he couldn't think about anything else but his skin color." About Amy Tan's mother who speaks broken English, some students said, "If she wants to live in America, why doesn't she make some effort to speak the language better so people can understand her?" Other students immediately pointed out that racial discrimination was more than just in Staples' head. "Didn't the office manager take him for a burglar when he walked into his own office and didn't the security guards chase after him until he reached someone who knew him? Didn't the woman in the jewelry store let out a dog on him when he strolled in to kill time before an interview? And wasn't his colleague, also a Black man and a journalist, taken for the killer by the police and held at gunpoint when he went to a neighboring town to work on a story about a murderer who was born there? As for Amy Tan's mother," the students continued, "just because her English isn't good enough, is the hospital justified in losing her CAT scan without apologizing when she was suffering from a tumor in her brain? If this is not discrimination then what is?"

Discussions like this made me glad to be a writing teacher. I didn't need to take sides for neither side was wrong. Nevertheless, those students who said "It's all in his head" would benefit from knowing that, from a social constructionist view of self and other, what is in Staples' head may not be Staples' sheer imagination but the internalization of his interactions with the people around him. As Corey Anton (2001) points out, this view maintains that since "When I see you your face is all, mine nothing" and vice versa, "others are the source of an objective presence of myself in the mode of not being me" (66). In many cases, "encountering others is a kind of 'trial,' including meanings such as 'judgment,' 'guilty,' and perhaps even 'sentencing'" (67). Anton cites Sartre's *Being and Nothingness* as an example of "powerfully [showing] how I become an object before myself in the gaze of the Other" and how "others' abilities to locate me 'amidst-the-things-of-the-world' easily transforms me into either a tool for their possibilities or an object for their possession" (67). In the case of Staples, his being seen as a threatening object on urban American streets may well be the possibility of his being eliminated, a possibility that is anything but a fantasy he created to keep himself amused. For those students who readily see the dark side of reality, Mikhail Bakhtin's theory of aesthetic consummation would provide a positive outlet for their encounter with others, including the others in their readings as well as in the classroom. In Anton's succinct rendering of Bakhtin's thinking, "others are necessary for aesthetizing lived-through world-experience." In other words, "others consummate me, and this provides the conditions in which my selfhood can be artistically manifest and experienced by others" (Anton 2001, 67). The examples of this consummation are too many to list here. Brent Staples and Amy Tan have achieved this consummation through writing. So has Keith Gilyard. And so has Gao Xingjian. Only through writing can the tragedy, the comedy, and the beauty of encountering others be captured and become a source of transformation for self and for the culture at large.

Writing this essay has thus compelled me to articulate my once tacit commitments as a writing teacher, intellectual, and citizen. Writing this essay also has helped me to crystalize my dream: that the next Chinese Nobel laureate will live and write in China, and that one day every human on earth will have the freedom to write and be encouraged to write about their personal experience of encountering and living with others.

Works Cited

Anton, Corey. 2001. *Selfhood and Authenticity*. Albany: State University of New York Press.

Gao, Xingjian. 1999. *The Other Shore*. Translated by Gilbert C. F. Fong. Hong Kong: Chinese University Press.

Gilyard, Keith. 1991. *Voices of the Self: A Study of Language Competence*. Detroit: Wayne State University Press.

11

Personal Narratives and Rhetorics of Black Womanhood in Hip-Hop

Gwendolyn D. Pough

Rap music and hip-hop culture's quest to "keep it real" and "represent" the real has led to the creation of a vast array of lyrics from the grit of gangsta rap to the playful nostalgia of Will Smith. Rappers use rap music as their initial entry into the public sphere. Often criticized for its harsh lyrics and negative images, rap music has been praised on the other hand for representing clearly what is wrong with society so that something can be done to change it. Rappers view representation or "representin'" as their role to speak for the people and voice their concerns. Michael Eric Dyson (1995) described the hip-hop generation's use of representation in a talk given at Brown University titled, "Material Witness: Race, Identity and the Politics of Gangsta Rap":

> Within hip-hop culture, representation signifies privileged persons speaking for less visible or vocal peers. At their best rappers shape the torturous twist of urban fate into lyrical elegies. The act of representing that is much ballyhooed in hip-hop is the witness of those left to tell the afflicted's story. They represent lives swallowed by too little love or opportunity. They represent themselves and their peers with aggrandizing anthems that boast of ingenuity and luck in surviving.

Dyson no doubt arrives at this stance by taking into consideration the numerous rappers that have gone on record in interviews saying that they are the voice of their respective "hoods." Whether they all actually perform this task is arguable. But suffice it to say that some rappers do articulate community issues and concerns via their lyrics, the most available verbal vehicle they have for attracting public attention. They are self-designated tellers of the people's suffering and deliver messages that otherwise might not be heard. However, most examinations of rap music and hip-hop culture view rap as a masculine discursive space and seldom consider the relevance of the Black woman's experience. With the exception of a few critiques of misogyny and sexism in rap music and hip-hop culture, issues of Black womanhood and how rap as rhetoric influences Black womanhood remain unexplored. This essay attempts to help fill the void by exploring briefly several coming-of-age stories that focus on what it means to grow up Black and female in an era of hip-hop. I will examine how these women add to the lineage of Black autobiography in America, then discuss how stereotypes like the *strong Black woman* and the *domineering Black mother* influence the identities of these authors.

Let's begin with some questions: What does it mean to define oneself within and against stereotypical images and constructions? How can one develop a rhetoric of Black womanhood against these contemporary and historical representations? How can one begin to tell the truth of one's own life? To address these questions, I will examine Sister Souljah's *No Disrespect* (1996), Queen Latifah's *Ladies First: Revelations of a Strong Woman* (1999), Veronica Chambers' *Mama's Girl* (1996), and Joan Morgan's *When Chickenheads Come Home to Roost . . . My Life as a Hip-Hop Feminist* (1999). My goal is to indicate how these women use the language of the past and present to construct their identities as Black women and create a rhetoric of agency and self-definition.

The autobiographies of Black women who have come of age in an era of hip-hop, like the African-American autobiographies before them, provide entries into the public sphere and offer the women a chance to tell their stories while making social commentary. The texts serve dual functions as life stories and message texts, with each author attempting to uplift and heal others through the telling of her story. For Sister Souljah, it is the entire "African race" she wishes to uplift and indeed save with her message. For Queen Latifah it is other young Black women that she hopes to make strong by the telling of her tale. Veronica Chambers aims to illumine the plight of the strong Black woman and speak directly to other mama's girls who yearn for a mother's love and touch. Joan Morgan seeks the empowerment of Black women in general. In addition to trying to heal others, these women present critiques of society and comment on how society impacts both their own lives and the lives of others.

For example, Sister Souljah writes in *No Disrespect*, "No matter how backward and negative the mainstream view and image of Black people, I feel compelled to reshape that image and to explore our many positive angles because I love my own people" (1996, x). She notes:

> It is with this kind of spirit and that kind of love that I live my life and
> offer this book, which deals with the African man and woman in America
> and our ability to relate to and love one another in healthy life-giving

relationships. I am especially concerned with the African female in America, the ghetto girl whom nobody ever tells the definition of womanhood, or manhood for that matter" (1996, xiv).

Similarly, Queen Latifah dedicates her book "[t]o every woman who has ever felt like less than royalty." And she writes:

> I am writing this book to let every woman know that she, too—no matter what her status or her place in life—is royalty. This is particularly important for African-American women to know inside out, upside down, and right side up. For so long in this society, we have been given—and we allowed ourselves to take the role of slave, concubine, mammy, second-class citizen, bitch, ho" (1999, 2).

Both Queen Latifah and Sister Souljah have a goal for writing their autobiographies that is rooted in the old spiritual tradition of "if I can help somebody." Just as the slave narratives were written to help those who remained in bondage, these contemporary hip-hop autobiographies are intended to instigate progressive social struggle.

Along with critiquing society and giving advice on how to enact new possibilities, these autobiographies are concerned with issues of identity construction as they pertain to Black womanhood. The preceding quote from Queen Latifah offers a list of the kinds of images and misconceptions that Black women confront. She lists "slave, concubine, mammy, second-class citizen, bitch, ho." The images function alongside notions of the *strong Black woman* and the *domineering Black mother,* and some have reached new heights of popularity due to contemporary rap music. I might add that the focus on identity construction and Black womanhood is not new to Black autobiography. In the nineteenth century, Harriet Jacobs was concerned with these misconceptions and stereotypes surrounding Black womanhood. In the twentieth century, well-known figures like Angela Davis and Elaine Brown expressed similar misgivings. The struggle is represented now with women like Queen Latifah and Sister Souljah actually embracing the controversial label, say, of the strong Black woman—so much so in fact that Latifah's subtitle is "revelations of a strong woman." Similarly, Sister Souljah notes throughout her text that she is a strong African woman out to save the race and make them strong. It might be worthwhile to note that as female rappers in the masculine discursive space of hip-hop, Queen Latifah and Sister Souljah may have found being a strong Black woman a necessity in ways not as pressing for journalists such as Joan Morgan and Veronica Chambers.

Both Morgan and Chambers grapple with and eventually reject the label of strong Black woman. Both of these women reach a point in their lives where they can no longer be Black superwomen. Each suffers near-emotional breakdowns when coming to that realization. Chambers likens the strong Black woman to a magic act. She writes:

> I remember seeing a magic act when I was little in which the magician would repeat over and over: "The closer you get, the less you can see." And oddly enough, it was true. The people in the front row couldn't see through the deception; they were so close, yet they were looking for the wrong thing while the trick was being pulled right before their eye. Black women are masters of emotional sleight of hand. The closer you get, the less you can see. It was true of my mother. It is also true of me. (1996, 75–76)

Chambers realizes that the strong Black woman is a false image, a magic act that Black women perform so well even the people closest to them do not realize that a trick, an "emotional sleight of hand" is being performed.

Morgan takes the realization one step further by symbolically giving her resignation. She explains:

> Since sistas are quick to call themselves STRONGBLACKWOMEN and loathe to call themselves feminists, I realize my retirement requires explanation. This is not to be confused with being strong, black, and a woman. I'm still alla that. I draw strength daily from the history of struggle and survival that is a black woman's spiritual legacy. What I kicked to the curb was the years of social conditioning that told me it was my destiny to live my life as BLACKSUPERWOMAN emeritus. That by the sole virtues of my race and gender I was supposed to be the consummate professional, handle any life crisis, be the dependable rock for every soul who needed me, and yes, the classic—require less from my lovers than they did from me because after all, I was STRONGBLACKWOMAN and they were just ENDANGEREDBLACKMEN. Retirement was ultimately an act of salvation. Being a SBW was killing me slowly. Cutting off my air supply. (1999, 87)

Morgan had the job of her dreams, was working hard, and tried to save the world. Then she realized that she could not do it all. Like anyone raised to believe that a Black woman has to be strong enough to take on and bear the world, indeed be the "mule of the world," the realization that one is not strong in that mythical sense can be maddening. This is especially true when Black women all around you are performing that "emotional slight of hand" with effortless ease and when one of those women is your very own Black supermother.

"Dear Mama" or "Mother, Mother": Depending on Your Generational Shift[1]

Jo Malin (2000) maintains that, "every woman autobiographer is a daughter who writes and establishes her identity through her autobiographical narrative. . . . many twentieth-century autobiographical texts by women contain an intertext, an embedded narrative, which is a biography of the writer/daughter's mother" (1). This is especially true in the autobiographies of young Black women coming of age in an era of hip-hop. The Black mother in all her glory and controversy is the key to the identity construction of the women discussed in this essay. The image of the domineering Black mother a la Daniel Patrick Moynihan plays an interesting role in their autobiographies. Moynihan's report, written in the 1960s, was a government-funded study on the state of the Black family. What Moynihan found, in his view, were too many single/female headed Black families and domineering Black mothers who metaphorically castrated their Black sons. Although I will not enter the debate concerning whether Black mothers are more domineering in the lives of their sons or daughters, or take up at length the pathological bent of the Moynihan report, I will say that issues surrounding Black women, motherhood, and Black sons have been analyzed *ad infinitum;* whereas, until recently, the interaction between Black mothers and daughters has been largely ignored. Therefore, I would like to explore the images of Black motherhood that surface in these autobiographies and examine how they influence the identities of the writers.

The mother's strength or lack of strength shapes each writer. Each weaves her mother's story through her own. Where Queen Latifah becomes a strong woman because her mother was a strong woman, Sister Souljah becomes a strong African woman because her mother was not. Whereas Queen Latifah, Chambers, and Morgan grew up wanting to emulate the strong Black women that they believed their mothers to be, Sister Souljah creates an image of Black womanhood that was denied her because of poverty and racism. Sister Souljah's mother fell victim to the trappings of a racist and materialist society, finding worth only in her body and looks. She hit rock bottom in Souljah's eyes when she began to date a White man, an act that signals to Souljah that her mother no longer possesses the strength to help them survive the projects. She writes, "It was as though body snatchers had somehow invaded her body and turned her heart cold. Life was too much and too harsh for her." Yet she thanks God for her mother and the fact that:

> [S]he had the strength to save us and secure us from the projects, the danger, the hunger, and the mental devastation . . . I thanked God for allowing me to know her before the world took her . . . But I had come to believe that the woman walking around the house posing as my mother was not my mother. She was America's creation and that did not belong to me. (1996, 50)

Interestingly, Souljah's depiction is inherently contradictory, for it presents the dual images of the strong Black woman and the domineering, and damaging, Black mother coexisting and contradicting each other.

This dual representation surfaces again in Veronica Chambers's book *Mama's Girl,* which is the autobiography of Chambers and the biography of her strong Black mother. Watching her mother's strength and ability to remain calm after being hit in the head with a hammer by an abusive husband and take herself to the hospital has a tremendous impact on Chambers. She writes:

> When the hammer connects, my mother doesn't scream. Her head is gouged . . . My mother sees me watching and tells me to go to my room, she is going to the hospital. She says it in a calm, grown-up, don't worry voice . . . She presses the towel against the hole in her head. The towel is white, which she isn't thinking about as she bleeds into the snowy terry cloth. . . . My mother grabs her purse off the kitchen table and goes out the front door. She is bleeding so much, but she doesn't cry. (1996, 25–26)

Just like Sister Souljah's, Queen Latifah's, and Joan Morgan's mothers, Chambers' mother holds her life together and maintains a strong façade in order to raise her children. But just as for Sister Souljah's mother, the strong façade crumbles when she meets and marries a man that she places before her children. Chambers ends up leaving her mother's house and going to live with her father and then her aunt because she cannot get along with her mother's new husband. But unlike Souljah, Chambers does not write her mother off, refusing to reject her mother at the first sign that she is just a "reglar" Black woman.[2] She still longs for her mother's love and appreciates all that her mother has endured. Her ability to appreciate her regular Black mother and give up on the superblackmom comes from the vision she receives when she realizes that the superwoman is a magic trick. When she suffers a near-nervous breakdown from trying to do it all, she writes that her mother:

> . . . reached over and hugged me and did not let go. This was not how we hugged. Our hugs were quick . . . This hug was different . . . It felt so strange . . . Was I dying . . . Then my mother started to rock me, rock me like I wanted her to when I was seven and terrified of my father . . . I never thought she'd do it. I never thought she'd see how much I needed it. I started to cry, I figured it was okay to cry now. (1996, 166–67)

It is the mother's touch and the mother's story embedded within this autobiography that frees the writer from the misconceptions surrounding Black womanhood and allows her to try to free others.

When read separately, these autobiographies extend, in various ways, the tradition of Black autobiography in America. Separately they offer the kind of insights that Patricia Bell-Scott (1998) writes of in *Flat-footed Truths: Telling Black Women's Lives*. They tell stories that are "straightforward, unshakable, and unembellished" (xix). And they join the lineage of women who always "insisted on speaking truths in the face of disbelief and public criticism" (xix). However, when they are read together, as I have hopefully shown, they offer much more. Together, they help us to understand the narratives and images that influence us and to prepare for the new rhetorics of Black womanhood. When read in conversation with one another, these autobiographies highlight not only what it means to come of age as a Black woman in an era of hip-hop, but also how to grapple successfully with all the historical and contemporary baggage that comes along with it.

Notes

1. In his essay "Generational Shifts and the Recent Criticism of Afro-American Literature," Houston Baker defines "generational shifts" as "ideologically motivated movement overseen by young or newly emergent intellectuals who are dedicated to refuting the work of their intellectual predecessors and establishing a new framework of intellectual inquiry" (282). For the purposes of this essay, however, generational shifts represent the way Black women of the hip-hop generation build on and reject the images that historically and socially defined their mothers and foremothers.

2. "Reglar" as used here refers to Ntozake Shange's "Lady in Red" who goes out of her way to adorn her self in sequins and sweet perfumes in an attempt to escape the pain and ordinariness of her life. All of her efforts are washed away with a simple bath and she becomes the "ordinary/brown braided woman/with big legs and full lips" (34). She becomes in fact like any other regular Black woman.

Works Cited

Baker, Houston A. 1994. "Generational Shifts and the Recent Criticism of Afro-American Literature." In *Within the Circle: An Anthology of African-American Literary Criticism from the Harlem Renaissance to the Present,* edited by Angelyn Mitchell. Durham: Duke University Press.

Beanie, Sigel. 2000. "Remember Them Days." *The Truth.* Def Jam.

Bell-Scott, Patricia. ed. 1998. *Flat-Footed Truths: Telling Black Women's Lives.* New York: Henry Holt and Company.

Braxton, Joanne M. 1989. *Black Women Writing Autobiography: A Tradition Within a Tradition.* Philadelphia: Temple University Press.

Chambers, Veronica. 1996. *Mama's Girl.* New York: Riverhead Books.

Dyson, Michael Eric, perf. 1995. "Material Witness: Race, Identity and the Politics of Gangsta Rap." Dir. Sut Jhalley. Videocassette. The Media Education Foundation.

Franklin, V. P. 1995. *Living Our Stories, Telling Our Truths: Autobiography and the Making of the African-American Intellectual Tradition.* New York: Oxford University Press.

Kunjufu, Jawanza. "Turning Boys into Men," *Essence,* November 1988: 112.

Malin, Jo. 2000. *The Voice of the Mother: Embedded Maternal Narratives in Twentieth-Century Women's Autobiographies.* Carbondale: Southern Illinois University Press.

Morgan, Joan. 1999. *When Chickenheads Come Home to Roost: My Life as a Hip-Hop Feminist.* New York: Simon & Schuster.

Queen Latifah. 1999. *Ladies First: Revelations of a Strong Woman.* New York: William Morrow and Company.

Shange, Ntozake. 1975. *For Colored Girls Who Have Considered Suicide When the Rainbow Is Enuf.* New York: Collier Books.

Souljah, Sister. 1996. *No Disrespect.* New York: Vintage Books.

12

Narratives of Ethnicity:
A Tale of Two Nonnys

Marie J. Secor

I have two stories to tell: one from each side of my family. They are certainly ethnic, and reflection will suggest some ways in which they can be considered rhetorical.

My name is Marie J. Secor, the J standing for my maiden name, Jennette. It sounds like a middle name, and in combination with Marie it certainly sounds French. My college poetry professor pointed out to me that my name was perfect iambic dimeter, which helped me to learn metrics. Jennette is actually a common Italian name that can be spelled and pronounced many ways: Jannette, Genetti, Jannetta, Giannetti, Iannetti. The variants attest to the indifference to spelling by Ellis Island officials and among the immigrants who passed through there. In fact, Jennette, pronounced like the woman's name, may reflect the most accurate pronunciation, belying the assumption that Italian names end in vowels, because in some dialects the last syllable of a word is often clipped.

I have recently been going through family papers ever since moving my aged parents from Waterbury, Connecticut, where they spent their lives, to State College, Pennsylvania, where they ended their days in a nursing home—my mother, Olga, at 93, with severe dementia and two broken hips, and my father, Michael, at 102, of sound mind and body up to the end. I knew that my father was an American citizen born in Italy on a return trip by his mother in 1899, though he didn't know that until 1976 when he applied for a passport to visit me and my family when we lived in England. He then found that he was born in Montagano, province of Campobasso, not in Elizabeth, New Jersey, as he had thought. Around the time of his one hundredth birthday I was also surprised to learn that I had been mistaken my whole life about his exact birthday, which he and I had always celebrated together on September 22, as we joked about me being his birthday present. My mother informed me that his birthday was actually September 7, but at that point she was unable to explain why we were confused or whether somebody had just lied.

Two documents among the papers confused me further. The first was a naturalization certificate stating that Angelo Vitullo had become an American citizen on March 10, 1897, in Elizabeth, New Jersey. More precisely: "Angelo Vitullo, an Alien, personally appeared in open Court, and prayed to be admitted to become a Citizen of the United States." The surprise is the name. This had to be my grandfather, so the name should have been some variant of Jennette. I knew—or thought I knew—that my grandmother's maiden name was Maria Vitullo and that her husband was Angelo Jennette— spelled any way you like. And I knew that Angelo had become an American citizen before my father was born, so the document definitely refers to my grandfather.

The second piece of paper, tattered, was my father's birth certificate. It is written in Italian, which I decipher only laboriously. It states that Giuseppe Antonio Michele Vitullo was born in Montagano, in the province of Campobasso, on "ventotto settembre," 1899. Notice that the date is September 28. So not only was Dad's birthday not September 22, it was also not even September 7, when we threw his one hundredth birthday party. That small mystery was solvable. A quick glance might have led people to place the birthdate on the 7th because his is registered as birth number 97 of the year. But apparently his name was never Michael Jennette, in any variant. And his parents were Angelo Vitullo and Maria Iannitto. What was being hidden from me? And how did Giuseppe Antonio Michele Vitullo become Mike Jennette? Why did Maria and Angelo—not wealthy people who could travel on a whim—return to Italy for the birth of their youngest child after they had emigrated here and become citizens?

I also found a newspaper clipping about my father's sister Isabelle's 105th birthday party. In the article she talks about her early childhood and the poverty her family knew. She recalls going to work as a child, sewing hooks and eyes onto pieces of cardboard. She earned ten cents after completing twenty-five dozen of the cards. The article also mentioned that Isabelle's maiden name was Vitullo, and it mentioned that she had two brothers, John Jennett and Michael Jennette. No one commented on the oddity.

Dad always said that his mother was a Vitullo and that his father had died at the age of thirty-four of a ruptured appendix, leaving a widow and three children: Isabelle, John, and himself, the youngest, only two years old. I called my cousin Christine to find out whether she could tell some stories, and she confirmed that her mother had always used Vitullo as her maiden name. Christine figured that Isabelle had simply taken her mother's maiden name as her own, whereas the two boys had kept their father's name. It didn't seem strange to her because Spanish families often did that and maybe

Italians did too in earlier times. When I read her my two certificates, that was the first she ever heard about the reversal. There had to be a reason why the two boys had reverted to their mother's maiden name after their father died.

I quizzed Christine, a generation older than me, for more family stories. She said that our grandfather, Angelo, who died in 1901, was a literate man (in Italian, of course), very smart, who liked to read to his young wife to inform her about the world. Long before the invention of the airplane, he had predicted wonders to our Nonny, that some day there would be "machines flying in the sky," and she never forgot that. I asked how Nonny Neddy (which was what I always called her as a child) managed to survive in America with three children and no husband and no English. Of course the children worked, my father and his brother gathering scraps of wood in winter to keep the stove going at home and in factories from the age of twelve, Isabelle sewing hooks and eyes and later assembling the gears of watches at the Waterbury Clock Shop. Nonny worked too—cleaning houses for Irish people, taking in laundry and boarders, one of whom was Frank Iacovino, an immigrant, who ended up marrying Isabelle and joining the family. Frank treated Nonny like his own mother, handing over his paycheck to her every week of his life to support the entire family. He was a hard worker—he had started out in the steel mills of Pittsburgh—and eventually became a supervisor at Scovill's, the biggest factory in Waterbury. He made enough money to buy the three-family house on Platt Street, where the family lived for over eighty years.

Christine also recalled hearing about an earlier time when Nonny and her three children had lived with an uncle who used to beat her boys. Nonny had moved out of his house to get away from him. She vowed that she would never marry again because she was never going to let any man mistreat her children. This uncle was a Vitullo, and, true to her word, Nonny remained a widow for sixty-five years, a tiny woman with thick white hair, a black dress, and a permanent bronchial cough. She never achieved five feet or a hundred pounds, and she spoke a dialect comprehensible only to others from her village. I can't prove it, but I think that Maria Ianitto Vitullo bestowed her own name on her sons when she left the household of that uncle and severed ties with that family in order to establish an independent home where she could protect her two boys. She claimed her sons and removed them from the uncle's control. Her daughter, a little older, kept the family name. Apparently Nonny never felt it necessary to explain to anyone what she did or why.

Mike loved school and he got to attend Webster Elementary School on the North End, a rough Italian neighborhood, of Waterbury until he was twelve. He was proud of being known as the smartest boy in his class. I have only one picture of my father as a child. It is a class photograph of the first grade at Webster School in 1905. Most of the children look poor and unhealthy. The little girls wear sagging stockings, soiled dresses, and worn shoes, and boys look snuffly and adenoidal. In the second row of children, at the end, there is one very small boy wearing clothes that are too big for him. He has a bowl haircut, a big smile, and bright eyes. He didn't look much different ninety-six years later.

The Vitullos/Jennettes/Iacovinos—Maria Iannitto Vitullo, her daughter and son-in-law Isabelle and Frank Iacovino, and their four daughters (Mary, Inez, Christine, and Corinne) all lived together in one house, and Mike lived there until he married at the age of thirty-five. Christine remembers her Uncle Mike playing word games with her and her sisters when they were children and playing baseball and pinochle with the Irish boys and young men from the neighborhood. He proudly drove a Model T Ford and took his nieces for rides to buy Eskimo Pies on payday and cellophane-wrapped baskets of chocolate at Easter. Christine recalls sitting on the bathroom sink watching him shave before he went out on dates with my mother. He smelled good and liked to kid around. He always called her and her sister Tootsie and Tilly, and the names stuck to this day. The family struggled during the depression, and there were times when Mike had no work. He was in his early thirties, and he and my mother had postponed their marriage for five years (until 1934) because of the hard times. During one particularly difficult period he would go down to Waterbury Farrell Foundry's employment office and just sit there stubbornly all day, day after day, until they finally hired him. He worked as a machinist at Farrell's until 1967, operating a boring mill that made the machine equipment that other factories ordered. I have a picture of him in the factory, dwarfed by a massive machine he had tooled but proud of his handiwork. When I showed it to him recently, he smiled and said "1945." He was always precise about numbers, but he never wanted to be a machinist. He said, "I was a half-baked mechanic. I wanted to go to Wall Street."

My mother's family, the delPo's, lived in Town Plot on the other side of town, and the two families were not close. Evidently some quarrel occurred when my parents got married, and my two Nonnys spoke such different dialects that they could hardly understand each other. The children of my generation were addressed in Italian by our grandparents' generation and expected to answer in English. I get stories about the delPo's from my cousin Lenny, who is the family memory and furniture collector. My maternal grandfather, Giuseppe delPo, came from the town of Celenza val Forte, in Foggia. The family was—and in fact still is—prominent there in a small-town way—mayors, judges, artists, people of substance. When Lenny retraced our roots a few years ago, the town mayor and many officials still bore the delPo name, all of them just as proudly glum, says Lenny, as the delPo's on this side of the Atlantic. The family had been pushed south by Napoleon's armies when they swept through the Po River valley in the north—hence, the name referring to their northern origin.

Giuseppe delPo—tall and red-headed like many of my uncles—was the youngest son. He had entered the army, in which his uncle was a general, but he proved unsuitable for a military career (no one knows the details, but he seems to have had a reputation for being headstrong). I inherited the family photograph album—red velvet, with brass binding and a half-moon mirror on the cover—and as a child I spent hours in my Nonny's living room making up stories about pictures of unidentifiable relatives. My favorite was the blurry picture of the General, complete with plumes and epaulets and looking as if he stepped out of a Gilbert and Sullivan operetta. That's the uncle. Giuseppe's military career having foundered, it was decided that he should marry, and it was arranged—as proper families did in those days— that he would wed the eldest daughter of the deMasi family from the town of Airola, not far from Naples. But Giuseppe the Headstrong took a fancy to the youngest daughter, Maria, who was only seventeen. At that point it was determined that he could marry the youngest daughter if he insisted, and the couple was given a one-way ticket to America as a wedding gift.

The deMasi's were prominent in government circles. Maria was raised by an aunt while her parents, Michele and Sarah Lombard deMasi, traveled on government business. (The name Lombard suggests that they too were a northern family pushed south.) So the young couple sailed to America in 1900 on their honeymoon and, says my Aunt Rena with pride, they came tourist class, not steerage. But Giuseppe did not find great success in the New World. He went to work for Scovill's, in the dip room, and he died in 1939 from liver cancer contracted from the chemicals he worked with. The family struggled. None of Giuseppe's and Maria's six children—Fred, Chiarina (Rena), Olga, Bill, Armand, and Mike—were educated through high school. The youngest, Mike, proved a talented tool and die maker and became the first Italian allowed to take up that skilled trade at Scovill's. He eventually struck out on his own, started his own factory, and did well. Fred, Bill, and Armand worked as laborers in local factories. Armand— handsome, charming, generous, barely literate—lived with Nonny and never married. Rena is the mother of Lenny and a profoundly retarded daughter, for whom she cared all her life. My mother Olga (the unusual name because Giuseppe admired a Polish woman at the time she was born) was pretty and flirtatious.

My grandmother—Nonny delPo to me—presided as matriarch of her three-flat, a large, imposing woman and a great bountiful cook. The family paid homage to her on Sundays and holidays, and she always gave me an extra nickel whenever I went to the grocery store for her. I bought Dixie Cups with pictures of movie stars under waxed paper on the inside of the cover. She was full of largesse, recycling all gifts to the next person who entered her house, accepting and proud of the ethnic stew that resulted from the marriages of her children and grandchildren. "I got all kind," she would proclaim. Uncle Armand put red roses on her grave for years after she died.

There was another branch of the delPo family in Waterbury, descended from Giuseppe's more proper brother Dominic. They were also a big family. Bill, Josephine, Mary, Mario, John, Clara, and Ida were the cousins on that side. Bill—another charming, handsome bachelor—still lives in Woodbury, a nearby village, and is prominent in local politics. Aunt Jo (my mother's cousin) was an elegant woman who always wore hats and beautiful Chanel-style suits that she knitted herself. Whenever she visited (she learned to drive at the age of sixty-five) she would take out her needles and work on next year's outfit. She insisted that the delPo's were of high lineage, and once she gave me a silver pendant with a crowned eagle on it and a hook at the end. She said the hook was for a lady to loop her yarn over when she crocheted and that the closed crest on the crown symbolized the family's noble ances-try. I was skeptical. Aunt Jo had a lot of pretensions. But my cousin Tweetie, an artist, found in one of her college textbooks a Renaissance painting of a young noblewoman named Lucia delPo, so maybe there was some justifica-tion for Aunt Jo's pride. There have always been artistic people in the fam-ily. I have a newspaper clipping from the New York Italian language newspaper, *Il Progresso,* of a poem that my grandfather wrote. From what I can make out, it is an effusive reminiscence about the bounty of Christmas in Naples. He must have been homesick. Another uncle, Carl delTufo, painted a mountain scene that always hung over the mantel in my parents' house and now hangs in mine, and everyone in the family got one of his paintings as a wedding gift. I must have lost the pendant.

My mother Olga worked as a secretary at Scovill's and married Mike Jennette in 1934. She was lively and social and liked to travel. She prided herself and her mother on being ladies who did not plant vegetables (a dig at my other Nonny, who tended her tomatoes and peppers until she died at ninety-eight). My mom broke her hips because she kept trying to walk even though she should have stayed in her wheelchair.

What makes this narrative of ethnic experience rhetorical? It resembles many stories told in many families, though the details and the conclusions drawn from such tales will vary depending on who tells them for what reasons. In the most general way, the analytic language of rhetoric offers a toolbox to parse its components and aid understanding of how and why the story came to be told. This particular tale of two nonnys came about because of a *kairotic* moment, a time and place that this discourse answers. After having left Waterbury for good at the age of seventeen, I unexpectedly spent my most recent sabbatical leave taking care of my frail parents, closing up their house, and seeing to their final needs. At no other time could I have told this story, because at no other time did I know it. It was not purposefully kept from me; it's just that the pieces that I had heard in the past served different func-tions. People in my family don't reminisce a lot, and when they do they never dwell on past hardships or relive old quarrels. Forgetting and silence are often preferable to articulation. My recovery and partial invention of this story in this form answer a particular rhetorical situation, one that offers an audience opportunities and constraints for a certain kind of discourse and certain kinds of reflections that challenge us to figure out what we mean by ethnic rhetoric. There is, of course, also a personal exigence, my need to sort and shape my own experiences.

Certainly my story is rhetorical to the extent that it "observes the available means of persuasion," and its development can be traced through the traditional offices of rhetoric: invention, arrangement, style, memory, and delivery. Rhetorical theory from Aristotle through Cicero to Burke acknowledges narrative as a means of inducing belief and identification. *Narratio* is part of a classical oration, and stories abound in handbooks like *De Inventione,* the treatise that introduces stasis theory. A different story would have conveyed different meanings and forged different connections. This one is cobbled out of some testimony and what Aristotle would call some "inartistic proofs": certificates, clippings, photographs, objects treasured, lost, and remembered. Someone else, given different materials, situations, and interests would doubtless contrive a different story. It is arranged as extended parallel tales with commentary at the end, combining narrative and discursive genres. I had to fuss some over the words and style because I have never considered myself a storyteller. It is certainly drawn from the places of memory, both my own and that of others, and has often been delivered orally, but here in writing.

In addition to being rhetorically situated and constructed, this ethnic narrative makes an argument that depends on its reader's participation to complete its meaning. The ethos, logos, and pathos of my tale of two nonnys make meanings that I cannot wholly articulate or control. Stories are rhetorical just as direct arguments are because audiences draw conclusions from what is said, what is assumed, and even—perhaps especially—what is elided. But although narratives make arguments and can be part of arguments, the meanings of such narratives are not wholly propositional. They are composed out of little arcs of human experience that describe incomplete trajectories. How this tale makes meaning depends on who takes it up and on how those arcs of experience are traced to form larger, more recognizable patterns. Narratives are thus just as enthymemic as propositional arguments.

The assumptions that can be extracted from narratives, however, are not determined by syllogistic rules of exclusion and inclusion. Thus the meanings conveyed by this story might not be wholly consistent. My story might confirm some ethnic stereotypes and explode others. Not all Italians resemble each other in culture, class, or language. Not all of us resemble the Sopranos (the Mafia connections in my household are not on the Italian side). Not everyone came to this country for the same reasons or for the reasons offered by politicians, historians, or sociologists; and maybe the first ethnic stew occurred on the other side of the ocean rather than this one. Some generations

of immigrants did little to preserve their histories and their language, pre-
ferring the future to the past. In my family we were expected to understand
but not reproduce our grandparents' culture. You can trace lines in this story
that illustrate the power of patriarchy—the Vitullo uncle who tried to abuse
his nephews, the virtual exile of the impetuous Giuseppe delPo—or the
courage of women who found agency—the destitute Maria Vitullo who saved
her sons and the young Maria delPo who learned how to raise a family and
anchor a clan.

It is a story that includes narratives of both literacy and illiteracy, that
conjures names rich in history and names that just happened, that draws on
records preserved and records lost, that uses language that reveals and language that conceals. It is a story of progress achieved over several generations—both families would insist on that, though others might read it
differently—and it is a story of hardship almost unimaginable to my fortu-
nate generation. It is a story of assimilation, as history has been forgotten,
rewritten, or erased. Other immigrants and other generations have handled
the issue of assimilation differently, and authenticity is not limited to one
way of becoming American. But it is also a story of continuity. The rem-
nants of the past left traces, both material and discursive, and my generation
and the next still want to know who they were and are as well as what they
can become. Some meanings of this story are constrained by calling it an
"ethnic rhetoric," whereas others emerge and open for further deliberation.
And not all the questions it raises can be answered.

As I have told this story, I assume that readers have framed it in a historical context. Narratives activate story schema, frames, and patterns that
enable us to make sense of them. Without such interpretive schema, this tale
would be only a collection of data about people you have never met. This
ethnic narrative sends out social and political ripples. It can be understood
as an episode in the history of immigration, a phenomenon that continues in
this country, and it stands in relation to the stories told by other ethnic groups
in other times and places. Though as I have offered it, it is completely particular, it must also be in some ways typical. And it harbors implications that
I have left unexplored. From one perspective it is a chapter in the history of
industrial development and decline in a New England mill town. An oral history, *Brass Valley,* tells more of that story—in fact, with the help of one of
my cousins and my aunt, who proudly donated to the local museum the fine
tweezers that she used when she worked on the gears of watches in the Clock
Shop. Family members were active in unions that organized in the factories,
and my Aunt Isabelle had such passionate political convictions that she never
cared about cooking dinner—much to the dismay of my very domestic
mother. I always picture Isabelle stabbing the stickpin through her hat, on
the way downtown to City Hall to "give the politicians hell." Populated by
Marias and Giuseppes, this story has a submerged religious dimension,
though every family obituary speaks of the church societies that my parents,

grandmothers, and aunts founded and attended. Some pathways were cut off by the decisions I made in selecting and emphasizing elements of this story. No rhetoric of ethnicity is all-encompassing.

What is to be done with such stories? I can only suggest that we listen to them all and allow them to resonate against each other. Our identities as Americans are varied and cross-cutting as we claim multiple and even competing affiliations. There are many ways of being ethnic in America, and I would not like them all to be dominated by the imaginations of those who fix and commodify ethnicity—whether the creators of "Life with Luigi"— which I listened to in delighted innocence as a child, though the memory of it makes me cringe now—or those of "The Sopranos"—whose moral complexity I find fascinating even though the family and the home décor resemble none I ever experienced. No list of distinguished hyphenated-Americans can capture the full texture of ethnic experience. I sold my parents' house, by the way, to a nephew of Judge John Sirica of Watergate fame. If commodification is inescapable, it makes the recovery, creation, and dispersion of multiple narratives of ethnicity even more important. If such activity raises the question of "who should be doing it?" the only answer must be "everyone," in every genre and with every voice one can imagine. I recently read a novel by Rita Ciresi, who earned her MFA at Penn State, *Sometimes I Dream in Italian,* a collection of stories about growing up Italian in New Haven, just down the road from where I lived. I recognize its New England–Italian–American speech tune and its small-scale-urban landscape, though not the details of its experience. I think I've lost most of that accent, though I can fall back into it when talking with my Connecticut family. When one of my daughters was in college in Providence, Rhode Island, she spent some time in the infirmary, and as she feverishly and half asleep listened to the conversation of the nurses, she heard the voices of my mother and her best friend chatting in the kitchen. Having lived in central Pennsylvania for a long time, I just bought an Italian cookbook written by one of my State College neighbors. The recipes have a ring of familiarity, but they are a little more Sicilian in style than I am accustomed to.

I often experiment in the kitchen, trying to adapt recipes so that what I cook tastes like my grandmother's, though I never capture the exact flavor memory. The rhetorics of ethnicity come in many flavors, and no one of them appeals to every palate. Unlike Plato, I relish analogies between rhetoric and cookery: both are productive arts vital to physical and psychic sustenance. Plato is uneasy about the basic condition of rhetoric, which, like cookery, must aim to please, but that doesn't bother me at all. It is only a grudging asceticism that cannot delight in language or food that gives fleeting pleasure to the palate. If we are aware of what we are ingesting and take care to consume a wide variety of nourishment, we can see to our health and well-being. Although my cooking aims to please, it cannot please everyone. I'm not catering to the whole world. Some people might simply be unattuned to the peculiar blend of flavors in my cookery, whereas others might savor some elements of it. Like any argument, a narrative can please only those who are prepared to appreciate where it is coming from and what has gone into it.

The language issues raised by narratives of ethnicity are similarly thorny. I don't know what anyone's "real" name is any more, least of all my own, and there is no one to dictate authenticity. I worry a lot about what I will be called when and if I have grandchildren. Will I have grandchildren who call me Nonny, as I called my grandmothers and my children called my mother, or will that seem embarrassingly foreign to them? Indeed, what will I *want* them to call me? Names matter in the ways that language always matters— and when their significance is lost we often find that there is good reason for that too. When I offered this story to my daughter, Laura J. (for Jennette) Secor, she responded that she thought she should change her name to Laura Vitullo Shachanovsky, in honor of her ethnically diverse heritage. How the Shachanovskys became Secors is another tale for another time.

13

Challenging the Constraints of First-Year Composition Through Ethnic Women's Narratives

Janice Chernekoff

If we lived in a democratic state our language would have to hurtle, fly, curse, and sing, in all the common American names, all the undeniable and representative and participating voices of everybody here. We would not tolerate the language of the powerful and, thereby, lose all respect for words, *per se*. We would make our language lead us into the equality of power that a democratic state must represent.

June Jordan

By now, most of us accept the precept, phrased so clearly by James Berlin, that "a way of teaching is never innocent" (1988, 492). I carefully select authors such as Angela Davis, bell hooks, and June Jordan for my composition students because I want them to see words hurtling, flying, cursing, and singing, I want them to understand that people use academic discourse for a variety of purposes, and I want them to begin thinking about the potential capaciousness of academic writing. I also want them to experiment with language, to get to know themselves as language users beyond being producers of the well-behaved academic essay. I deliberately assign these authors and others who have written about the civil rights movement, including White SNCC participants Sally Belfrage and Florence Howe, to offer models of interested political writers who approach their subject variously. And because we discuss the rhetorical strategies and writing purposes of these authors, we are obliged later to discuss rhetorical strategies and purposes in other kinds of writing—such as academic writing, for instance. In her "Preface," Angela Davis (1974) declares that she has written a *"political* autobiography," and bell hooks, in "Building a Teaching Community" (1994), informs readers that she has chosen to engage in a dialogue with White male colleague Ron Scapp to present a "model of possibility" for the kind of border crossing that it is popular to promote (hooks, 129–31). The fact that these writers use language so deliberately and politically—challenging established notions of good writing—means that we must talk about not only what they say but also how and why. My not-innocent text selections also let students know where my political sympathies lie, and I continue, throughout the semester, to try to be clear without making them feel like they must agree with me. We read hooks' and Scapp's dialogue at the beginning of the semester and frankly discuss their concept of professors returning "to a state of embodiment in order to deconstruct the way power has traditionally been orchestrated in the class-room" (hooks 1994, 139). I emphasize to my students that they have a lot to teach me (and each other) because my perspective is certainly influenced by my race, age, and a host of other factors.

It is no easy task to bring students to the point of feeling comfortable enough to disagree with a professor and to take each other seriously. However, it is profoundly important to make the effort in order to disrupt the alarming effects of traditional education that are spelled out by June Jordan, "So I would say that our schools have served most of us extremely well. We have silenced or eliminated minority children. We have pacified white children into barely competent imitations of their fear-ridden parents" (1985, 30). If Jordan is correct in her analysis, writing instructors should aim to *not* please society (or some of our students, for that matter) so well. While a first-year composition professor's sense of duty may tell her that she must prepare her students for the academic world, and that there is little enough time to do that properly, it's possible that she would better serve her students by helping them understand the assumptions and politics of such training. This knowledge is essential for our students, Lillian Bridwell-Bowles tells us, if we wish to "invent a truly pluralistic society" (1992, 349). I am not suggesting that the composition professor abandon the teaching of academic discourse; in fact, that is impossible, according to Linda Brodkey, given that the professor's position in the classroom is authorized by academic discourse (1989, 140). This professor can, however, engage in an ongoing evaluation of activities and goals with her students, and teaching authors such as Davis, Jordan, and hooks enables that goal for me. These authors awaken students to the politics of language and prompt them to question me about my text selection. Thus, we find ourselves in the situation that Brodkey describes when she writes, "Resistance inside educational discourse is then a practice in cooperative articulation on the part of students and teachers who actively seek to construct and understand the differences as well as the similarities between their respective subject positions" (140).

The learning situation that I endeavor to establish is not always a comfortable place to occupy. Sometimes students simply resist my efforts to actively involve them in whatever we're doing, and sometimes the classroom is fraught with the tension identified by Mary Louise Pratt (1991) as being typical of a "contact zone" where "cultures meet, clash, and grapple with each other" (215). Making the politics of the classroom—what are students' roles and responsibilities? what are mine? what are we trying to do and why?—one of the initial topics of discussion, students quickly get the idea that they're not going to be able to nap through this one. By the time we begin to read and discuss civil rights narratives, they also understand that I expect to hear their voices and opinions on a regular basis. Having established the importance of their participation, they turn cautious again as soon as we begin to discuss race, gender, or sexual orientation, but most especially race. In the last few years, I have worked with classes that are almost entirely White, and I have learned that when it comes to race, they do not want to offend. As is to be expected, the one or two students of color quite rightly refuse to place themselves in the position of speaking for all Blacks or Latinos. However, approaching race issues through the civil rights movement minimizes their resistance because most students know very little about the movement yet are interested in it, and so are willing to approach the topic of racism through this nonthreatening historical "window." Reading about Davis' experiences with police and court systems, students are righteously outraged by the police brutality and the unjust justice system that she describes. They take seriously the argument in her narrative that she is a *political* prisoner along with many other Black activists whose names and circumstances she briefly describes. In other words, Davis's narrative opens students up to a discussion of racism and also simultaneously suggests that there are legitimate versions or aspects of U.S. history that are typically neglected by educators.

In fact, when we begin to study civil rights narratives, students ask why they learned nothing of this history except for the name "Martin Luther King." They are shocked to learn from White college student Sally Belfrage (someone many identify with) that John Kennedy—the only other name associated with the civil rights movement that they know—was not necessarily a civil rights hero. In the first level of discussion of these narratives, I ask students to talk about what interests, confuses, surprises, and upsets them. Following this, we spend considerable time talking about *how* Belfrage wrote her narrative. For example, we discuss her purpose in employing a journalistic, third-person narrator at the beginning of her story, and her inclusion of "actual" conversations among SNCC participants as well as the set of affidavits documenting the treatment of SNCC workers by local police. We talk about how this narrative breaks with the conventions of autobiography, and why Belfrage may have chosen to write this text in this fashion. By the time we've finished studying Belfrage's narrative, students are questioning their belief that justice is always meted out for everyone, that police always treat everyone fairly, that history, as they know it, is complete and accurate, that effective writing always follows the rules, and that studying writing is just about learning the rules.

When we move on to studying Davis' autobiography, we carefully compare her narrative to newspaper and magazine articles written about her at the time. Patricia Bizzell (1994) modifies Pratt's concept of a contact zone to cover situations like this where a *rhetorical study* of the texts of a particular historical moment allows one to evaluate them in terms of their communicative effectiveness (167). And it certainly helps in understanding Davis' style and rhetorical strategies to look at what was said about her in mainstream media. I provide classes with copies of an article from a 1970 issue of *Life* titled "The Path of Angela Davis," but I instruct them to find other news stories in order to help them gain a clearer sense of the political and social context in which Davis was writing.

Of course, when we compare media portrayals of Davis to her own story of her life, politics, and beliefs, we discover that we seem to be reading about two very different people. *Life's* incriminating pictorial narrative epitomizes the mainstream view of Davis. From the front-cover photograph, apparently one of the FBI mug shots, to an actual copy of the FBI Wanted Poster, to several photos of Davis with her "afro" speaking at rallies, to the final photograph of the attempted kidnapping scene in San Rafael in which the guns being wielded by Jonathan Jackson are purportedly registered to Davis, the impression created is of Davis as a radical, influential, and violent activist. Interspersed among these photographs are others of her with her family, showing how she grew up in a "normal" middle-class Black family with good American values. There is the sixth-grade class picture and a photo of the entire smiling family with a special mention of brother Ben's success with the Cleveland Browns. The message of the article and accompanying photographs is that Davis is a good girl who, unfortunately, has been led astray— whether by the Communists, the Black Panthers, or perhaps by some personal weakness. We learn that, at the urging of her mentor Herbert Marcuse, she went to Germany to "study under his old collaborator, Theodor Adorno" (23). We also learn that she has one unforgivable personal defect and that is inattention to her social life. According to the article, she is oblivious to the attentions of young men attracted to her, "Her beauty was so striking that men followed her down Paris streets and stumbled over each other to light her cigarettes. She seemed not to notice them" (22).

While *Life* portrays Angela Davis as a woman unable to think for herself, she quite carefully constructs a self-portrait of a cautious, savvy, inquisitive learner, thinker, and activist. For example, she writes about attending a conference in London in 1967 titled "The Dialectics of Freedom" (Davis 1974, 147), where she hears Stokely Carmichael and other influential political organizers speak. Interestingly, the focus of her commentary is her disagreement with their proposed response to racism. She admits that she "felt the cathartic power" of Stokely Carmichael's speech but is left unsatisfied because he dismisses socialism and Marxism as possible remedies and fails to draw appropriate connections between the situations of Blacks in England and Blacks in the United States (148). And contrary to *Life's* portrayal of her as a hater of Whites, she writes that, "When white people are indiscriminately viewed as the enemy, it is virtually impossible to develop a political solution" (148). Davis also claims that Carmichael's speech appeals to emotions rather than to reason, but in her opinion, their anger "would go nowhere" in terms of changing society (148).

Davis' thoughtful narrative encourages many students to seriously think about the effects of and solutions to racism, but there are always some students who hang on to the belief that it either does not exist any more or else that everyone is racist now. Because these comments pop up while we're in the middle of this analysis of civil rights texts, I can respond to them with questions that return them to the texts: How do you define racism and how does Davis define it? Does it have something to do with power and privilege? Do the authors in this contact zone have equal power and voice? After having studied this sampling of civil rights narratives, I can then ask students to think about the effects of that moment on current race relations and about whether things have changed that much—and how they could imaginatively express their own thoughts on racism. One student from a recent course notes in the reflective essay written for his final portfolio that this study made him more aware that writing presents arguments and that writers really need to address particular audiences: "Studying their books made me realize the power writing can have for social change. They defined their audiences and presented their writing to the reader. After this semester, I see writing just as much as a tool as an art form" (Kennedy 2000, 1).

With the final writing assignment of the semester, I give students the opportunity to practice thinking of writing as a tool to creatively express an opinion on one of the issues raised by the texts we've studied. Earlier in the semester, they do a traditional research project on something related to Davis' narrative—the Black Panthers, the Communist Party, and Political Prisoners are popular topics—but now their task is to craft an essay using personal experience to present an argument. Some students are able to eloquently write thoughts that they could not or would not say aloud in class. And other students come to a new understanding of the issue that they are writing about. For example, Lauren Maxwell, a young biracial woman in the class, did not speak very often, and even less during our discussions of race issues, but in her personal essay, she described two racist incidents. One was a childhood memory, the other was more recent. During a visit to a college in Connecticut that was trying to recruit her for its track team, Lauren was accosted by White men who drove by and yelled racial slurs at her. Describing this event in her essay, she overcomes the quiet almost-meek attitude that was characteristic of her and writes powerfully that, "The people of this nation are so engulfed in their work and their own life that if they are not personally impacted they think that nothing is wrong. THAT is wrong. People in this country must realize that just because something doesn't happen to them, there can be things that aren't right, and there is something that they can do about it" (Maxwell 2000, 1–2). In an incident that mirrors the second incident that Maxwell describes, White male student Eric Koopman describes being harassed by a small group of young Black "'thugs'"—a word that he puts in quotation marks in his essay. The interesting point of the story for him (and the reader) is, though, that he was in the company of twenty or more White guys all walking down a New York City street when the three young Black men drove by, threw a beer bottle at them and yelled "racial epithets" (Koopman 2000, 2). Eric admits to being terrified but wonders about this fear, ". . . why were we so scared? There were three guys and about thirty of us, but for some reason we walked in silence and ignored their actions. In retrospect, the reason for our fear seems to stem from the stereotype of Black men being violent animals, validated by their aggressive behavior, i.e. chucking forties at us" (Koopman 2). Maxwell's and Koopman's essays engaged each other so interestingly, and in such an important and contemporary race question, that I placed them together when I distributed the packet of all the final essays to everyone. Essentially, this final packet of writings, a literal contact zone, provides all the students with the opportunity to have their own last word on their chosen topics.

In general, these texts provide a provocative and interesting way to discuss crucial social issues, including education and the place of writing in society. However, I have been thinking about also using some of Davis' current, more academic, work *in addition to* her earlier narrative. This would reinforce the fact that people can have very different writing voices and styles for different purposes and audiences. Whereas the voice in Davis' autobiographical narrative sometimes seems hyperbolic, inflammatory, dramatic, and angry, the voice in her recent academic work—from the *Angela Y. Davis Reader* (1998), for example—is passionate, but her arguments are researched and documented in the manner expected for academic writing. This work evidences her ongoing interest in "the punishment industry" and how institutionalized racism now supports an assumption of the inherent criminality of people of color (61–73). Additionally, she has included pieces on both Blues and Black Feminism, and on photography, art, and popular culture as related to the representation of African Americans. Davis' current work would also exemplify committed scholarship in action; academic writing need not be, indeed should not be, deadly boring.

Traditionally, composition students have been led to believe that academic writing is more about form than content, and that they should not let their passion for their writing topics show. The possibilities for expression open to them have been limited by the constraints of academic writing and Standardized English taught in an a-contextual manner—as if this language and this kind of writing always existed or dropped down from the heavens. In my classes, academic writing, like the very setup of the class itself, comes under scrutiny. By examining the rhetorical strategies of various writers who forthrightly declare that their writing is political, I hope students better understand that all writing is political whether acknowledged by writers or not. I want them to understand that when they accept the task of learning academic discourse(s), they also accept a particular politics embodied in the kind of writing that they are doing. However, I hope to demonstrate to them that this political perspective can be "accepted" and resisted at the same time—through writing. Compositionists have the rare opportunity, as noted by Toby Fulwiler, "to examine the nature and validity" of the values held dear by the university in our writing classes (1990, 28). By working closely with students, we may discover what they can get from our writing classes, and perhaps we can also expand the boundaries of what is acceptable in the context of the writing classroom and in academic discourse.

Works Cited

Belfrage, Sally. 1965. *Freedom Summer*. New York: Viking.

Berlin, James. 1988. "Rhetoric and Ideology in the Writing Class." *College English* 50 (5): 477–94.

Bizzell, Patricia. 1994. "'Contact Zones' and English Studies." *College English* 56 (2): 163–69.

Bridwell-Bowles, Lillian. 1992. "Discourse and Diversity: Experimental Writing Within the Academy." *College Composition, and Communication* 43 (3): 349–68.

Brodkey, Linda. 1989. "On the Subjects of Class and Gender in 'The Literacy Letters.'" *College English* 51 (2): 125–41.

Davis, Angela. 1974. *Angela Davis: An Autobiography*. New York: Bantam.

———. 1998. *The Angela Y. Davis Reader*. Edited by Joy James. Malden, MA: Blackwell.

Fulwiler, Toby. 1990. "Writing as an Extra-Disciplinary Activity." "Writing Within and Against the Academy: What do We Really Want Our Students to Do? A Symposium" edited by Joseph Harris. *Journal of Education* 172 (1): 26–28.

hooks, bell. 1994. "Building a Teaching Community." In *Teaching to Transgress: Education as the Practice of Freedom*, 129–65. New York: Routledge.

———. 1995. "Culture to Culture: Ethnography and Cultural Studies as Critical Intervention." In *Rhetoric: Concepts, Definitions, Boundaries*, edited by William A. Covino and David A. Jolliffe, 328–35. Boston: Allyn and Bacon.

Howe, Florence. 1984. "Mississippi's Freedom Schools: The Politics of Education."
In *Myths of Coeducation: Selected Essays, 1964–1983,* 1–17. Bloomington:
Indiana University Press.

Jordan, June. 1985. "Problems of Language in a Democratic State." In *On Call: Political Essays,* 27–36. Boston: South End.

Kennedy, Matthew. 2000. "Reflective Essay." Honors Composition. Fall 2000. 1–4.

Koopman, Eric. 2000. "Lessons From Brooklyn." Honors Composition. Fall 2000.
1–4.

Maxwell, Lauren. 2000. "Personal Essay." Honors Composition. Fall 2000. 1–6.
"The Path of Angela Davis." *Life,* September 11, 1970.

Pratt, Mary Louise. 1991. "Arts of the Contact Zone." In *Profession 1991,* 33–40.
New York: MLA.

14

Race, Rhetoric, and *Sesame Street*: Learning to See Ourselves Reading

Deborah M. Williams

In an episode of *Sesame Street,* Elmo, and everyone else, learns to do the Salsa and to pronounce "Puerto Rico" properly, and then dances happily at the Sesame Street Salsa Party. Many of us would like multiculturalism in the college classroom to be something more than the celebration of diversity encouraged by well-intended anthologies and course requirements—a celebration that, like the *Sesame Street* episode, somehow seems to comodify, re-colonize, and re-essentialize at the same moment that it brings diverse voices into the classroom; but often we're not sure just what to do. One of the premises of this essay is that contemporary rhetorical theory and recent work in postmodern narrative theory has much to offer those of us interested in improving the multicultural classroom.

This essay has grown out of my attempts to teach an American Studies course entitled "American Lives" to a predominantly White, suburban, middle-class group of students at Temple University's Ambler Campus—in a way that challenged both our tendency to package multiculturalism and the pervasive neoconservative critique of "identity" politics that sees it as a dysfunction from which only misguided feminists and minorities suffer. In a reversal of the familiar Women's Movement slogan, for many students, the task often is to learn how the political might become personal—to learn how we might become responsible, or at least aware of, the politics of our own complicated relationships with others. For White students this often means learning to see Whiteness and coming to terms with our own complicity in creating and maintaining race privilege.

"American Lives" is a core course at Temple, taught by a broad mix of graduate students, adjuncts, and professors from different departments and disciplines. To provide some consistency, the American Studies Department publishes a set of guidelines for teachers. Texts must be autobiographic; Ben Franklin is required; texts must cover three centuries and must include works by women and African Americans, and one other minority. Of course rules like this are born of the desire to include narratives that have previously been excluded and that speak to and about experiences other than the White male experience. And there is nothing necessarily wrong with rules like this—just as there is nothing necessarily wrong with learning the salsa. (In fact, including the so-called minority texts in a class called American Lives rather than segregating them in African-American Studies or Women's Studies or Native-American Studies is perhaps an improvement over the practice of considering the White male experience the norm—the "American" experience—and everything else an area of specialization.) However, if we read these texts only in the Elmo spirit of "celebrating diversity" and "understanding and including the minority experience," we are missing a large part of what they might teach us and running the risk of "perpetrating a new orientalism" (Spivak 1993).

Students often tend to read texts, especially autobiographical texts, as unproblematic reflections of experience. This kind of reading can easily lead to neoconservative stances around issues of identity politics. Only those texts by women or minorities or working-class people will be seen as having to do with issues of race, gender, or class, and only those texts that announce a political motive will be seen as political. Whiteness generally is not recognized as having either an identity politics or a history. Another related problem has to do with students' attempts to perform the kind of reading academia generally encourages. These readings tend to position the reader as a detached, distanced, objective, scientific observer. For much of their academic lives, students have been told (explicitly and by our example) that this kind of reading is good because it is rational and impartial. It allows us to analyze and evaluate, without prejudice, experiences foreign to us. But unfortunately, this kind of reading also has a tendency to relieve the reader of responsibility for examining the politics of that evaluating gaze.

So a large part of the effort for me and my students goes into trying to see texts as socially constructed—both at the time of their writing and at the time of subsequent readings. And, as we learned in this particular course, in shaping a reading of any given text, readers "produce" that text out of their own relationship to available discourse(s).

In this class, as we read through Ben Franklin, Davy Crockett, Frederick Douglass, Harriet Jacobs, Black Elk, Kate Simon, and Anne Moody, we kept a collective list of the narrative patterns we found and tried to think critically as a group about how they come to shape our expectations and our experience. We tried to read the autobiographies as cultural products, produced by the discourse communities of a particular time and place, asking questions such as "How does this narrative reveal the culture that produced it? How does this narrative work within or against the conventions it inherits?"

As a group we identified what we came to call Great American Stories—narratives that appeared repeatedly in the autobiographies. These were primarily narratives of progress:

The Story of the Self-made Man.

The Story of the Lesson Well Learned.

The Story of Success through Perseverance (or, its variations—the Story of Virtue Rewarded, and the Story of Good Triumphing over Evil).

By mid-semester, things were going along rather smoothly. Although some students do resist when asked to read multicultural texts, many college students today are already quite skilled at performing in the typical multicultural classroom. Many White students have been trained to express appropriate respect for African-American authors, for example. They can give the politically appropriate response to the history of slavery. So we were all wonderful, and wonderfully self-congratulatory as we discussed how Fredrick Douglass skillfully deploys the rhetoric of enlightenment rationality.

Then we hit *Black Elk Speaks*. It was like hitting a brick wall. Here are some student responses:

"It doesn't make any sense."

"It's really strange; I can't understand it."

"What are we supposed to *get* out of this?"

"What's his point?"

"I think he was smoking too much of the good stuff."

These were responses to the sections where Black Elk describes his spiritual visions. Most of us could "understand" and "appreciate" the sections telling of events in a shared history between Whites and the Sioux because this was a kind of multicultural text we "knew" how to interpret and appreciate.

Of course, all these responses—and the tendency to look to me, the White English teacher, to explain what Black Elk meant—participate in a racist imperialist narrative that positions Native-American culture as the incoherent, irrational, uncivilized "Other" to a White culture that is constructed as coolly rational, scientifically objective and—most importantly—unraced (see Barnett 2000; Comfort 2000; Goodburn 1999 ; Keating 1995). And these responses were made by the very same students who described the behavior of the Whites in *Black Elk Speaks* as revoltingly racist, irrational, and barbaric. How does one begin to respond to the complex issues raised here?

I decided to view my strong urge to *explain* Black Elk with suspicion. We turned instead to our list of Great American Stories; and, no surprise, one student observed that the stories Black Elk tells don't seem to belong to the list. This discovery made possible two things: (1) Having allowed that Black Elk was speaking from a narrative tradition different from the one we had been tracing, we could begin the work of trying to recover or uncover the tradition that would give meaning to his stories. We no longer could think of them as not "meaning" anything; and we had to begin to consider our own responsibility for generating "meaning." (2) Having discovered that the assumptions and expectations the White Western narrative tradition creates are what gives meaning to narratives within that tradition (or denies meaning to narratives that don't speak the right way), we could begin to admit the imperative to interrogate that narrative tradition and the ideological work it does. We could begin to think about what is erased, silenced, or simply not allowed by the narrative—what the narrative "negates" (Vitanza 1997). And we could begin to think about what happens when a woman or a minority writer writes inside or outside that tradition, accepting it or resisting it, or both, and what it might mean to claim or reject that tradition at different times and places and for different peoples. By thinking of these Great American Stories rhetorically, we could begin to think of them as narrative choices (conscious or unconscious) that at least implied the possibility of other narratives.

As Hayden White (1987) argues, ideology is most masked in our narrative conventions and, because it is most masked, it is most powerful. We could readily admit that not all cultures find it necessary that a history have a "point," a lesson, a moral, or a "plot" that the historical narrative reveals. The students could even entertain the idea that White Western culture had not always needed to tell history this way; and they could see that forcing events into a Great American Story did erase, deny, or make ridiculous or irrelevant the things that didn't fit. But we could not all become Victor Vitanza overnight. Doing something new was much harder than it sounded. When it came to our own autobiographies and oral history reports, we discovered that "ideology, like halitosis, is something the other person has" (Eagleton 1991).

Student autobiographical narratives were almost uniformly progress stories. These are not naïve students. They had been cynical, even sarcastic about the Great American Stories we had put on our list. They would say that self-made men are largely mythical, that virtue is not often rewarded, that people do not always learn lessons from history. What is going on when students who cynically admit they have no faith in Great American Stories still tell them? One student: "We can only tell the stories we know how to tell." Another: "If we tell it differently, then we end up like Black Elk and no one gets it."

Or, in rhet/comp language: speaking outside the meanings authorized by the discourse community means running the risk of being the incoherent Other. We learned how the narrative traditions we inherit cause us to see certain events in our lives and the lives of others as inherently worthy of being narrated, while other events are classified as unimportant, irrelevant, meaningless. But we also learned that the normalizing power of the narrative (Bernard-Donals 1998) is sometimes the power to bring the reader into the world of the writer, as Michael Halloran suggests we need to do if we are to build an effective ethos (1994). We learned that no narrative or reading can ever be unraced (Goodburn 1999) or politically neutral and that the appearance of pure unmediated perception in traditional narrative or in academic writing is simply a mirage that, unchallenged, serves to perpetuate race privilege.

As a composition teacher, I learned to rethink those student narratives that begin by announcing, for example, that they are about "the most important lesson I ever learned" and then have trouble sticking to the story. What I might once have classified as a problem in the student—perhaps the student "lacks organizational skills?"—might now be a problem caused by how the traditional narrative shoe fits—or doesn't fit—the story the student wants to tell. As one student observed, the story sometimes "slops over." If I had this course to teach over again, I would like to add one more assignment to the syllabus. After the students had done their own autobiographical writing, I'd have them go back and rethink the areas where their stories "slop over" and take another look at things that don't fit. Perhaps I'd have them do some writing about what is being silenced and why, to have them better explore those areas where the normalizing narrative both does its work and doesn't work.

I don't want to tell this particular story as a New American Success Story—yet another Lesson Well Learned. Although a number of apparently progressive things happened in this class, what should I make of the fact that one Mexican student (who had worked as a sports announcer and arguably was not shy), simply did not show up for class on the three different days he was scheduled for class presentations? How should I explain the fact that one Jewish lesbian felt comfortable talking about her Jewish heritage but told me privately she felt the class as a whole was too homophobic to risk outing herself? Because of my desire to make the class as democratic as possible, I did not respond to racist and homophobic remarks forcefully enough. As a result, at least two students were silenced. If the politically neutral narrative and the politically neutral reading are myths, so is the politically neutral pedagogy.

I wonder, also, if my undisguised enjoyment of the Douglass and Jacobs autobiographies cued the students that they, too, should respond with appreciation, while my confession that I found *Black Elk Speaks* difficult reading gave them the opening they needed to voice their resistance to the text. If I believe that getting racist assumptions out in the open is an important first step in combating them, I have to wonder if we missed an opportunity. I have to wonder if our scholarly "appreciation" of the Douglass and Jacobs autobiographies participates in an Elmo-esque celebration of someone else's exoticized ethnicity, or, perhaps worse, performs what Donna Haraway (1988) calls the "God-trick"—positioning us as detached, distanced, disinterested, objective, and unraced observers/readers. With Douglass and Jacobs, our scholarly approach prevented us from making the political personal—and prevented us from taking responsibility for our reading. The lesson here is that, when the work of the multicultural classroom seems just a bit too easy, maybe we're not looking closely enough at our own participation in constructions of race.

Works Cited

Barnett, Timothy. 2000. "Reading 'Whiteness' in English Studies." *College English* 63 (1): 9–37.

Bernard-Donals, Michael. 1998. *The Practice of Theory: Rhetoric, Knowledge, and Pedagogy in the Academy*. Cambridge, MA: Cambridge University Press.

Comfort, Juanita Rogers. 2000. "Becoming a Writerly Self: College Writers Engaging Black Feminist Essays." *College Composition and Communication* 51 (4): 540–59.

Eagleton, Terry. 1991. *Ideology: An Introduction*. New York: Verso.

Goodburn, Amy. 1999. "Racing (Erasing) White Privilege in Teacher/Research Writing about Race." In *Race, Rhetoric, and Composition*, edited by Keith Gilyard, 67–86. Portsmouth, NH: Boynton/Cook.

Halloran, S. Michael. 1994. "On the End of Rhetoric, Classical and Modern." In *Professing the New Rhetorics: A Sourcebook*, edited by Theresa Enos and Stuart Brown, 331–43. Englewood Cliffs, NJ: Prentice Hall.

Haraway, Donna. 1988. "Situated Knowledges: The Science Question in Feminism and the Privilige of Partial Perspective." *Feminist Studies* 14: 575–99.

hooks, bell. 1994. *Teaching to Transgress: Education as the Practice of Freedom*. New York: Routledge.

Keating, Ann Louise. 1995. "Interrogating 'Whiteness,' (De)Constructing 'Race.' " *College English* 57 (8): 901–18.

Lu, Min-Zhan. 1998. "Reading and Writing Differences: The Problematic of Experience." In *Feminism and Composition Studies: In Other Words*, edited by Susan Jarratt and Lynn Worsham, 239–51. New York: MLA.

Spivak, Gayatri Chakravorty. 1993. *Outside in the Teaching Machine*. New York: Routledge.

Vitanza, Victor. 1997. *Negation, Subjectivity, and the History of Rhetoric*. Albany: State University of New York Press.

White, Hayden. 1987. *The Content of the Form: Narrative Discourse and Historical Representation*. Baltimore: John Hopkins University Press.

15

Lessons From the Turtle Grandparents: American Indian Literature and the Teaching of Writing

Linda Cullum

Several years ago, I left a teaching job at a small rural college in northern Michigan's Indian Country to come East. My new position, as a compositionist in a Pennsylvania university smack in the middle of cornfields and buggies, was a far cry from the reservation. Further still were the realities and sensibilities of my new students, who are mostly White, middle class, usually the first generation in their families to go to college; and born and bred nearby in a county that has the unfortunate claim to being the hate-group capital of the United States. As one student described her class, they are "just a bunch of average White kids." These were good kids as well, for the most part, but ones frequently oblivious to life's rich variety and suspicious of learning too much about themselves, let alone the mysterious "others" who lurked around the corner, waiting to complicate their already stress-fraught project of figuring out college life. What they expected from a composition class was to find out where their commas belonged, or as Robert Connors has said, to "Tell Me How To Build It . . . so I can give it to you, you can judge it, and we can both be on our way" (1996, 150). If my students' interest did happen to extend beyond surface correctness, they felt sure that all good writing fit one of three molds: it described; it compared and contrasted; or it persuaded—and never in the first person!

The question was clear: How could I move my students away from this restrictive, personally and culturally limiting mindset toward a genuine relationship with language and the chance to harness some of that power to

explore their own realities and that of others? Looking for guidance, I turned
to the writing that I had come to know best—American Indian texts, both
historical and contemporary. As do most who are not tied to a Eurocentric
framework, Native writers and speakers draw from a very different and more
expansive set of cultural norms while formulating and describing their relationships to language, to the world around them, and to self and other. As
such, their work can offer us, as composition teachers, a fresh way of looking at our students, what we want to offer them, and how best to accomplish
our goals.

Throughout Native discourse, one finds a deep respect for the power of
language. As N. Scott Momaday has said, "Words are powerful beyond our
knowledge . . . intrinsically powerful. . . . And there is magic in that.
Words . . . are created in the imagination and given life on the human voice
(1993, 183). However, as a people who have for so long experienced this
power in such negative ways, ways that have silenced and constricted them,
it is no wonder that the abuse of language by those in power is a recurring
theme. For example, In "Columbus Day," Jimmie Durham, a contemporary
Cherokee writer, reminds us of the devastating damage that language, in the
form of recorded history, can do:

> In school I learned of heroic discoveries
> Made by liars and crooks.
> The courage
> Of millions of sweet and true people
> Was not commemorated. (1988, 130)

Bay of Quinte Mohawk writer and critic Beth Brant (Degonwadonti) also
writes of the damage done by imposed silences, but on a more personal level.
For example, in "A Long Story," from her collection *Mohawk Trail* (1985),
she interweaves two tales—one a century old and the other modern—to offer
two separate realities, both of which show how words can become tools of
the majority, used to distort and control. The first story tells of the pain of a
Native mother whose children are taken away from her and sent to Indian
school. It is introduced by an actual 1892 newspaper headline which reports,
"About 40 Indian children took the train . . . for the Philadelphia Indian
School. . . . They were accompanied by the government agent, and seemed
a bright looking lot (1985, 77).

Once at the school, the children change; braids shorn and identities sup-
pressed, they write messages sanctioned by the boarding school—itself a
familiar metaphor for patriarchal control[1]—in a foreign language filled with
false words their mother cannot comprehend:

> The agent was here to deliver a letter. . . . This letter hurts my hand. It is
> written in their hateful language. It is evil. . . . I am confused. This letter
> is from two strangers with the names Martha and Daniel. They say they are
> learning civilized ways. . . . (Brant 1985, 79)

Interrelated with this story is a parallel, contemporary one, in which a lesbian mother loses custody of her daughter to her ex-husband. Again, the mother senses coercion and falsehood in her child's written expression: "I imagine her father standing over her, watching the words painstakingly being printed. Coaxing her. Coaching her. The letter becomes ugly" (Brant 1985, 82). These are two different worlds, and yet the message becomes one: Our language—indeed, our very selves—become false and ugly when the words we speak are not our own, when they are forced on us, external to our real center, silencing our own truths. This message has direct application to our classrooms, which students experience, all too often, as a site of extreme powerlessness. As the helpless Others, regardless of whatever status bonus they enjoy in the larger culture, they must surely reel from our invasive actions, our presumptive "understanding" of what they need to express, very much as so many Native protagonists in stories and novels recoil from the oppressive behaviors of the White man.

A second Brant short story, "The Fifth Floor, 1967," offers, in the form of a mentally unstable Native woman, a frightening metaphor for just such an overwhelmed and "undervoiced" student. In this autobiographical narrative, the Native wife and mother has tried desperately to imitate and fit in with her White husband's way of life, losing touch with her own heritage and sense of self in the process. Alienated from her identity, her culture, and her former vitality of "blood, muscle, electric pulses, and rage" (Brant 1985, 75), she has forgotten her story and lost her ability to tell it. Like a blank page in someone else's book, she feels "useless with no pattern . . . ready to be folded into fours, tucked away in a drawer" (72).

Eventually she trades one deadening institution for another when her husband signs her over to a mental hospital. In this chillingly sterile and antiseptically "White" environment (where "milk is the perfect food"), she now experiences complete absence from self. Nonetheless, she is "a good girl" (1985, 71), passively playing the hospital's game while inwardly recognizing the futility of the situation:

> In occupational therapy I am told I have a choice of making a trivet or an ashtray. The therapist is young and white. Her face is filled with school optimism. . . . We are uncooperative and strange. But she knows how to handle us: she talks in a perky, determined manner and ignores the strangeness. (Brant 1985, 73)

How many of our students, we might ask ourselves, have sat in class feeling like the woman on the fifth floor: alienated and silent, betrayed by the institution or co-opted into making "trivets or ashtrays"?

These monitory images remind us of our obligation to break our students' silence in positive and restorative ways. Indeed, both Durham and Brant move beyond their despair to offer celebrations of the power of language when used in service to this end. Jimmie Durham, after unearthing the stories of some of the "sweet and true" fallen heroes—from Chaske, to Many Deeds, to Laughing Otter the Taino—concludes "Columbus Day" with this powerful exhortation:

> Let us then declare a holiday
> For ourselves, and make a parade that begins
> With Columbus's victims and continues
> Even to our grandchildren who will be named
> In their honor.
>
> Because isn't it true that even the summer
> Grass here in this land whispers those names.
> And every creek has accepted the responsibility
> Of singing those names? And nothing can stop
> The wind from howling those names around
> The corners of the school. (1983)

And Brant, in a third selection from *Mohawk Trail*, also pays tribute to the generative power of words. Her description of her ability, her need, to write— and to write what she needs to say—is central for all writers, professional and student, beginning and seasoned:

> I write because to not write is a breach of faith.
> Out of a past where amnesia was the expected.
> Out of a past occupied with quiet.
> Out of a past, I make truth for a future. . . .
> Leaving my mark, my footprints, my sign.
> I write what I know (1985, 93–94).

As these excerpts demonstrate, language holds the key both for self-discovery and the discovery of others. In fact, many Indian texts link words with existence itself, revealing a deep understanding of the connection between language and life—both of which have been repeatedly stolen away. Because words are seen as inextricably linked to the continuance and renewal of the Indian people, the stories fashioned from these words become the key to one's connection with the world, one's heritage, and one's very being. Because of this, it is crucial that these stories be remembered and given voice, as Leslie Marmon Silko explains in "Language and Literature from a Pueblo Indian Perspective":

> . . . with the story we know who we are. . . . The stories are always bring-
> ing us together, keeping this whole together. . . . These occasions of story-
> telling are continuous; they are a way of life . . . Whatever . . . we received
> at school (which was damn little), at home the storytelling, the special
> regard for telling and bringing together through the telling, was going on
> constantly. . . . As the old people say, "If you can remember the stories,
> you will be all right. Just remember the stories." (1981, 57, 59, 67–68)

Because Native rhetoric is rooted so strongly in an oral tradition, the stories are never distanced from the speakers and writers, who are celebrated for their eloquence and the uniqueness of their personal vision. But they also remember that any personal vision—no matter how unique—is always dependent on, and the product of, one's ancestry, traditions, and relationships.[2] Far from subscribing to the EuroAmerican myth of the "self-made man," who can create and recreate himself independently at will, Native discourse conveys an abiding reverence for the interrelatedness of the human community—past, present and future. Using this understanding, we can encourage our students, as Nancy Sommers has said, to "begin to see for themselves their own complicated legacy, their own trail of authority" (1992, 31), and to understand how this legacy is situated in other, larger—and sometimes hostile—cultures.

This vision of language as dependent on, and safeguarding, the connections that potentially exist for all of us is often expressed in Native writings through central, though varying, metaphors. For example, Silko and Paula Gunn Allen favor the image of the spider's web for words and stories, with many little threads radiating from a center, criss-crossing each other. Silko maintains that, as with the actual web, the structure of a story will emerge as it is made, and one must simply listen and trust.

Images of lesbian lovemaking are also offered up regularly by Native women writers as models of the tender probing and gentle respect—so unlike the intrusive and potentially violent phallocentric sexual style—that remind us, as teachers, to encourage our students to locate their stories and personal meaning from within, rather than to attempt to thrust our topics, our models, and our culture forcefully on them. This passage, from the conclusion of Brant's "A Long Story," demonstrates the joy and ease of summoning up words in an atmosphere of security:

> She comes to me full in flesh. . . . She covers me with the beating of her heart. . . . Our bodies join. Our hair braids together on the pillow. . . . Her mouth, moving over my body, stopping at curves and swells of skin, kissing, removing pain. . . . the center of my soul is speaking to her, I am sliding into her, her mouth is medicine, her heart is the earth, we are dancing with flying arms, I shout, I sing, I weep salty liquid, sweet and warm. . . . (1985, 104)

It is a circular and highly integrated vision: Words are brought forth in a climate of comfort, and through their very expression, they reify and continue the atmosphere of love and safety from which they issued.

This passage also speaks of how the lovers' "hair braids together on the pillow" (104), capturing another central metaphor, for hair is often imagistically connected with words, stories, heritage, and cultural identity. When these are taken away, desperation and hollowness ensue. Listen, for example, to how Zitkala-Sa (Gertrude Bonnin), born on the Pine Ridge Reservation in 1876 and taken to Indian School at age eight, describes her shearing:

> I remember being dragged out. . . . I felt the cold blades of the scissors against my neck, and heard them gnaw off one of my thick braids. Then I lost my spirit. . . . now I was only one of many little animals driven by a herder. (2002, 58).

And again, in a more contemporary expression, this by Cheryl Savageau:

> And Grandmother, they wouldn't tell me
> Your name.
> Grandmother, Grandmother,
> I was singing to you,
> and they cut off,
> my hair. (1995, 15–16)

Hair imagery also holds optimism, however. Braids are formed of individual strands, the hairs—the words—recovered and fashioned together with love and patience, as in Brant's "For All My Grandmothers":

> with no words, quietly
> the hair fell out
> formed webs on the dresser
> on the pillow
> in your brush.
> These tangled strands
> pushed to the back of a drawer
> wait for me
> to untangle
> to comb through
> to weave the split fibers
> and make a material
> strong enough
> to encompass our lives. (1985, 24)

Inspired by these images and so many other wonderful tropes that fill American-Indian language and literature, I have developed my own governing metaphor for teaching. Of course, our learning-centered paradigm has furnished us with many possibilities. No longer "bankers," who deposit chunks of information into passive students' mental accounts, or warriors in a blackboard jungle, we are now the "guides," the nurturing "midwives" (Belenky et al. 1986, 217), even the "tricksters" (Murphy 1991, 163). But what does this make our students? The lost and confused? The helpless babies? The tricked? I offer instead the image of the "turtle grandparent" as an alternative metaphor for the composition teacher.

Throughout Native writings, the turtle—on whose back the earth has been built, according to many familiar creation myths—provides security, protection, and a sense of a past that is inextricably connected to the present and future. As Cheryl Savageau writes in "All Night She Dreams," it is on "turtle's back" that "she can talk to fire, to stone" (1995, 92). We can connect this image with that of the grandmother—a central force in so many American-Indian texts. Like the turtle, the grandmother offers security and comfort. She is the caretaker who makes the quilts and covers us with them; the one who "sets the pot over the fire that has never gone out" (Brant 1985, 15); the one who "listens through a thick blanket of years"

(Chrystos 1989, 30). Patient and serene, she is the trusted member of the family who maintains her connection with her heritage even when others have lost themselves to the vices of the White world. Moreover, as the oldest member of the earthly family but soon to be the newest of the ancestors (to which she will return for her future), the grandmother stands for transition and connection, a bridge between the old and the new, whose "spirit stands obdurate before [our] door" (Cardiff 1984, 59). In this way, she is very much like our stories themselves, drawing sustenance from all that has come before, while enabling future connections and strength through their very being.

She also, like the turtle, symbolizes home—another essential concept in Native-American writings. For example, in "Indian Boarding School: The Runaways," Louise Erdrich writes that "Home's the place we head for in our sleep," 1988, 334 whereas Brant's character Sweet William in "Turtle Gal" says: "Home was where you were somebody. Your name was real, and the people knew your name and called you by that name. It was when you left home that your name became an invisible thing" (1991, 107). I believe that as turtle grandmothers and grandfathers, we can reconfigure our classroom as a home, a nonthreatening and natural site where students trust that connections can be made and the pieces come together. Our students, then, become the turtle grandchildren, perhaps younger or less experienced in the ways of language, but members of the same family of teachers and learners.

I have watched this vision bear fruit over the last several years, although, certainly, not always. I am reminded, for example, of the young White male who wondered loudly, as prelude to a class discussion of Chief Seattle's "My People," why he was constantly subjected to reading about these kinds of things. He was tired of being made to feel guilty; he was sick of reading about things that happened so long ago; he wanted to read and talk about people like him; and he could tell us plenty of stories about injustices done to him by minorities! Happily, though, much more often, students have welcomed the chance to explore—through language—their own truths and discover those of others, to reject, as Macedo and Bartolome have written, "the social construction of images that dehumanize the other,'. . . [seeing that] by dehumanizing the other we become dehumanized ourselves" (1999, 29).

We've come a long way from teaching about commas, from replicating old paradigms of writing instruction, and from reinforcing hegemonic notions of what constitutes an American "reality." These days, the borders of our classrooms are becoming a bit more contested and we realize, as Robert Brooke has said, that "the process of building identity is the business we are in" (1987, 152). And so I offer American-Indian texts, which speak so compellingly about the potential to balance and create through language, as a guide in this process. For what finer gift could we give to our students than the opportunity to discover themselves; to understand their relationship to their cultures; to share their stories; and to learn those of others in honor and respect?

Notes

1. I have found that teaching around such historical moments as Columbus' arrival, the movement West and the creation of reservations, and the phenomenon of the Indian School opens students' eyes to other versions of "reality" and shows how language has shaped their cultural and historical relationships. By reading Indian and Euro-American texts and government legislation, they can see how language, rather than simply recording events, is the tool for advancing certain realities and suppressing others.

2. Sherman Alexie's short story "A Drug Called Tradition" offers a literal interpretation of the interrelatedness of the human spirit when his three protagonists, Junior, Victor, and Thomas, each has a vision not of his own future but of that of one of the others.

Works Cited

Belenky, Mary Field et al. 1986. *Women's Ways of Knowing.* New York: Basic Books.

Brant, Beth. 1991. *Food & Spirits.* Ithaca, NY: Firebrand Books.

———. 1985. *Mohawk Trail.* Ithaca, NY: Firebrand Books.

Brooke, Robert. 1987. "Underlife and Writing Instruction." *College Composition and Communication* 38 (2): 141–53.

Cardiff, Gladys. 1984. "Grey Woman." In *That's What She Said; Contemporary Poetry and Fiction by Native American Women,* edited by Rayna Green. Bloomington: Indiana University Press.

Chrystos. 1989. *Not Vanishing.* Vancover, B.C.: Press Gang, p. 30.

Connors, Robert. 1996. "Teaching and Learning as a Man." *College English* 58: 137–57.

Durham, Jimmie. 1983. *Columbus Day.* Albuquerque: University of New Mexico Press.

Erdrich, Louise. 1988. "Indian Boarding School: The Runaways." In *Harper's Anthology of 20th Century Native American Poetry,* edited by Duane Niatum, 334–35. San Francisco: Harper San Francisco.

Macedo, Donaldo, and Lilla Bartolome. 1999. *Dancing with Bigotry.* New York: St. Martin's.

Momaday, N. Scott. 1983. "The Magic of Words: An Interview with N. Scott Momaday." In *Survival This Way: Interviews with American Indian Poets,* edited by Joseph Bruchac. Greenfield Center, NY: Greenfield Review Press.

Murphy, Patrick. 1991. "Coyote Midwife in the Classroom: Introducing Literature with Feminist Dialogics." In *Practicing Theory in Introductory College*

Literature Courses, edited by James M. Cahalan and David B. Downing. Urbana, IL: National Council of Teachers of English.

Savageau, Cheryl. 1995. *Dirt Road Home.* Willimantic, CT: Curbstone Press.

Silko, Leslie Marmon. 1981. "Language and Literature from a Pueblo Indian Perspective." In *English Literature: Opening Up the Canon,* edited by Leslie A. Fiedler and Houston A. Baker, Jr., 54–72. Baltimore: Johns Hopkins University Press.

Sommers, Nancy. 1992. "Between the Drafts." *College Composition and Communication* 43 (1): 23–31.

Zitkala-Sa. 2002. "The School Days of an Indian Girl." In *Literature, Race, and Ethnicity: Contested American Identities,* edited by Joseph Skerrett, 55–63. New York: Longman.

16

Challenging Racial Authority, Rewriting Racial Authority: Multicultural Rhetorics in Literary Studies and Composition

Laurie Grobman

Patricia Bizzell (1987) argues that multicultural rhetorics—the language of texts written by African Americans, Asian Americans, Latinos/as, Native Americans, and other ethnic minorities, and taught in both literature and composition classrooms—collapse distinctions between the disciplines, as both kinds of classrooms have become anti-racist, anti-sexist locations for social change. Certainly, multiculturalism has irrevocably altered the objectives and methods of literary study, whereas the composition classroom, with its proliferation of multicultural readers, is itself viewed as a multicultural "contact zone." Such changes in emphasis reflect a shared understanding that ethnic texts are rhetorical objects that can be studied in an effort to curb injustice.

Lately, however, I have been wondering about the intersections of literary studies, composition, and multiculturalism, about the objectives and methods of teaching in literature and composition from a multicultural perspective and with multicultural texts. As composition entrenches itself in cultural critique and as literary studies embrace the politicized, rhetorical nature of literary texts, do they undermine their integrity as distinct disciplines?

For Bizzell, the distinction between composition and literature no longer makes sense. She writes, "What I want students [in both courses] to do is to study rhetorical strategies of persuasion in readings from a variety of genres, fiction and non-fiction ('literature'), and also to practice rhetorical strategies in a variety of writings of their own ('composition')" (1997, 167). Bizzell argues that her composition course based around multicultural literature is distinguished from literature courses she teaches "only by the proportion of reading to writing: in writing courses, we write more and read less, and in literature courses, vice versa" (172). But is there more to the distinction than the quantity of reading and writing?

This essay explores this important question, suggesting that multicultural rhetorics offer important ways of teaching students about human understanding in both composition and literary studies as separate disciplines, each with its own pedagogical and political work to do. As I use them in my literature classes, ethnic texts such as Toni Morrison's *Beloved* or Sandra Cisneros' *The House on Mango Street* provide opportunities for students to challenge dominant modes of racial authority, whereas in composition, these texts provide a pedagogical space for students to rewrite such authority.

The Changing Relationship Between Literature and Composition

I entered Lehigh University as a graduate student in the early 1990s, when Lehigh had a two-semester first-year composition requirement. The second semester was literature based, although it was a *composition* course, a course in which we were instructed to use literature to teach writing. It was not until I began my dissertation on the teaching of literature by women of color that I began to question the wisdom of using literature in composition.

At that time, I turned to the research on the topic, most notably the Tate–Lindemann debate in *College English*. Gary Tate, a proponent of literature-in-composition, points to literature's potential to effect personal, moral, and political growth, and sees this as composition's objective as well: composition instructors should prepare our students to join the "'community'" of the "conversations [that] will take place *outside the academy*" (1993, 320). Erika Lindemann, an opponent of using literary texts in composition, held that a writing course should make students more effective academic writers, introducing them to generalized and discipline-specific discourse conventions, so literature is at best irrelevant, at worst detrimental. Asserting that first-year English should "provide opportunities to master the genres, styles, audiences, and purposes of college writing" and offer "guided practice in reading and writing the discourses of the academy and the professions," Lindemann claimed that writing about literature "amounts to collapsing the discourses of the academy into one genre" (1993, 312).

But this debate has largely disappeared from our disciplinary conversation, and the proliferation of multicultural readers for composition classes suggests that many compositionists welcome multicultural literature into their classrooms. However, they do so by adopting multicultural readers specifically put together for composition classes, whereas literature classes still seem to stick to the more traditional (however multiculturally transformed) literary anthology, such as *The Heath Anthology of American Literature* and its succesors (Norton, Prentice-Hall, etc.).

One possibility for the disappearance of the literature-in-composition debate is that the distinction between literary and nonliterary texts has collapsed, and therefore we no longer need to address the role of literature in composition. This seems to be the case in Wayne Booth's *College English* article on the ethics of teaching literature (1998). Without any mention that literature's role in composition may be distinct from literature classes, Booth premises his argument that teaching literature is about building character on a *College Composition and Communication* article by Elisabeth Anne Leonard, an article about teaching writing (1997). Nevertheless, Booth focuses on students' reading, not writing, and on teaching. Booth only addresses the issue of literature in writing in this way: "Although [Leonard] avoids the words 'ethics,' 'ethos,' 'morality,' and 'character,' and although she never uses the word 'literature,' she obviously teaches literature, in my broad definition—the world of story—and in doing so she hopes to produce results of the kind we all *ought* to hope for" (1998, 43). By broadening "literature" in this way, we can avoid discussing the issue of imaginative literature's role in composition. However, if we include such a distinction in practice, then we have made a mistake in ignoring it in theory. Booth's section on practical suggestions largely includes examples of imaginative literature. Indeed, if Booth is right about the power of story to influence ethics and values, we would be foolish to omit it from multicultural-oriented composition classes, which have at their core (as much as some are averse to the suggestion) the transformation of students' belief systems. We should not ignore the particular power of multicultural texts to address and redress the social, political, and economic injustices in American society.

A further possible explanation for the disappearance of the literature-in-composition debate has to do with the theoretical bridges that have been created between these two subdisciplines of English studies. Increasingly, compositionists and literary specialists are forging connections, recognizing the ways the work in each discipline informs the other. John Clifford and John Schilb's *Writing Theory and Critical Theory* (1994) is, in my view, the most comprehensive account of these productive associations. Significantly, Clifford and Schilb reject the term "literary theory" in favor of "critical theory," arguing that the latter involves a "critique of current discursive practices and social structures," including but not limited to the "literary," a notion which has itself been critiqued by the very schools of thought critical theory encapsulates (1–2). Moreover, Clifford and Schilb point out that while the hostilities or tensions between the two subdisciplines of English have lessened, rather than merge literature and composition, many scholars seek a rubric to embrace them both: *cultural studies* or *rhetoric,* for example (3). What is clear in their collection and in other work in English studies is the effort to bring critical theory to bear on writing theory and practice, and vice versa, in fruitful ways.

In discussing his pedagogy of "cultural rhetoric" in a multicultural literature class, for example, John Alberti (1997) makes the important connection between literary and composition theory, with "rhetoric" as its bridge. Rhetoric, he argues, has been "revived, transformed, and modified by developments in both composition and literary theory" (204). "Composition," he writes, "whether we mean the encoding process we call writing or the decoding process we call reading" involves "a dialectical process that is inherently social, diverse, and dynamic" (204). Because all language is imbued with ideology, rhetoric—language negotiation in reading and writing—involves negotiating among intersecting political, social, economic, and cultural forces (206).

Multiculturalism, Literature, and Composition: Complementary Disciplines

There is no doubt in my mind that some of the most important transformations in the ways we understand and teach—in both composition and literary studies—have been deeply influenced by the multicultural commitment to justice and equality. The blending of literature and composition within multicultural rhetorics intrigues me because I regularly teach introductory-level courses as well as conduct research in both disciplines, with multiculturalism and multicultural texts as the bridge between these possibly separate worlds. Certainly, for the most part, my articles on writing and on literature have separate venues, with differing sets of expectations. For example, when I received a rejection of an article on using *Beloved* in composition, both reviewers praised my article, but they insisted it belonged in a journal about literature, not writing. At the same time, one reviewer wrote this:

> While I found this all quite informative as a teacher of literary texts, I failed to see how it pertained specifically to the composition classroom. Perhaps such a distinction between the literature and writing classroom should no longer be made. Reading and writing are joined at the hip and the head, after all. Nevertheless, the existence of composition classrooms and the myriad journals devoted to teaching literature in literature courses suggests that the distinction is very much alive and very much necessary.

When I read these comments, I realized that I had not clearly articulated my argument for how to use a literary text in composition in a way that would distinguish it from literature. But then I wondered what that meant, particularly given the reviewer's contradiction between suggesting that we might not want to make the distinction any longer, but then the recognition that we do make it, *and* that it's "necessary" to make it.

In literary studies, multiculturalism takes many forms, but what is most evident is how multiculturalism has influenced canon issues: recovering previously excluded texts and reevaluating and revaluing traditional texts as well as criteria for literary excellence and canonization. Such cultural and intellectual work has led to a broadened literary canon and broadened criteria for literary excellence, but is by no means complete, as many questions remain as to how we are to make judgments about all texts, including multicultural texts. As Reed Way Dasenbrock (1999) observes, "Despite the fact that a conventionalist critique of literary value dominates literary theory today, nonetheless as we read and teach individual literary texts we generally invoke the old language of evaluative criticism and aesthetic judgment" (693). Dasenbrock argues that we teach what we like and we like what we think is good; even if we teach a very different set of texts than we were taught: "few of us eschew aesthetic evaluation in the way we should if we truly accepted the critique of canonicity itself in the way we claim" (694). The 2001 MELUS (The Society of the Study of the Multi-Ethnic Literature of the United States) Conference focused on aesthetic judgment of multicultural literature with MELUS President Bonnie TuSmith calling on scholars of multiethnic literatures to be more critical in their aesthetic and artistic evaluations of ethnic literature.[1]

Approaches to the texts themselves have also changed. Many instructors conceive of literary texts as rhetorical arguments that arise out of the cultural constructions that produce them rather than as insular aesthetic expressions. They no longer believe that teaching literature is equivalent to transmitting a sacred set of texts (and values) to students. Although numerous scholars claim that literary studies is experiencing a period of skepticism and uncertainty about its objectives and purposes (see, for example, Bérubé 1998; Goodheart 1999; Levine 2001), I believe there is great consensus about teaching multicultural texts. They inform students about difference, promote an understanding of the destructive effects of racist and other kinds of oppression, work to achieve social and economic justice, encourage a rethinking of value systems, introduce students to alternative discourses, foster close reading of and critical thinking about texts, and encourage reflective, thoughtful writing.

Certainly, much of the same can be said about multicultural perspectives and the use of multicultural texts in composition. Although compositionists may not specifically deal with canonization, we frequently include issues involving power relations, ideology, and language's inextricable connection with both. Multicultural perspectives in composition intend to expose students to difference, to foster thoughtful consideration of the devastating impact of oppression, to work toward a more just and equal society, to invite reflection on value systems, to introduce students to unfamiliar language practices and epistemological assumptions, to promote close reading of and critical thinking about texts, and to provide the opportunity for practice in serious, engaged writing. We want students to see themselves as creators of knowledge who have the power and agency to influence how our society defines significant concepts like value, justice, equality, democracy, and difference. By using multicultural readers, compositionists also choose to expose students to the idea of a pluralistic U.S. society, while providing them opportunities to connect to their own backgrounds and experiences.

In both literature and composition, I use multicultural texts as examples of overlapping, intersecting, competing discursive systems; in both disciplines, this approach underscores language's power and provides students with an opportunity to examine their own language practices as they relate to larger cultural forces. I teach students to consider the ways their writing (and all writing) is culturally situated, as well as the ways students can use writing to revise and resist cultural constructions and structures. As Umeeta Sadarangani (1994) suggests:

> Upon learning that discourses vary in different contexts, students are more likely to realize that the dominant discourse does not represent "Reality" but rather a "reality," and that if the students' own worlds are not represented by this discourse, it does not necessarily mean those worlds are any less valid. Undertaking this critique encourages students to see how the dominant discourse attempts to control their world; knowing this they may become less subject to the way that discourse defines them. (41)

I use what I have learned from the scholarship in multicultural studies in literature and in composition to inform my approach in each discipline, in ways that seem to bridge them. For me, both courses are about students' involvement in the making of meaning, whether through reading, writing, and/or discussion.

Nevertheless, I want to explore a potential fundamental difference between these subdisciplines of English studies. In one sense, Bizzell is accurate in that the quantity of reading and writing is at issue. But more importantly, while there are shared objectives and methods between literature and composition courses integrating multicultural texts and perspectives, the emphases are, in my view, distinct. In literature classes, my students' activities are centered on challenging dominant modes of racial and other hegemonic authority through a focus on multicultural texts. In composition, however, I use multicultural texts as a springboard for addressing the larger issues raised by the text; thus, in composition, multicultural texts provide a pedagogical space for students to rewrite hegemonic authority.

The Ethics of Multiculturalism in Literature and Composition

In the introduction to *The Ethics in Literature* (1999), Andrew Hadfield, Dominic Rainsford, and Tim Woods observe the recent (re)attention to ethics in literature, and they argue that the "famous question on which Aristotle based his ethical philosophy, how shall we live life, has been transformed into the question, how can we respect the other? What responsibilities do we owe to our fellows?" (9). Gary Olson (1998) echoes these assertions vis-à-vis the composition classroom. Building on the work of several postmodern thinkers, Olson argues that we can productively conceive of ethics as "*the encounter with the Other*" (46). These scholars' ideas are also echoed by Booth's observation that ethical concerns remain at the heart of English studies, despite the turn from traditional ethics and foundational values (1998, 41). It is clear that both literature and composition, in their embrace of multiculturalism, can have enormous impact on our students as they develop intellectually and ethically. It is incumbent on all of us in English studies to continue to define the work we do, to seek ways to bridge the sometimes contentious, sometimes convoluted differences between the sub-disciplines, to assist our students as they grow as reflective, engaged, and caring people.

Notes

1. The Conference Call for Proposals sought papers addressing the "second wave" of the struggle to broaden American literature: "assessing the value of the uncovered and recovered texts and sharing judgments" (see Rodier 2001).

Works Cited

Alberti, John. 1997. "Teaching the Rhetoric of Race: A Rhetorical Approach to Multi-cultural Pedagogy." *Rethinking American Literature,* edited by Lil Brannon and Brenda M. Greene, 203–15. Urbana: National Council of Teachers of English.

Bérubé, Michael. 1998. *The Employment of English: Theory, Jobs, and the Future of Literary Studies.* New York: New York University Press.

Bizzell, Patricia. 1997. "Negotiating Difference: Teaching Multicultural Literature." *Rethinking American Literature,* edited by Lil Brannon and Brenda M. Greene, 163–74. Urbana: National Council of Teachers of English.

Booth, Wayne C. 1998. "The Ethics of Teaching Literature." *College English* 61.1: 41–55.

Cisneros, Sandra. 1984/1991. *The House on Mango Street.* New York: Vintage.

Clifford, John, and John Schilb. 1994. Introduction. *Writing Theory and Critical Theory,* edited by John Clifford and John Schilb, 1–15. New York: MLA.

Dasenbrock, Reed Way. 1999. "Why Read Multicultural Literature? An Arnoldian Perspective." *College English* 61.6: 691–701.

Goodheart, Eugene. 1999. *Does Literary Studies Have a Future?* Madison: University of Wisconsin Press.

Graff, Gerald. 1992. *Beyond the Culture Wars: How Teaching the Conflicts Can Revitalize American Education.* New York: Norton.

Grobman, Laurie. (Forthcoming.) "Rhetorizing the Contact Zone: Multicultural Texts in Writing Classrooms." *Reading Sites,* edited by Elizabeth Flynn and Patsy Schweickart. New York: MLA.

———. 2001. *Teaching at the Crossroads: Cultures and Critical Perspectives in Literature By Women of Color.* San Francisco: Aunt Lute Books.

Hadfield, Andrew, Dominic Rainsford, and Tim Woods. 1999. *The Ethics in Literature.* New York: St. Martin's.

Leonard, Elisabeth Anne. 1997. "Assignment #9—A Text Which Engages the Socially Constructed Identity of Its Writer." *College Composition and Communication* 48.2: 215–30.

Levine, George. 2001. "The Two Nations." *Pedagogy: Critical Approaches to Teaching Literature, Language, Composition, and Culture* 1.1: 7–19.

Lindemann, Erika. 1993. "Freshman Composition: No Place for Literature." *College English* 55.3: 311–16.

———. 1995. "Three Views of English 101." *College English* 57.3: 287–302.

Morrison, Toni. 1987/1988. *Beloved.* New York: Penguin.

Olson, Gary. 1999. "Encountering the Other: Postcolonial Theory and Composition Scholarship." *JAC: Journal of Composition Theory* 18.1: 45–56.

Rodier, Katharine. "'Taking Stock of Multiethnic Literatures': Call for Papers." *NewsNotes, E-Publication for the Society for the Study of the Multi-Ethnic Literature of the United States.* Winter/MLA 2001 Special Issue. (Accessed 4 March 2001.) http://www.marshall.edu/melus/newsnotes/

Sadarangani, Umeeta. 1994. "Teaching Multicultural Issues in the Composition Classroom: A Review of Recent Practice." *Journal of Teaching Writing* 13.1-2: 33–54.

Tate, Gary. 1995. "Notes on the Dying of a Conversation." *College English* 57.3: 303–09.

———. 1993. "A Place for Literature in Freshman Composition." *College English* 55.3: 317–21.

Afterword

Immigration to the United States was severely limited with the passage of the anti-immigrant, anti-ethnic, Johnson-Reed Act of 1924. The passage of the Johnson-Reed Act attempted to codify, naturalize, and entangle Whiteness and Americanness through a policy that privileged those of western and northern European backgrounds. Ultimately, however, this containment of ethnicity gave way to an onslaught of immigration and ethnic diversity. In fact, all kinds of ethnicity are embraced and widely celebrated these days. The 2000 census reflects the new state of affairs: The number of ethnic categories was increased from five to fifteen. For instance, where Asians and Pacific Islanders were once a single categorical shelf in the ethnic aisle, they are now located on two separate shelves marked "Asian" and "Native Hawaiian and Other Pacific Islander."

Ethnicity is so entrenched in the American imagination that Marilyn Halter's *Shopping for Identity: The Marketing of Ethnicity* (2002) is just one of a spate of books on the corporate targeting of ethnicity to sell a variety of products. Halter illustrates how business is capitalizing on the fascination of consumers with ethnicity, particularly with respect to fashion, food, music, literature, and other expressive culture. But shopping for identity in this manner increases the fetishizing of ethnicity as a commodity.

Rhetoric and Ethnicity is important in an era where, for some, depth and meaning are jettisoned in favor of surface and play, enabling the claiming of ethnicity (I am part Mexican, Indian, Zulu, Hui, Dutch, Jamaican, etc., etc.) with the cavalier ease of a shopper with a no-limit American Express card. Of course, one should avoid a kind of vulgar analysis that denigrates any market activity around ethnicity as corrupt or inauthentic. After all, many immigrants from countries such as Mali, Nigeria, Senegal, and Gambia made a living and ensured the survival of their families by selling ethnic artifacts at the Malcolm Shabazz Harlem Market. Mexicans, El Salvadorans, and Guatemalans have followed similar pursuit in the cities and suburbs of Los Angeles. The problem occurs when ethnic identity is thought of as just one more easily obtainable commodity. For example, Joycelyn Moody's "Enslaved Women as Autobiographical Narrators: The Case of Louisa Picquet" and Jessica Enoch's " 'Semblances of Civilization': Zitkala-Za's Resistance to White Education" remind us how ethnicity and subjectivity are often forged in crucibles of displacement, struggle, and sacrifice. To claim an ethnic allegiance to an abstract Irishness is one thing. As a "Nunley" I could do just that. But it is quite another matter to have ancestors who starved during the Irish potato famine, dwelled in the squalor of New York tenement housing at the turn of the twentieth century, or who currently reside in Ireland and hear themselves referred to as the "niggers of Europe." I hear some things said about me, but I don't hear that. In other words, my idea of ethnicity centers on issues of history, politics, and commitment.

Rhetoric and Ethnicity is not only up on the social and linguistic nature of epistemology, but it is also aware of the spatial turn in many disciplines and the role that the spatial as social and ideological plays in the mediation of ethnicity and rhetorical performance. Like Quintillian before them, scholars in this volume recognize that the "where" of rhetorical performances and artifacts is just as important as the message of a rhetorical situation. It is not by accident that in a text that takes ethnicity seriously spatial tropes are pervasive. For example, Geneva Smitherman deploys the trope of the "hood" to discuss the continuous denigration of Ebonics as a language variety despite volumes of research. Malea Powell theorizes on the ground of a spatial trope as she alludes to the "territory" of empire to examine colonial discourse and its construction of the "Indian problem."

Finally, *Rhetoric and Ethnicity* returns us to primary concerns of rhetoric: democracy, citizenship, and the construction of subjectivity. Ethnicity, like democracy, is not easily found while shopping for music, clothes, or identity. And, like democracy, ethnicity is contested ground. Whereas some shop for ethnicity, others are profiled into theirs. Whereas some bask in the light of democracy, others struggle to illuminate its darker recesses to enhance democracy's meaning. Lives hang in the balance. *Rhetoric and Ethnicity*, anchored in *phronesis*—practical wisdom and intelligence—tries, as a whole, to articulate ethnicity through a critical, spatial, and experiential lens that can serve well rhetoric, democracy, and America.

—Vorris Nunley

Works Cited

Halter, Marilyn. 2002. *Shopping for Identity: The Marketing of Ethnicity.* New York: Schocken Books.

Contributors

Janice Chernekoff is an associate professor of English at Kutztown University of Pennsylvania. Her research interests include composition studies, pedagogical arts, and the rhetorics of alternative discourses.

Marilyn M. Cooper is an associate professor of Humanities at Michigan Technological University. She is working on a book that looks at the implications of ecosocial theory and ethical subjectivity for teaching writing.

Linda Cullum is an assistant profesor of English and director of the University Writing Center at Kutztown University of Pennsylvania. She is the editor of *Breaking the Cycle: Gender, Literacy, and Learning* and the forthcoming *Contemporary Ethnic American Poets*.

Jessica Enoch is an assistant professor at the University of New Hampshire. She has published essays in *College English* and *Nineteenth-Century Prose* and is revising her dissertation project, "Women's Resistant Pedagogies in Turn-of-the-Century America: Lydia Maria Child, Zitkala Sa, Jovita Idar, Marta Pena, and Leonor Villegas de Magnon.

Xin Liu Gale was an assistant professor of writing and rhetoric at Syracuse University at the time of the conference. She is the author of *Teachers, Discourses and Authority in the Postmodern Composition Classroom* and coeditor of *(Re) Revisioning Composition Textbooks*. In 2001, Gale left academe to pursue fiction and nonfiction writing full time.

Keith Gilyard is a professor of English at Penn State. His books include *Voices of the Self: A Study of Language Competence, Let's Flip the Script: An African American Discourse on Language, Literature, and Learning*, and *Liberation Memories: The Rhetoric and Poetics of John Oliver Killens*. He also has edited *Race, Rhetoric, and Composition, Rhetorical Choices: A Reader for Writers* (with Deborah Holdstein and Chuck Schuster), and *African American Literature* (with Anissa Wardi). Gilyard is a former Chair of CCCC.

Laurie Grobman is an associate professor of English and Co-Coordinator of the B.A. in Professional Writing at Penn State University, Berks-Lehigh Valley. She is the author of *Teaching at the Crossroads: Cultures and Critical Perspectives in Literature by Women of Color* as well as of numerous articles on multicultural theory and pedagogy in both literature and composition. Her most recent pedagogical and research interests integrate service-learning with multicultural and women's literature.

LuMing Mao is an associate professor of English at Miami University of Ohio. His work in comparative rhetoric and discourse analysis has been published in *Rhetoric Review, Rhetoric Society Quarterly, Journal of Asian-Pacific Communication,* and *Journal of Pragmatics,* among others. He is currently finishing a monograph on comparative rhetoric, and he is co-editing, with Susan Jarratt, Andrea Lunsford, Jacqueline Jones Royster, and John Ruszkiewicz, a Norton anthology on rhetoric and writing.

Richard Marback is an associate professor of English at Wayne State University. His research focuses on the social organization of rhetoric and race in urban environments in the United States and South Africa.

Jaime Armin Mejía is an associate professor of English at Texas State University in San Marcos, Texas, where his research and teaching attempt to bring Rhetoric and Composition Studies together with Chicano/a Studies.

Joycelyn K. Moody is an associate professor of English at the University of Washington. She specializes in African-American literature, autobiography, and women's issues, and has published *Sentimental Confessions: Spiritual Narratives of Nineteenth-Century African American Women.* Her work in progress explores intersections of literacy and power in dictated narratives by antebellum U.S. Black women.

Vorris Nunley is a student at Penn State completing doctoral work in rhetoric, composition, and literature. He was the coordinator of the Conference on American Ethnic Rhetorics held at Penn State.

Gwendolyn D. Pough is an assistant professor of Women's Studies at the University of Minnesota. She is author of a book on Black womanhood, hip-hop culture, and the public sphere.

Malea Powell is a mixed-blood of Indiana Miami, Eastern Shawnee, and Euroamerican ancestry. She is an associate professor of Writing, Rhetoric and American Culture and American Indian Studies at Michigan State University, where she teaches graduate and undergraduate courses in writing, rhetoric, critical theory, and American-Indian Studies. Her research focuses on examining the rhetorics of survivance used by nineteenth-century American-Indian intellectuals. She has published essays in *CCC, Paradoxa, Race, Rhetoric & Composition, AltDis,* and in other essay collections; she is also the editor of *Of Color: Native American Literatures* (forthcoming) as well as editor of *SAIL: Studies in American Indian Literatures,* a quarterly journal devoted to the study of American-Indian writing.

Marie J. Secor teaches rhetoric and composition at Penn State University. She is the co-author of *A Rhetoric of Argument* (Third Edition) and articles on nineteenth-century history of rhetoric, rhetorical theory, and argumentation. She is an associate professor and Associate Head of Penn State's English Department.

Geneva Smitherman, University Distinguished Professor of English and Director of the African American Language and Literacy program at Michigan State University, has written more than one hundred essays on language, literature, education, and public policy. Her books include *Talkin and Testifyin: The Language of Black America, Black Talk: Words and Phrases from the Hood to the Amen Corner,* and *Talkin that Talk: Language, Culture, and Education in African America.* Smitherman has chaired the CCCC Language Policy Committee since 1987. She received the CCCC Exemplar Award in 1999 and NCTE Russell Award for Distinguished Research in 2001.

Barry Thatcher is an assistant professor of rhetoric and professional communication at New Mexico State University. His research focuses on Latin American and U.S. intercultural communication, the history of rhetoric in Latin America, and U.S./Mexico border rhetoric.

Deborah M. Williams is a Ph.D. student in rhetoric and cultural studies at Temple University. She lives in Mumbai, India, with her husband and two children.